D1460650

# A NOONTIDE BLAZING

WITHDRAWN FROM STOCK

In accordance with the wish of the late Dr Brigid Lyons Thornton
all royalties from the sale of this book are being contributed to
the Defence Forces Benevolent Fund,
Defence Forces HQ, Parkgate Street, Dublin 8.

# A Noontide Blazing

*Brigid Lyons Thornton*
*Rebel, Soldier, Doctor*

John Cowell

920/1Ho

LIMERICK 0046526l.
COUNTY LIBRARY

CURRACH
PRESS

First published in 2005 by
CURRACH PRESS
55A Spruce Avenue, Stillorgan Industrial Park, Blackrock, Co Dublin

www.currach.ie


Cover by Anú Design
Cover photograph of the Four Courts from Fáilte Ireland
Index by Therese Carrick
Origination by Currach Press
Printed by ColourBooks Ltd, Dublin


ISBN 1-85607-918-X

Copyright © John Cowell, 2005

# CONTENTS

# DEDICATION

IN THE SECOND decade of the twentieth century, the magistrates presiding in the Sligo Courthouse grew used to the face of a spirited young Irish Volunteer called Alec McCabe, who never flinched from showing his contempt for the Royal Irish Constabulary and everything for which that body stood. In 1918, while once again a prisoner, McCabe was elected an MP for Sinn Féin, with a sweeping majority. Politically he never looked back. He became a consistent poll-topper.

Sent to Sligo by Sinn Féin headquarters to nominate candidates for the 1921 general election, Brigid Lyons made certain to include Alec McCabe, that most distinguished Volunteer, then once more in prison. She missed his presence as well as the wise advice he might have given at that nomination meeting. Besides, Alec was 'a neighbour's child'. He came from Kesh in south Sligo, while she hailed from Scramogue in nearby north Roscommon.

Both Lyons and McCabe supported the Treaty, and both afterwards served in the new Free State Army. As a soldier, McCabe was once faced with an almost insoluble problem — that of dislodging the enemy from a stronghold on a peninsula unapproachable by land. With his usual initiative, Colonel McCabe commandeered the SS Lily, a cross-channel freighter in Sligo Bay, and from her decks a little marksmanship soon solved his problem.

Alec McCabe's popularity flourished on his retirement from the army when, in 1935, he founded the Educational Building Society, enabling thousands of newlyweds to acquire their own homes speedily.

This book is dedicated to the memory of a man whose inspiration, vision and dynamism helped in so many practical ways to create our modern history.

# FOREWORD

*A NOONTIDE BLAZING* tells the story of Brigid Lyons Thornton, a woman described by her biographer as a rebel, soldier and a doctor. Brigid's story, written by John Cowell, is a biography but often reads like an autobiography, as Brigid's voice is evident throughout the narrative.

The book tells of a woman who lived through Ireland's revolutionary period; the rebel who took part in the 1916 Rising and the War of Independence; the soldier who was the first women commissioned officer in the Irish Free State Army during the Civil War; and as Dr Lyons Thornton, worked in the medical field both as a doctor, as a medical librarian and lecturer in addition to being a practitioner.

The affection that Dr Cowell has for his subject shines through. Working in the field of Irish women's history, I am aware of the magnitude of this painstaking reconstruction of Brigid's life, the hours of recording and interviewing, and the difficulty of contextualising of this material into an engaging narrative that takes the reader from the final years of the nineteenth century to the 1940s and beyond, charting this often complex historical period with its multitude of events. This book will be of benefit to social, political and medical historians as well as the general reader.

Brigid Lyons Thornton has been previously mention in books dealing with the history of the Revolutionary period; indeed I included her in my book on Irish women political activists 1900-1923 *No Ordinary Women*. I used the available published sources but now this full record of her life is available and her contribution can be fully assessed.

Sometimes the subject of the biography is not at the epicentre of historic events – not so with Brigid. She was active in the area of the greatest fight at the Four Courts in 1916, she took part in electioneering in 1917 when her Uncle Joe MacGuinness was voted into parliament and she was a key member of the silent army of women who made possible the guerrilla war that became known as the War of Independence. She was one of Michael Collins' most trusted couriers. Supporting the Treaty, she was a medical officer when her former comrades were imprisoned in Kilmainham Gaol in 1923 for their opposition to the new Irish Free State. Her observances as a female member of the Irish Free State Army are unique and her account of her meeting with her former comrades in prison gives a new perspective on the divisions in the Civil War. This book will be welcomed by scholars of this period.

*A Noontide Blazing* is first and foremost a human story. Brigid was a good storyteller; observing and recording the details of events that make you feel like you were there, she does not omit the fact that during the Rising she was referred to as 'the fat girl from the country'. Her pen portraits of W. T. Cosgrave, Michael Collins, Seán Mac Eoin and Kathleen Clarke, known to Brigid as Mrs Tom Clarke, give us new insights into the personalities of well-known activists. In her recounting of her medical career, Brigid's descriptions of the suffering and medical cures for TB are informative, but hers is no text book analysis, she gives the reader a real insight into the social stigma of the disease described as the plague of her generation. John Cowell tells us that Brigid did not talk as much of her time working as a doctor from the 1930s onwards and when I read this I was profoundly sorry – approaching the end of the book, I wanted to read more.

Reading those final pages, I was travelling on a train from Mayo to Dublin and glancing up, noted I was passing through Foxford, I smiled as I read that she was buried nearby. I call it historical serendipity when the lives of those in the past touch, even fleetingly, those in the present. I hope this book will touch you as it has touched me.

Sinéad McCoole,
February 2005

# INTRODUCTION

IN THE SECOND and third decades of the twentieth century, Ireland was still very much a man's world. Her heroes, of course, she lauded, but her heroines were given scant consideration. On that April day in 1916, when a patriotic bunch of men in cloth caps and trilbies wheeled into Sackville Street (now O'Connell Street), antique rifles on their shoulders and newly burnished purpose in their hearts, a group of equally patriotic, long-skirted, long-haired women followed with only common sense in their heads — the sense that told them that men must eat and have their wounds dressed, even while they waited to die. In later years, the men of 1916 found many a niche in the Irish pantheon, but sadly the memory of the valiant deeds of the women was mostly lost in the mists of time.

This book is not a history book recounting Ireland's twentieth-century wars in pursuit of freedom. It is a tribute to a family whose members suffered greatly as active participants in those wars, yet even at the worst of times never lost their faith in the future of their country. In particular, it is a tribute to one member of that family. Nurtured in Fenianism, she graduated through Sinn Féin and Cumann na mBan to become a significant cog in the war machine known as The Movement. As a teenage medical student, Brigid Lyons first saw active service, and subsequent imprisonment, in 1916. This was to be followed by years of trials and tribulations, her eventual reward being a lengthy period of inactivity for the treatment of pulmonary tuberculosis, the plague of the time.

After an energetic life as a public health doctor, Bridgie did not take kindly to the comparative idleness of retirement. She lived at 41 Fitzwilliam Place, Dublin, while I worked for the Irish Medical Association at 10 Fitzwilliam Place. Boredom often drove her across the street for a chat. Her opening words were often, 'Did I ever tell you about?' to be followed by another exciting story of the Troubled Times. One day, I suggested that she use her new liberty to write it all down, and so preserve her experiences for posterity. On subsequent visits, I enquired as to her progress. Eventually my repeated enquiries caused irritation.

'You know well I couldn't apply myself to writing,' she said. 'And anyway, nobody'd be interested, so I'll take it to the grave with me.'

There was an air of defeat in the way she spoke. As so many of our distinguished patriots had already taken their stories to the grave, I offered to help. My offer was instantly and gladly accepted, and thus we spent many happy evenings, and many fruitful hours while I recorded Bridgie's answers to all my questions. She imparted a knowledge and understanding of the Troubled Times which I, like a lot of my generation, did not possess.

Looking back from an Ireland of freedom and opulence, the revisionists may deride the emotional intensity of nationalism as expressed and acted out by those who had suffered under colonial suppression. To say that they felt strongly about Ireland's woes would be to understate the case. Nor must feminine revisionists be critical of the form of address used for women. Brigid Lyons observed the usage of her time. No diminishment of a woman's standing was intended by linking her name with that of her husband. Most liked it that way. Mrs Tom Clarke, for instance, preferred it, as indeed did people like Mrs Henry Wood, the popular novelist.

Although she held the strongest possible political views Dr Brigid Lyons Thornton was never a politician. Her views were black or white, with no grey areas. She took the pro-Treaty side in 1922, and thereafter served as the first-ever female commissioned officer in the Irish Army. Thus she served her country in war and peace.

Personally, I look back with a modicum of pride to that day when

I encouraged Bridgie to get her story down on paper. I hope there may be readers somewhere who will agree that it was worthwhile.

One point that needs to be made here is in relation to the spelling of her name. She is recorded in other publications as Brighid Lyons Thornton. However, in her dealings with me, she invariably spelt her first name as Brigid. This is the form I have used here.

# 1

# A FENIAN FATHER

ON A MAY day in 1917, an upper window of the Longford courthouse was thrown open. A man appeared. Excited, he tried to speak. He raised his voice. He shouted, but still his words were lost in the clamour of the crowd jamming the main street. They had waited through long, tense hours. Now they were too emotionally overcome even to listen. Reaching out, the man unfurled a tricolour. He had no further need of speech.

In reply, Longford's Main Street became a human tide, a heaving swell of green, white and orange. Exultant whoops topped the tumult to greet the successful result of Ireland's first Republican by-election.

It had been a cliffhanger from the start: an unwilling prisoner-candidate still languishing in a British jail, the first-ever candidate to dare stand against the British abhorrence of an Irish Republic. Even a recount had been necessary, adding to the already unbearable hours of tension. But the result was to have an impact so great it changed the course of Anglo-Irish history. The first Irish Republican MP had been elected to Westminster, and it had been achieved by a majority of thirty-seven votes.

Longford erupted in an orgy of jubilation. Rebel songs were sung and bonfires blazed on the hills. Tricolours appeared at every vantage point. In their joy and disbelief, the happy throng lingered into that mild May night — one to be remembered, like the night of The Big Wind. The significance of the occasion was clear: 1917, the year of

15

Ireland's hopeless gloom, had suddenly given way to the first great clarion call in Ireland's post-1916 resurgence.

The shock of the Longford by-election reverberated through the British press. Questions were asked. How could this have happened in the light of the Government's Irish policy? Where had been the might of the British forces in Ireland? Questions continued to be asked. Questions are asked to this day.

Many had helped the 'jail-bird' candidate, reluctant Joe McGuinness, to become a member of the Mother of Parliaments. But somewhere in that crowd in the Main Street of Longford, there were two young people who had helped, each in a peculiarly special way. Time was to prove them special people. In their different ways, each was deeply dedicated to 'The Cause'. In Longford, they had collaborated politically. In the future, their lives would cross again when each was even more intensely preoccupied with the fight for Irish freedom.

The first was a young man of twenty-five. It had been the unshakable decision of Michael Collins that had resulted in the reluctant prisoner becoming Longford's most famous candidate. It was Collins' first great political decision, turning the tide of Irish history.

The second was a teenage girl, a medical student called Brigid Lyons who, as a woman, lived before her time. After weeks of intensive campaigning, her first reaction to the news of success was to run to the nearest post office to dispatch a tart telegram to Lloyd George telling him that Ireland had now given him his answer.

To Collins, Joe McGuinness was a soldier of the Republic proclaimed in 1916. He was a Republican prisoner of war in a British jail, so his election in 1917 would represent a political achievement of incalculable measure. By ignoring his political elders, and by determinedly sticking to his own decision to nominate McGuinness, Collins first marked himself as the pragmatist he was to remain.

With Brigid Lyons, the motives were different. The new MP happened to be her uncle. But, more importantly, to the teenager he was the embodiment of everything an Irish patriot should be. Of the many influences which had shaped her nationalism, none had been greater than that of her Uncle Joe. Not that his task had been difficult.

She was an apt pupil, having come of Fenian stock. She was long familiar with Ireland's woes, for the seeds of her patriotism had been sown as a small child.

Born in Northyard, Scramogue, Co Roscommon, Brigid was the eldest child of Patrick Lyons, a farmer and a lifelong Fenian. Her memory of him reflected the frustrated Irishman of his time. Reserved, he was methodical and he never drank. Apart from his pipe, he had one indulgence: his horses. He kept brood mares and their progeny won him prizes.

Pat Lyons should have been an average citizen of a normal country, earning his living from the land, enjoying the good life, content in the happy embrace of a wife and family. But the conquest of Ireland had made Ireland different, had made Irishmen different. Centuries of oppression had imposed a sort of mass dichotomy. Many Irish boys grew to manhood accepting they had two lives to lead: the one, by day, that earned them a livelihood; the other, by night, plotting and planning, sooner or later, to rid their country of the conqueror.

Pat grew up in the darkened shadows of a land laid waste by famine. At the age of seventeen, he was one of the thousands of Fenians who waited for the call from James Stephens for the rising of 1867. And when that call came — for 5 March — Pat Lyons watched the first flurry of snowflakes that heralded twelve days and nights of one of the greatest snowstorms ever known in Ireland. An Act of God, some called it. Others said the Devil was at work.

Like his neighbours, Pat Lyons fought in the Land War. He was arrested and imprisoned. One of Brigid's earliest memories was of listening to her father talking to Barney Dolan, who lived beside the local church, about their prison days in Sligo Jail. His most treasured possession was his Land League membership card. Coloured green, it had a picture of Robert Emmett on it. Around his head were emblazoned the words 'Who fears to speak of 98?'

In the 1880s, a brightening star shed a new light, bringing a guarded hope that some measure of freedom might be at hand, this time by constitutional methods. In the driving wind and the soaking rain, Pat Lyons travelled tiresome miles in pursuit of the buoyancy —

the conviction — that flowed from the speeches of Charles Stuart Parnell. But by 1890, that once-bright star was flickering, the hero discredited by the bishops of Ireland for his love of a married woman. By 1891, death had taken Parnell, and Ireland was in mourning again.

Marriage should have brought a compensating happiness to Pat Lyons. And so it did — for four brief years. Pat had always been a lonely man. Destiny, it seemed, had meant it that way. At the birth of her third child, his wife died suddenly, and Pat was alone again, a widower with three small children.

In Brigid's memory of those November days, sadness predominates — her mother's hands, white and cold as stone, with rosary beads glinting in the candlelight; Uncle Frank on his knees, proving that even strong men wept; people, known and unknown, coming and going. And when all the fuss was over, there was no mother any more. Even the new baby had gone — taken by an aunt with whom she grew up, never knowing her father as her father, but only as Uncle Pat. Annie Lyons, Pat's sister, came to live with him, and cared for his children with a unique devotion. There was never need for stricture, unless it was for overindulgence.

At the age of five, Brigid went to Northyard National School. The short way was across the fields. In summer, she made daisy chains and picked honeysuckle. In winter, there might be snowballing, but that was horseplay for boys. Soon, she led her young brother along the same path. By then, she was a 'senior infant', already showing an unusual curiosity about everything. With a teacher's observation, James O'Dowd had noticed.

Brigid Lyons felt little debt to her reserved father for her lifelong sense of patriotism. He talked little of whatever he may have done for Ireland. It was to James O'Dowd, her first teacher, and later to her Uncle Frank, that she attributed her awakening to all that Ireland was to mean to her.

Senior girls learned Irish voluntarily. Always ambitious where learning was concerned, little Brigid Lyons begged to be included. In yielding to her wishes, her teacher could hardly have foreseen the results. At the Strokestown Feis, she won the most coveted prize, that for spoken Irish. She displayed the same facility in other school subjects, and James O'Dowd continued his encouragement. Where her learning might lead was never discussed. But to her the answer was clear. She wanted to be a teacher because teachers knew everything.

However, on the day when Miss Parr, the beautiful domestic economy instructress, came to Northyard School, Brigid Lyons' ambition became more focused. Hugging herself in a corner, she told herself, 'That's what I'd like to be — not an ordinary teacher, but a special teacher like Miss Parr.'

Brigid confided her secret to her aunt. Her father was remote and aloof — she sensed his loneliness. For her he seemed always to move in an air of sadness. 'Don't mind him,' Aunt Annie would say of her brother. 'He thinks more of his horses than he does of us.' Sadly, Pat Lyons was one of nature's strong, silent men. However, Brigid could talk to Aunt Annie — tell her all the exciting things that happened in school.

Brigid was nine when, recognising her potential, Frank McGuinness and his wife, Kate, approached her father. They were childless, they were well off, and they could give her an education matching her promise. She loved her Uncle Frank. His nationalism fascinated her. True, he didn't speak Irish, but she assumed you could still do a lot for Ireland, even if you could do it only in English. The prospect he opened up was too exciting to think about.

However, when she looked at her father, and at Aunt Annie, a sense of disloyalty struck Brigid. There was that look again — her father's look of suppressed sadness. And now she was about to add to his silent misery. But Pat Lyons, the man of few words, spoke unequivocally that day. 'I won't stand in Bridgie's way,' he asserted, and that was that. Whatever his private feelings, the decision was made. Life for the future was to be mainly a matter of moving on. For the rest of her childhood, apart from short visits, Brigid Lyons was to see little of her father or her brother or of Northyard, Scramogue, County Roscommon.

# 2

# BANDS AND BUSBIES

IN 1905, LONGFORD was a British garrison town. It had all the colourful contrasts to fascinate a child. A main street filled with big shops, two of the biggest being those of Uncle Frank McGuinness, over one of which Brigid now lived. For her it was the outstanding building, for spread across its front was the name of its proprietor. On market day, Longford awoke early. By seven, it was filled with farmers with whinnying horses and cartloads of squealing pigs. The farmers would celebrate on the strength of their sales, and some would get so drunk, it was often the horse that found the way home.

Sunday mornings brought a different kind of excitement. From an upstairs window, Brigid would watch the British Army's church parade. First she would hear the music. Then the parade would come swinging out of the barracks at the north end of the town. It would pass up the Main Street, led by a military band. All those colourful uniforms — blue and silver and red — and the precision of the marching fascinated her. But the busbies beat all, making those tall soldiers look like creatures in a picture book — half-bear, half-man.

Brigid couldn't understand why the grown-ups were so disinterested in all this colour and spectacle. Her uncle explained that it was an army of occupation; he spoke of them not being 'our people'. They were our conquerors, he said, the ascendancy. Brigid wasn't sure what all that meant, but she accepted Uncle Frank's explanation because, as far as she was concerned, what he said was always right.

Uncle Frank was a jolly, happy man and told his stories with gusto. He liked a drink and had a reputation for chivalry: he danced with every wallflower. Aunt Kate, his wife, was his opposite: religious and retiring, she abhorred everything to do with drink. Because they had no children, they filled their house with 'adoptions'. As well as Brigid Lyons, there was Rose McGuinness, a brother's child, whom they educated. Later, there were Maureen, Bríd and Peg, daughters of Frank's brother Tom, who had died leaving ten children. Nurtured in the patriotism of Frank and Kate McGuinness, all of these girls distinguished themselves in the National Movement.

Aunt Kate was known as Aunt Frank; because there were three Aunt Kates in the family, each was known by her husband's name. Aunt Frank hadn't always been a nationalist, but having married Frank McGuinness, she had had little choice in the matter. She was the stabilising influence. Her husband's political interests ranged widely — too widely she sometimes thought for the good of his business. He was Chairman of the Urban District Council, Chairman of the County Council, and a Justice of the Peace. Then there were his political activities. He supported John Redmond and the Irish Parliamentary Party, and believed in the coming of Home Rule. Although he couldn't speak the language himself, he inspired Aunt Frank to learn Irish. Her sympathies for the Nationalist Movement grew, and her place in the Main Street was to become an open house for those who worked for Ireland.

To Brigid Lyons, the convent school was an immense institution. The classes too were huge. Any other child might well have lost her identity in the crowd. Not so with Brigid. Her proficiency in Irish had marked her out. Habitually, she was top of that class. Her ambition was to be top of every class, but as that was not possible, she set her sights on one other. Christian Doctrine was encouraged by the award of a holy picture to the girl who was best. Brigid was upset on the rare occasion when she went home without a holy picture. Her ambition was always to be at the head of the class.

There were some 'British' children in the school, children of the local garrison. They spoke with what were called 'superior accents'. While there was no obvious resentment, neither was there fraternising.

0046526l.
LIMERICK
COUNTY LIBRARY

The girls never met outside school. The English girls played tennis, never camogie. In fact, the 'barracks people' kept themselves to themselves, with little social intercourse with the locals. The officer class, of course, mingled with the local gentry, but Brigid saw nothing of that side of life. She belonged to 'business', and Longford observed its own social code.

Her inquisitive nature didn't stop at school subjects. There were the newspapers. Brigid began to read odd bits and pieces. Sometimes they were about things of which she'd heard people talking: what John Redmond had said in the House of Commons; the respectable people who were getting themselves arrested for cattle-driving; and then the excitement in 1910 when two general elections came in quick succession, each with Home Rule in its programme. The Liberals were returned, with the Irish Party holding the balance of power. John Redmond summed it up: 'This is not only a Home Rule election, but *the* great Home Rule election.' Uncle Frank became wildly excited. Brigid asked what it all meant, and he explained: our own parliament in Dublin; our own police; our own civil service; the freedom of Ireland at last.

The young Brigid hesitated. Would we have our own king? Uncle Frank didn't immediately attempt to unravel that one. Her interest in kings and queens, while a little contradictory, was understandable. Those gorgeous pictures in the papers: Queen Alexandra, tall and elegant and beautiful, with a tight little wasp-waist and great big hats as big as cartwheels. She wondered whether the queen ever ate plain bread, or whether it would always be rich cake. And did she wear a crown of diamonds all day long? Or was it a tiara? She ventured to enquire of Uncle Frank, but he grew tetchy at this wanton interest in royalty. The royals were, he explained with some emphasis, like ordinary human beings. She thought she knew what he meant, but it was very disappointing. She had imagined that a king and queen would be different. She had had a soft spot for them, especially for Queen Alexandra's hats. However, it was clear that Uncle Frank disapproved thoroughly. But then, Uncle Frank was even a spoilsport over Lady Longford's party.

It was a tradition in the convent school that, once a year, Lord and

Lady Longford drove in a coach from Castlepollard and gave the pupils a slap-up celebration. Preparations began weeks beforehand, including the nuns' admonishments that the girls behave well because this was the only school so favoured by the Longfords. Classes were suspended, party dresses came out, and there were gallons of tea and mounds of biscuits. Lady Longford gave the head girls presents of workboxes. When she left school, Brigid had four, one for each year.

However, Uncle Frank's attitude to the Longfords' party was just like when he told her about the royals. It mystified her. When she was all dressed up and ready for off he'd begin to sneer. 'Going to the party again?' he'd enquire, knowing well where she was going. A party was a party and a gift was a gift. 'It's a disgrace,' he'd say, 'taking presents from the gentry.'

These adult attitudes confused her. There was another occasion when Uncle Frank became furious. On the death of King Edward VII in 1910, the nuns closed the school. When Brigid arrived home, her uncle fumed because the nuns had shown such respect to an English king. A free day was a free day, though, as far as Brigid was concerned, and she thought Uncle Frank unreasonable.

However, it made her think. Uncle Frank read the *Leader* and the *Independent* and the *Freeman's Journal*. He must know what one should and should not do if one wanted to be a nationalist like him. He talked about Sinn Féin and Arthur Griffith and the Abbey Theatre, and while she didn't understand these things, she was prepared to believe that Uncle Frank was probably right in his attitude. Shortly she was to redress the situation, regaining her uncle's approval. Lord Longford sent a consignment of memorial cards for King Edward, asking the nuns to distribute them. Now, a holy picture was a holy picture, but Brigid Lyons refused to accept a royal memorial card. She walked home proudly and proudly informed Uncle Frank. Who is to know whether in that moment Frank McGuinness recognised another Irish rebel in the making?

Meanwhile, Uncle Joe McGuinness, Frank's younger brother, had returned to Longford after many years in the United States where he had worked with John Devoy and Joe McGarrity. He surprised everybody because he hadn't acquired an American accent. In fact, he had been an organiser of Gaelic activities in New York and had learnt fluent Irish there. As a patriot, he quite eclipsed Uncle Frank. They often disagreed on what was best for Ireland. Frank was a constitutionalist, a Redmond man, a Home Ruler. Joe was a separatist, extremely anti-British, and spoke Irish whenever possible. Brigid thought him an ideal patriot. He was a Republican and the first man she heard use the expression: 'Break the connection with England.'

In looks, Joe McGuinness was tall, dark and handsome — every girl's dream. In time, he became known as 'the husband of Cumann na mBan.' He was a boyish extrovert who sang and danced and played the fiddle. His tunes were traditional and his songs ranged from 'The Rattling Bog' to 'The Darlin' Girl from Clare'. In Longford they used to say 'Joe's great at a party', and there was no better tribute to a man's popularity. In New York too, he had been the darlin' boy of the Irish colony. To prove it, he came home sporting an inscribed gold watch, presented in recognition of his services to the Gaelic League.

Longford was soon to see the results of Joe McGuinness' ideas in making Ireland Gaelic again. With Tom Bannon, a local teacher, he organised a branch of the Gaelic League. The separatist movement was actively aided by Irish women, notably Maud Gonne and the members of Inghínidhe na hÉireann — the Daughters of Ireland — a society she had founded in 1900. Uncle Joe established a branch in Longford. He was also responsible for having the banner in English across the front of the family business painted out and replaced in Irish. It was still to be seen in recent years as you approached Longford Main Street from the Dublin Road.

Brigid developed tremendous admiration for her Uncle Joe. He was more like a big brother than an uncle, and his separatist ideas attracted her. 'Break the connection with England.' It seemed more practical, more positive, than waiting indefinitely, like Uncle Frank and John Redmond, for a measure of Home Rule, if and when Asquith thought well of giving it. Brigid was bitterly disappointed when Uncle Joe decided to leave Longford to live in Dublin. With his new wife (another Aunt Kate who had to be known as Aunt Joe), he opened a business in Camden Street. Although she couldn't know it at the time, it was to be *au revoir*, and not *adieu*.

As in the rest of the country, the land agitation in Co Longford continued. For generations, the large properties had been owned by Protestants, many of them absentee landlords living in England, while among Catholics, there was a land hunger which no Act of Parliament had sufficed to appease. The aim of the agitators was to have the large ranch-like farms divided to provide economic holdings for local small farmers. Their demand for land was part and parcel of their demand for Home Rule, or for the complete independence of Ireland. The form which the land agitation demonstrations took varied — from public meetings, with brass bands, torchlight processions and placards, to what was known as cattle-driving. Cattle were driven from the ranches on to the roads, and the gates closed behind them. It was a gesture, but it caused confusion for the owners. The catch-cry became 'The land for the people; the road for the bullocks.'

Otherwise respectable citizens lent their support, sometimes actively, some indeed managing to get themselves arrested and prosecuted. But there was no disgrace. It was part of nationalist expression. J. P. Farrell, a local MP who represented Longford for the Irish Parliamentary Party at Westminster, was a friend of Uncle Frank's and had been responsible for his appointment as a Justice of the Peace. Both men supported the land agitation.

Local indignation was inflamed when Farrell was arrested and committed to Kilmainham Gaol. Uncle Frank's passions were greatly aroused, and at public meetings, he spoke out more forcefully than ever. As a tribute, local brass bands played outside his house. Frank McGuinness was becoming a force in the political life of Longford.

In 1912, a new era in Irish history commenced. In April, Asquith prepared to introduce his third Home Rule Bill. Strategically, the political position of the Irish Parliamentary Party in the house could not have been better. The Liberal Government had been returned, pledged to establish Home Rule. Redmond was optimistic as never before, for in holding the balance of power, he appeared to dominate the British political machine.

On 31 March, two weeks before the introduction of the Bill, a mass meeting took place in Sackville Street, Dublin. On the platform, two of the three wings of prevailing Irish public opinion were represented. For the Home Rulers, John Redmond spoke of the victory now so close at hand. Patrick Pearse for the separatists said: 'There are two sections of us — one that would be content to remain under the British Government in our own land, another that never paid, and never will pay, homage to the King of England.' The absent wing that day was the representative of the Loyal Ulster Orangemen. The intensity of the opposition against Home Rule which was then gathering in Belfast had been underestimated.

From 11 April, when Asquith introduced his Government of Ireland Bill, Edward Carson in Ulster intensified his campaign against the measure. 'Home Rule Means Rome Rule' became the battle-cry. In a flurry of Union Jacks and Bibles, Carson threatened that a mandate for Home Rule would be the signal for civil war. Asquith called this speech 'a declaration of war against constitutional government'. It 'furnished forth the complete grammar of anarchy'. But Asquith took no action against the anarchists. The British Government quailed at the threat of the Ulster Protestant backlash. The Home Rule Bill was rejected by the House of Commons.

The sellout in the face of the threats of Carson's Belfast bully boys brought immeasurable unrest to Ireland. Emotions ranged from bitter disappointment to a hardening of the resolve to make a complete break with England. The land agitation intensified and, in Longford, Frank McGuinness gave it his full and active support. In time, he was arrested on a charge of cattle-driving, and was taken away to prison. The event threw a dark shadow over his household. However, short of there being any indignity involved, to Brigid Lyons her uncle had become a hero. If every man were to do as much, Ireland would not always be in subjection — thus did she rationalise her first experience of seeing a relative taken away by the police.

Frank McGuinness was taken to Arklow for his trial. Back in Longford, the event held tremendous interest. Tension mounted as people waited to hear the verdict. With others on the same charge, he was acquitted. The night he returned to Longford, the town was ablaze with light. Lamps and candles shone in every window. In their triumph, the people made it a great occasion. The brass bands came out in force. Shoulder high, Frank McGuinness was escorted into the

Main Street by a torchlight procession — oil-soaked turf sods hoisted high on the prongs of pitchforks. Ireland was marching again. Ireland would never cease to march until England learned to have done with injustice.

At an open window, high above the surging crowd, Brigid listened to her uncle's speech, part of it drowned out again and again by the cheers. She feared he might be re-arrested, but he wasn't — not that night. With hindsight, she realised that the emotional experience of that night was another milestone on her own road to patriotism.

# 3

# SLIGO'S SCHOOL FRENCH

IN THE AUTUMN of 1911, Brigid became a boarder at the Ursuline Convent, Sligo. Of the daughters of St Ursula, Archdeacon O'Rourke, the Sligo historian, had said that they inculcated 'elevation of character, goodness of heart and grace of manner'. He had not mentioned patriotism. Nevertheless, the Ursuline convent was to throw up another powerful influence for a girl in search of an identity. Though Brigid's interest in teaching had waned, her interest in nationalism had grown. Small wonder, given the turbulent McGuinness background from which she came. But nationalism could not be a career. She hardly allowed herself to dream her truly cherished dream: she wanted to be a doctor. The idea had always lurked somewhere in her mind, but everything was against her: the strenuous study, the prohibitive cost, the bias against women. So, she had always smothered her dream.

There was nothing cloistered about life at the Ursuline convent. Brigid remembered it as the best years of her life. Amongst the excellent teachers, there was one with whom she formed an instant rapport. Mother Scholastica (Beatrice Dolan) was a woman of breadth and vision who never pushed the religious side of her vocation. Nor did she expect her girls to circulate on silent pads with haloes floating above them. She was as practical as she was frank. She told the girls they would be wives some day — and mothers; they would be privileged to hear children cry, and even more privileged to hear their laughter. In the meantime, her French, her Irish, and her mathematics were taught without tears. Not surprisingly, Mother Scholastica never lost touch with her past-pupils. She kept up a lifelong and ever-growing correspondence. 'That in itself is an apostolate,' she used to say.

Nor did she permit affairs in the outside world to pass her by, particularly those affecting Ireland. She communicated them and discussed them with her girls. That was necessary, she considered, for the preparation of future citizens. But it was when she discussed what she called 'The Irish Cause' that Mother Scholastica's enthusiasm burned even more brightly. In her path to a life devoted to nationalism, Brigid Lyons was destined to meet another influential mentor.

Increasing hours of study brought eyesight difficulties. During a school holiday, Brigid attended the Royal Victoria Eye and Ear Hospital in Dublin. She stayed with Uncle Joe and his wife. A shy person, Aunt Joe was lovable and generous, and very interested in fashion. But this never distracted her from her work for Ireland. She would have made a good mother, but alas, like Aunt Frank, she had no children. A founder-member of Cumann na mBan, the women's auxiliary force to the Irish Volunteers, Aunt Joe trained girls in semaphore and first-aid. She was an intimate friend of Mrs Tom Clarke, wife of the Fenian who had suffered fifteen years' imprisonment.

The McGuinness Dublin home was open and hospitable. In the evenings, there were many callers. Brigid met people with names she had often heard and had sometimes seen in the newspapers, among them Seán T. O'Kelly, Martin Conlon, Diarmuid Lynch and Michael Hayes, afterwards Professor of Irish at University College Dublin, and the first Ceann Comhairle in Dáil Éireann. The talk was always about Ireland, politics, the language and, of course, Sinn Féin and Arthur Griffith. Through it all ran an obvious hatred of British domination. The conversation was often punctuated by Uncle Joe's favourite expression: 'Break the connection with England.' Most of what she heard, Brigid did not understand, but she listened with growing interest. Some day, she hoped, the jigsaw might fit together.

Sinn Féin, for instance. What did it represent? And who exactly was Arthur Griffith? True, he was a pal of Uncle Joe's, but did that mean he also stood for breaking the connection with England? They all talked incessantly, but nobody ever stopped to explain. It was Mother Scholastica who came to the rescue. She it was who patiently sorted out the ravelled skeins of Ireland's woes for a confused pupil. The result was that every time young Miss Lyons returned to Longford, she was better able to converse on politics. She was even learning to contradict.

Mother Scholastica's faith was pinned on the Irish Volunteers. Founded in 1913, they were Eoin MacNeill's response to Carson's Ulster Volunteers who were arming to fight Home Rule. Mother Scholastica was not alone in her faith. The Volunteer movement had swept the country. Men of all ages rallied by the thousand and drilling was in progress everywhere.

On her next holiday, Brigid went to see her father. He was not at home — Brigid found the old Fenian drilling with the local Volunteers outside Scramogue chapel. Their commanding officer was the new teacher. Uncle Joe, of course, had joined at the famous Rotunda meeting. Uncle Frank was still a constitutionalist.

About that time, Brigid sounded out Uncle Frank about her dream of becoming a doctor. She got nowhere. The notion was pooh-poohed — indeed, it was stubbornly opposed. Women doctors! Who in their senses would go to a woman doctor? But nobody mentioned the expense — the one obstacle which stood between Brigid Lyons and her cherished dream. Uncle Frank had written her off, and, in any case, he was preoccupied with events of the time. The year was 1914.

In March, there was the Curragh Mutiny when Brigadier Hubert Gough and fifty-seven members of the British Army refused to enforce Home Rule in Ulster. They would accept dismissal rather than march on Belfast to call the bluff of Edward Carson and his armed Orangemen. Carson was still flagrantly defying the British Government, to which, at the same time, the Ulster Protestants claimed to give their loyalty. 'Drilling is illegal,' Carson said in Newry. 'The Volunteers are illegal and the Government know they are illegal, and the Government dare not interfere with them… Don't be afraid of illegalities,' he counselled the people of Ulster. And still the British Government wavered under the threat of the Ulster Protestant backlash.

On 24 April 1914, an illegal consignment of 35,000 German Mauser rifles and two-and-a-half million rounds of ammunition were landed in Bangor, Donaghadee and Larne to supplement the arming of the Ulster Volunteers against Home Rule. The police did not interfere, the Royal Navy looked the other way and, though Carson stated publicly that he took full responsibility for the enterprise, London remained silent. These events intensified the resolve of people like Uncle Frank and Uncle Joe and their friends. Carson's challenge must be met, if not by the British Government, then by Ireland herself. In many minds, plans began to evolve for the arming of the National Volunteers.

The final reading of the Home Rule Bill was moved in the House of Commons on 25 May. In the meantime, to appease Carson, the Government had introduced an amending bill to exclude Ulster from the operation of Home Rule. Carson's latest threat hung in the air: 'The day I shall like best is the day upon which I am compelled, if I am compelled, to tell my men, "You must mobilise".'

Dorothy Macardle summarised the situation thus:

Asquith had pledged himself to Home Rule for Ireland — not for three provinces of Ireland. He had also pledged himself to the Amending Bill. A complete deadlock had been contrived. Home Rule, as Carson boasted a few months later, had been rendered a nullity.

Mother Scholastica burned as heatedly in her frustrated indignation as did her patriot pupil. The idea of the division of Ireland was as unthinkable as it was abhorrent. But meantime, life had to go on. Too much attention to the monstrous cavorting of pigheaded politicians would not help a girl's examination results. Occasionally, however, the drudgery had its romantic compensations.

Pigeon O'Connell's family lived in Finisklin, close to the Ursuline convent. Pigeon had lovely auburn hair, but, more interestingly, she had a tall he-man brother called Ginger who also had patriotic notions. Brigid listened to what Pigeon had to tell about brother Ginger's capers. He had been to the United States, for instance, and now he was strongly pro-German and anti-English. To Brigid, being anti-English made sense … but pro-German? That was a new idea. In later years, Brigid Lyons came to know Ginger O'Connell very well. As General J. J. O'Connell, Deputy Chief of Staff to Michael Collins, he was kidnapped by Rory O'Connor's Four Courts men in June 1922. That kidnap helped to trigger the bombardment of the Four Courts and the outbreak of the Civil War.

In the summer of 1914, Brigid had another holiday in Dublin with Uncle and Aunt Joe. Both were very busy. Joseph McGuinness was an officer in the National Volunteers. Camps were being organised in the country, and strategy and tactics were being studied. With her comrades, Aunt Joe was busy perfecting the organisation of Cumann na mBan, preparing for ambulance work and to organise food supplies and equipment.

One June afternoon, Aunt Joe decided to take a few hours off. With Brigid, she set out for Howth. On the return journey, as the tram trundled along the shore of Dublin Bay, they heard the cries of the newsboys. A Stop Press announced that Archduke Franz Ferdinand of Austria had been assassinated in Sarajevo. Who was Franz Ferdinand anyway? And why all the commotion? Such were the immediate reactions of two women, sun-soaked and intoxicated with fresh sea air. In the streets of Dublin, there was an air of confusion. Some showed tension — those who thought they could foresee dire consequences from the assassination. But for most, the news was just another bit of foreign 'gas'. However, that night, Uncle Joe's callers had other ideas. If Austria declared war on the Balkans and if Germany mobilised, Britain would be in difficulty. They had no need to go further. Brigid understood. Every Irish schoolchild understood: England's difficulty was Ireland's opportunity. Brigid went to bed that night tired and confused — but her mind was still tugging at those theories thrown out by Uncle Joe's visitors.

She was back in Longford when, a month later, Irish men and Irish women boldly wrote another glowing page for the history books. The real thrill was the women's part in this great adventure. Erskine Childers, with his wife and the Hon. Mary Spring-Rice and Gordon Shepard, had landed 900 Mauser rifles and 29,000 rounds of ammunition from his yacht, *Asgard*, at Howth. Here was the answer to

Carson! But there was more to come, thanks to yachting enthusiasts like Conor O'Brien with his *Kelpe* and Sir Thomas Myles, a surgeon at the Richmond Hospital, with his *Chotah*. Although the landing was carried out safely, that Sunday ended in tragedy. The success of the manoeuvre made Dublin over-exuberant. That evening, a contingent of Scottish soldiers was hooted at and stoned at Bachelor's Walk. In reply, they fired on the jeering crowd. Thirty-two civilians were wounded and three shot dead.

The people of Longford besieged the railway station in search of news from Dublin. In the McGuinness household, it was assumed that Uncle Joe would have been with the Volunteers at Howth. He had been. He recounted later that apart from a few officers, the Volunteers ordered out that day knew nothing of what was afoot. To them, it was a routine Sunday march under the command of Cathal Brugha. Alongside his friend, Arthur Griffith, Joseph McGuinness marched, neither with any knowledge of the plan, which had been carefully arranged by Thomas MacDonagh and Bulmer Hobson.

Ten days later, Longford railway station was besieged again by a population hungry for news. Even if a newspaper could not be got, the guard on the Dublin train might have some information. The reason for the clamour for information? The First World War had begun.

On 4 August 1914, Britain — and that meant Ireland too — had declared war on Germany. Carson promised the support of the Unionist Party. John Redmond, too full of gratitude for the carrot of Home Rule, assured the Government it might with confidence withdraw its troops from Ireland: the National Volunteers would co-operate with the Unionists in protecting the Irish coasts. Six weeks later, on 18 September, the Home Rule Bill received the Royal Assent and went on the statute book, but its operation was frozen indefinitely by a suspensory Act passed on the same date. In so doing, the British Government had shirked a confrontation with Ulster Unionism.

In the days and weeks ahead, Brigid Lyons, like all young people of the time, was to continue, as Roger Casement put it, 'climbing the painful stairs of Irish history'. There were sharp divisions of opinion. On the one side, she heard sharp bitterness expressed against the British disposal of Home Rule, and against Redmond too for his servile offer of Irish help to Britain in her fight against Germany. On the other hand, she heard those, often called West-British patriots, who cried out about German atrocities and little Belgium, and women and children refugees fleeing through Flanders before the cruel Hun. In this turmoil of bitterly divided opinion, she was confused again. There was a crisis of conscience. Who was right and who wrong? Should she be sorry or glad now that England was in trouble?

Meantime, Longford had become a place of mass movement, like a sleepy ant-hill stirred into stinging activity. Trains left for Dublin packed with British troops bound for the expeditionary forces going to France. More troops arrived to replace them, for whatever difficulties the Huns might present, the British process of civilising the Irish must not be interrupted.

In the first surge of emotionalism ('the war to end wars'), huge numbers of Irish men rushed off to enlist in the British Army. Longford had long been a garrison town, and with little gainful employment about, there was a local tradition of fathers and sons joining the British militia. Longford's former British soldiers were always easily recognisable about the town, if only by their military bearing and their closely-shaven heads. Their wives had a reputation in some quarters of indulging in drunken binges and noisy rows when the British 'separation money' or the disability pension arrived.

As Brigid Lyons waited at Longford station for her train to Sligo, the strains of a mouth organ came from the opposite platform: 'Pack up your troubles in your old kit-bag and smile, smile, smile.' Khaki-clad soldiers — English, Irish, Scottish and Welsh, laden with rifles and greatcoats and tin mugs and kit, were waiting impatiently to be borne off to do their bit for the Empire. They were in a hurry, for, after all, the bloody war was going to be over by Christmas.

Brigid remembered again the theories she'd overheard from Uncle Joe's callers. What sense could a body make of it all?

# 4

# A PLACE OF PEACE

FOR ALL THE excitements of the summer months, Brigid found the Ursuline Convent still hedged around in its contradictions of timetables and tranquillity. The great trees on the front lawns had turned to russet. The cross on the high-peaked roof was still etched against the sky, and the daisies in the fields around Finisklin were less by millions than when she'd gone home in June.

She was back for her final year as a schoolgirl. Mother Scholastica spoke about careers and about ambition. A girl must be no less ambitious because she was a girl. There was nothing in life a woman could not do if she put her mind to it. She instanced some past pupils and their achievements. There was an immense rustle as one hundred girls turned over new leaves in answer to Mother Scholastica's clarion call. Everybody was going to be a credit to the school. This applied doubly to senior girls.

Brigid allowed herself that wild dream again. A girl could at least aspire to a career in medicine. Perhaps she might even become famous — discover some new and amazing cure, like Madame Curie; or go on the missions and give her life to the lepers; or maybe just bandage up wounded Volunteers when Uncle Joe's friends decided to rise against hated England. In a dazzling flash, she could see her photograph going up in the Ursuline Hall of Fame. In fact, the Hall of Fame was just a corridor where the nuns hung photographs of distinguished past pupils — suffragettes, for instance, like Katty Keane from Galway, who had had the courage to sling a brick through a window at Number 10 Downing Street.

If there were nothing in her way — if the choice were hers alone — Brigid Lyons would be a doctor. The practice of medicine was to her the very highest aspiration. But how would she go about it? She confronted the nun who had talked about ambition.

'But, Brigid, child, no Ursuline girl has ever yet gone for medicine,' was the response.

'Somebody must be the first,' Brigid said.

'And what about your relatives? What do they think?'

'They're opposed. They think women doctors couldn't be any good.'

That roused the suffragette in Mother Scholastica. 'That's not the point,' she said. 'Of course there's a place for women doctors. If your ambition is strong enough, you'll be a doctor, don't worry.'

That was the first encouragement Brigid had received. As always, Mother Scholastica had understood. A scholarship to the university would make her independent. After that, it would be up to herself. There and then, it was agreed: she would enter for a county council scholarship — provided by a halfpenny in the pound levied on the rates. Now her studies would have point and purpose. Life held exciting prospects.

Nonetheless, progress was interrupted periodically by the latest from the outside world. A sensation broke, for instance, on 20 September 1914, when Redmond, intent it seemed on political suicide, made his fatal speech to a parade of National Volunteers at Woodenbridge, Co Wicklow. 'Go on drilling,' he told them. 'And make yourselves efficient for the work and then assert yourselves as men, not only in Ireland itself, but wherever the firing line extends in defence of right, freedom and religion in this war.'

Redmond's speech was interpreted as a request to help the British war effort. Its immediate effect was to split the Volunteers. Four days later, the Central Committee was divided and the division went right through the ranks. The Volunteers repudiated Redmond and expelled his followers who became known as Redmondites. The episode was the political end of John Redmond.

Meanwhile, Belgian refugees had arrived in Sligo. The town was doing what it could to help. Public emotion was running high about 'little Belgium' and her refugees. As a charitable gesture, rather than a war effort, the Ursuline girls helped out as interpreters, using their Sligo school French. It worked! The refugees could understand them. The plight of the refugees made a deep impression. It reflected the worst features of war: the sufferings of the innocent. Here, before her, Brigid saw mothers and children lost to their homes, husbands and fathers, and to all that life had meant to them. She was aware of a new and deep compassion — a need to serve those in need. Her work with the Belgian refugees in Sligo inspired her with an even greater desire to be a doctor — 'my highest aspiration'.

Amongst the other girls, the experience generated heated political arguments. Until then, the war had been far away. The presence of the refugees had made it a reality. Some girls had fixed ideas on nationalism — like the Grays from Drumlish who had been at St Ita's, Pearse's school in Dublin. Others were not so much pro-British as anti-German. Now the anti-German faction multiplied because of the treatment meted out to Belgium.

England was Ireland's enemy, Brigid argued. Why hate England's enemy more than England? She quoted Arthur Griffith in Sinn Féin: 'Ireland is not at war with Germany. She is not at war with any continental power. England is at war with Germany.' A schoolgirl political crisis threatened, until Mother Scholastica intervened.

'But, Brigid child, there's no reason why we should be on England's side just because of what Germany has done to Belgium. It's the old, old story. The same relationship exists between Ireland and England.'

That was it! Ireland was forced to fight in England's war although England was her only enemy. Brigid had won her first political argument. Reassured, she went home for Christmas.

Uncle and Aunt Frank weren't all that excited about the Belgian refugees and her talking French to them. They thought that talking Irish might be preferable and they hoped she wasn't beginning 'to lean the wrong way,' as they put it. She wanted to tell them they were 'stuffy' — the in-word of the time. You could care for Belgian refugees without being any less Irish. If she became a doctor, she would have to care for anyone —Belgian, English or German. But she didn't argue the point.

Brigid discovered a kindred spirit. Daisy Foley, a classmate, also had ideas of studying medicine. Her brother was a medical student, and although her father was a Sligo brewer, she too hoped to win a university scholarship. Competition would be keen.

June arrived all too soon, and with it the examination, held in Galway. Daisy Foley's mother accompanied them. On the train, they saw two ravishingly beautiful girls in picture hats. Daisy's mother thought that there must be a theatrical company in the area, but she hadn't heard of it. At the end of the journey, they lost sight of these lovely girls. Next morning, there they were, in the examination hall — still in their picture hats. They too were sitting for the halfpenny in the pound examination.

The occasion was a challenge. Brigid passed but that proved to be only the first stage on the way to the university. Next, there was an interview in Irish. She was a little fearful — not that she doubted her ability, but the name of the examiner was famous in Gaelic circles, and she had little experience of facing people who were famous. Professor Seán McHenry, Professor of Irish and a Gaelic scholar, proved to be a charming, paternal man with a sense of humour. Afterwards, she wondered why she had expected that famous people would be any different from the unknowns. She had won the day! At last, the way was open. Her highest aspiration might yet become attainable.

To Mother Scholastica of Sligo, Brigid Lyons attributed her scholarship. Apart from her teaching and her encouragement, her ability to instil ambition in her pupils was a characteristic all too rare. Brigid was never to lose touch with the nun who had been her inspiration.

With a light heart, she faced the long summer of 1915. She was back in Dublin, staying with Uncle and Aunt Joe, who were even busier — her uncle with recruitment and training of the Volunteers, and her aunt with the training and organisation of Cumann na mBan. Recruitment to the British Army was active, particularly amongst those who had taken the side of Redmond in the Volunteer split. The National Volunteers, therefore, had to face increasing competition to bring forces back to their pre-split strength.

With Aunt Joe, a top-ranking officer, Brigid began to attend the meetings of the Dublin City branch of Cumann na mBan, on Friday nights, at 25 Parnell Square. There she met many of the women who were afterwards to figure in the fight for freedom, including Dr Kathleen Lynn. With Fiona Plunkett (sister of Joseph Plunkett) and Dot and Kitty Fleming, she did a course in first-aid and semaphore. (Years later, Kitty Fleming was to help Dan Breen after the Drumcondra ambush.) Occasionally a formidable lady officer of the Citizen Army 'blew in to see we were keeping up to scratch'.

In July, the death occurred in New York of the veteran Fenian leader, Jeremiah O'Donovan Rossa. The news, stirred Irish memories. All his life, O'Donovan Rossa had stood firmly for nothing less than full independence for Ireland. Six years' penal servitude in British jails confirmed his determination to win total Irish freedom. The name of O'Donovan Rossa was an honoured one. He must be brought to Dublin for burial. Not alone must his funeral be an occasion to honour the dead patriot, but it must also be made a reminder to the people of Ireland of all that the Fenian leader had striven for. Indeed, what he had failed to achieve in life, he might well achieve in death — a reawakening of the national consciousness. Defiance of British rule had been similarly demonstrated at the funerals of Daniel O'Connell, Terence Bellew McManus and Charles Stuart Parnell.

Feverish activity began in national organisations. Brigid worked with Cumann na mBan. Day and night, the women toiled, making haversacks and mourning badges, the latter to be sold on the streets, with programmes of the funeral arrangements, and souvenir brochures. As Brigid observed, 'Rossa's funeral was to be a massive public declaration of our faith, hope and nationality.'

On arrival in Dublin, the coffin was received at the Pro-Cathedral amidst a throng of mourners. That night, with Aunt Joe and Mrs Tom Clarke, Brigid went to the old Gresham Hotel (the one destroyed during the Civil War) and met O'Donovan Rossa's widow and daughter. Mrs Clarke had been a friend since she had lived in America. Mrs Rossa was overcome by Dublin's massive demonstration, something which took her by surprise. But that was only the beginning. After requiem mass the following day, the body was taken to the City Hall, where it lay in state with a guard of honour drawn from the Volunteers and the Citizen Army. Brigid saw, for the first time, her Uncle Joe wearing his Volunteer's uniform, on guard at the catafalque. Marshalled by soldiers of both armies and by boys from Fianna Éireann (the Irish scout movement founded by Countess Markievicz), vast crowds filed past a glass-lidded coffin.

The funeral took place on Sunday 1 August, a very hot day with the sun shining relentlessly from a cloudless sky. Brigid spent the morning in Sackville Street, selling souvenir brochures. There was no time for a meal, and that was where the contents of the haversacks came in. Meanwhile, special trains arrived, bringing thousands of spectators from all over the country until the streets were packed. At the fountain in James' Street, some 1,000 members of Cumann na mBan had mobilised. There Brigid joined Aunt Joe and had the unexpected privilege of leading the Cumann na mBan section. The parade took one-and-a-half hours to reach Glasnevin Cemetery.

Every organisation in the country, religious, military and political, was represented. Ten thousand Volunteers and 200 of the Citizen Army marched openly in military formation; as many as possessed rifles carried them on their shoulders. There were dozens of bands, and a large contingent of Fianna Éireann. As the funeral wended its way through the sun-baked city before the silent crowds, it was clear that as a massive demonstration of nationalism, nothing like it had ever been seen in Ireland. As a recruiting demonstration, its effect could never be calculated. Leslie Bean de Barra made a decision: 'It was strange to see all these armed men as if they were going to fight. Cumann na mBan were there too, and I felt that I had better be in it to help them, so I joined.'

Ernie O'Malley too was a bystander. 'I watched the funeral pass to Glasnevin Cemetery, company after company of Irish Volunteers marching by, some in uniform, some wearing uniform hats and bandoleers, others green ties only. I saw the ungainly side of the parade: irregular marching; faulty execution of commands; strange slouch hats turned up at one side; uniform caps wobbling; long single-shot Howth Mauser rifles. They provided an amusing topic of conversation at dinner.' For all his cynicism, O'Malley was converted, eventually becoming Commandant General of the IRA.

Brigid Lyons sometimes thought that everything in her life had happened through chance. That idea was certainly borne out on that Sunday afternoon in Glasnevin Cemetery when she found herself within a few yards of Pádraig Pearse. A teacher in Dublin, he was only a name to her, but she was interested in seeing the man. She knew girls who had been at his school, and they adored him. Just then, she thought, even in that huge crowd, he looked a lonely figure standing by O'Donovan Rossa's open grave, against a background of tall Celtic crosses and taller yew trees.

Pearse's tribute to Rossa was spoken quietly, but Brigid was near enough to hear his words, and his words soon attracted her attention. Then she listened with a new curiosity to what he had to say, and how he said it:

> This is a place of peace sacred to the dead where men should speak with all charity and with all restraint: but I hold it a Christian thing, as O'Donovan Rossa held it, to hate evil, to hate untruth, to hate oppression, and hating them, to strive to overthrow them. Our foes are strong and wise and wary, but, strong and wise and wary as they are, they cannot undo the miracles of God who ripens in the hearts of young men the seeds sown by the young men of a former generation…

Asked if there was anything she remembered about the man that suggested the future leader of a revolution, Brigid said: 'I wasn't competent to make a judgement like that. I was just happy that I happened to be there, and happier as the years have passed. His figure and his face are as vivid as if it was yesterday.'

Her haversack empty, and with weary feet, Brigid trudged in the evening heat to Aunt Joe's place. Feeling curiously elated, as she remembered the great occasion, she was far from realising that she had just lived through a day destined to become a date in Irish history. As a demonstration of increasing national solidarity, the O'Donovan Rossa funeral parade was an undoubted success. Recruitment increased rapidly. Within two months, 1,200 Volunteers marched openly in Dublin, carrying arms. Cumann na mBan was parading regularly in uniform, and James Connolly and Countess Markievicz, wearing the uniform of the Citizen Army, led a sham attack on Dublin Castle. Afterwards, it became known that the action of the Citizen Army was an attempt to goad the Volunteers into organising a rising without further delay.

O'Donovan Rossa had not lived and died in vain.

# 5

# GUNS IN GALWAY

ANTICIPATING HER ENTRY to University College Galway in the following October, Brigid obtained the college prospectus. The fees came as a shock. It was clear that she could not face the cost of the medical course on the finance provided by her scholarship. All that could be done — if she were to keep her financial independence — was an arts course. It was a grave disappointment. However, she took it philosophically, remembering the time when she had thought that the holder of a BA was some kind of supernatural being. Still, it was medicine she had really wanted.

When she arrived at Galway station in October 1915, Brigid was startled to be met by Fr Hynes, Dean of the University. This wasn't part of his duties, he explained. Mother Scholastica had written. Good old Mother Scholastica! She could never do enough for her girls. There were no taxis, so they walked across Eyre Square towards Francis Street. Miss Maud Kyne ran a 'digs' near the Franciscan Friary. Halfway there, Fr Hynes put her in charge of a Tom Fitzgerald. Embarrassed, she explained that she didn't know Galway. Miss Kyne's house turned out to be warm, hospitable and chatty. There was another girl in digs there, too, also about to begin the arts course. Brigid's heart sank when she thought of Daisy Foley about to start medicine, her scholarship supplemented by her father.

In conversation, she mentioned the O'Donovan Rossa funeral to Miss Kyne. Unwittingly, she had played a trump card. Miss Kyne was entranced and confided her ideas on local nationalism. Galway, she said, was West-British. It hadn't the fiery enthusiasm of Dublin. Miss Kyne almost implied that her new student might look into the matter.

Next morning, as Brigid made her way to the university, she felt lost, confused, apprehensive … and disappointed. The sight of the gracious building in its sylvan setting near the Corrib did nothing to lift her spirits. In the hall, she met her friend of four long years in Sligo, Daisy Foley (afterwards Mrs Roger Livesey of Mullaghmore, Co Sligo). Mind clear and quite made up, Daisy was waiting for the bell for the first lecture in the medical course.

'Have you made up your mind, Biddy? What's it to be?' she enquired light-heartedly.

'It must be Arts — that's all the scholarship will cover.'

'Don't be an ass; come and do medicine with me.' Daisy came from a wealthy background. She had never known the meaning of want.

The bell rang. Daisy moved off down the corridor. Slowly, Brigid followed. It was now a matter of turning right or turning left at the end of that corridor — and pretty quickly too because one way or the other, it was now three minutes to the hour. Impelled as if in a dream, she turned right and followed Daisy into the chemistry lecture theatre. In later life, Brigid Lyons always claimed that it was Daisy Foley who made that fateful decision, and to her she was eternally grateful. Daisy was a forceful character and a tremendous friend. The future was to be a struggle and a constant financial worry, but in the belief that the Lord and her Uncle Frank had a way of providing for those of sufficient faith, Brigid turned her immediate attention to Charles' Law and Boyle's Law and all that tiresome rigmarole of chemistry and physics which seemed to have nothing to do with curing human ailments.

Soon she was recruited into the Gaelic and the Debating Societies. Now a medical student, she was feeling heady — prepared to join in everything. She soon discovered that her academic Irish was no match for that spoken by the Galway natives. In the first week, the 'Gibs' (the first years) were invited by the Dean to a party in the Aula Maxima, a sort of getting-to-know-you affair. She received some attention from a handsome, well-spoken young man. He was terribly interested in organising things — and so was she. 'I say', he said grandly, 'we must organise a branch of the Red Cross in college. Will you help?'

'Red Cross? Not me!' Brigid replied.

'Oh, but you must,' he insisted. 'There's a war on — first-aid and all that!'

Amazed at herself, she decided to show this man the error of his ways. 'I'm willing to help organise a branch of Cumann na mBan in college,' she said. 'They do first-aid too.'

It was the young gentleman's turn to be amazed. So that was it! She was one of these rebels, an Irish nationalist. He would never have thought it. 'We'll see Professor McHenry about a branch of the Red Cross in college,' he persisted.

And they did — the following day. Professor McHenry, although Professor of Irish, happened to be a qualified medical doctor. He was the 'famous' person who had examined her in spoken Irish a few weeks earlier. The professor produced a nice inoffensive (as he thought!) academic compromise. There was a branch of the Red Cross in town and they could all go off and join that if they wished.

Brigid was shocked — amazed that a Professor of Irish in University College Galway would make such a suggestion when a branch of Cumann na mBan would be the answer in more ways than first-aid. But that was the way of it in Galway. Public opinion had not yet come round to her sense of nationalism.

Brigid got busy. With the backing of a few contemporaries, she set up a branch of Cumann na mBan, but it had to meet outside the college. The women got a room in the County Hall. There they drilled and paraded and made badges and organised first-aid lectures. There was a corps of Irish Volunteers in Galway, so, as in Dublin, they supported and co-operated with the corps as the auxiliary women's wing. Brigid was getting herself marked out as a rebel.

One night, she was approached, very sheepishly, by a chap who said he had three guns. He asked her if she would please take them out to 'the boys' at Atlantic Lodge. At first, she thought he was fooling. Then he produced three revolvers, explaining that the house might be under surveillance, but a girl would not be noticed. She remembered the college rules: females were forbidden to visit male digs, and vice versa. She decided to take a chance.

'I set out with my guns,' Brigid remembered. 'And with cold feet too. I wandered round the streets wondering how I'd brought this on myself and what was I to do about it. It was getting late, so finally I walked up to Atlantic Lodge, knocking timidly. The young man who answered looked as frightened as I felt.'

She indicated that she wanted to see 'the boys' privately. With obvious apprehension, she was admitted to a back room. There were three male occupants. With the minimum of chat, she handed over the guns. It was quite clear that the boys were surprised that she was the kind of woman who would carry guns. The business concluded, they all relaxed and the chat began. She was to be trusted. She was one of them. John Madden — he it was who had opened the door — saw her home that night. Next day, rumour was already rife in the college: a great romance was afoot — Madden and that first-year rebel, Lyons.

Also in digs at Maud Kyne's was Alf Monaghan from Belfast. He was said to be in Galway as a Gaelic League organiser, but in fact he was organising for the Volunteers. He was a friend of Liam Mellows who often used to visit Uncle Joe. Maud gave the occasional party, and John Madden and his friend Eddie Connolly, both medical students, used to come. Such parties where the sexes met were heavily frowned upon by the college authorities. As with most medical students, Brigid found chemistry and physics a tiresome bore. Nonetheless, she held her own in memorising equations and formulae under the threat of impending exams. Although she persisted in trying to interest her contemporaries, they did not take her activities with Cumann na mBan and the Volunteers too seriously. Nationalists were still a bit of a joke in Galway. Indeed, there were occasions when she was accused of being a rebel simply to get 'notice'. This probably arose from her noisy activities in heckling speakers at meetings held to recruit for the British Army. To Cumann na mBan, nuisance value alone was important and urgent work.

Meantime, she had met George Nicholls and his wife. George was the brother of the beautiful Evelyn, who was drowned on the Blasket Islands trying to save a fisherman. It was said that she had been the girlfriend of Pádraig Pearse. The Nicholls entertained Brigid at their home on University Road. George was strongly nationalistic, and was always in and out of jail for his principles.

Soon, he invoked Brigid's help. At first, his plot seemed involved, but she didn't ask too many questions. Sometimes it was better to be ignorant of what one was about than to be in possession of what could be embarrassing information. On a certain night, George Nicholls told her, she was to stay in her digs between 8 p.m. and 10 p.m. Miss Kyne would be out. Brigid related the story:

> Then he told me it would be a good idea if I could send the maid to the pictures. Somebody would be coming to the digs — a young country fellow dressed like a priest. I was to meet him and keep him in chat in the front room. After that, there'd be a few more, but they'd explain things as we went along. Well, the country boy arrived, and I chatted to him, though he didn't look much like a priest to me. Then two or three others arrived and took the young fellow to a back room. Soon there was another knock and when I opened the door, it was Liam Mellows. I had met him at Uncle Joe's. Just now he was like a vision. I thought he was still in jail. He had a reputation for telling funny stories, but that night he was very serious. He told me to watch the front door, and he went into the back room with the others. Presently the country boy left as a country boy and shortly after that Liam Mellows walked out dressed as a priest. And I'll say this for him: with his bushy blond hair and his pince-nez glasses and his scholarly face, he looked more like the part than the country boy.

Explanations came afterwards. Aware of the value of certain Volunteer leaders as organisers and instructors in strengthening the movement, the Government issued expulsion orders, banning them from certain areas. For refusal to obey these orders in July 1915, four leading Volunteers were imprisoned: Liam Mellows, Ernest Blythe, Denis McCullogh and Herbert Moore Pim. On his release, Mellows returned to Galway; his return drew the unwelcome attention of the British. His temporary 'ordination' was an emergency measure to evade the closing net of His Majesty's Forces. And it worked!

Even Maud Kyne's absence from her house that night had been prearranged. She too was loyal to 'The Cause', but because of her livelihood she could not afford to be seen to be active. Her sister was married to Frank Hardiman, an ardent Galway nationalist who spent time in jail on various occasions. They had a large family. Nevertheless, after the execution of James Connolly in 1916, Mrs Hardiman brought the Connolly children from Dublin and kept them together with her own. All her brothers in Kilcolgan were arrested after 1916 and taken to Frongoch. Maud Kyne eventually married Harry Sheils who lost an arm in 1916.

It was the Mellows escape that led to Brigid's closer friendship with George Nicholls and his wife. On her return to Galway after Christmas 1915, they invited her to stay with them. Thus she spent three happy years in the comfort of their luxurious house near the university. 'It was the first real home from home I knew,' she said. It suited her temperament, her finances and her way of life, for she didn't mix that much with the students. She never felt equal to their all-night binges and parties. Apart from the odd céilí or fund-raising function, hers were outside activities, more removed from the noisy student circles in college.

The home comforts provided by the Nicholls should have been conducive to study, but somehow patriotic duties kept calling. Every time British Army recruiting meetings took place, Brigid was out with the Cumann na mBan, interrupting the speakers, waving flags and heckling. Somebody called The O'Donoghue of the Glen (later the Lord Lieutenant) came to confer a title. This kind of thing had to be challenged — if not with guns, then with the nuisance tactics of a group of noisy women. The greater the activity of the British Army recruiters, the more the Cumann girls became active too. They thrived on opposition. It fed their sense of nationalism. Brigid noticed that at last there seemed to be a stirring of patriotic feeling in college. They had founded a college corps of the Volunteers.

It was in the spring of 1916 that a raffle was organised in aid of the Corps. This was what she wanted — a more lively patriotic interest from the students. She enthusiastically supported the raffle, for which the prize was a revolver. The printed tickets made no secret of the fact and, willingly, people bought them, at the same time wondering what they would do with a revolver if they won it.

Leaving for Longford at Easter, Brigid brought a consignment of these raffle tickets with her. They were to cause much anxiety to many people, but who was to anticipate that at the time? As far as Brigid was concerned, the cause was a worthy one, and, on a bicycle, she spent Holy Week on a vigorous sales campaign. She was surprised at the change of heart in Longford. The air was full of threats of coercion and conscription. People were disgusted at the postponement of Home Rule and outraged at the British hypocrisy which appealed to Irishmen to sacrifice themselves in Flanders for the cause of small nations. The result was that it was now the in-thing to belong to the Volunteers. Even politically uncommitted people bought her raffle tickets at three pence each. In Longford, it seemed, you no longer joined the British Army — you joined the Irish Volunteers. Nobody anticipated embarrassment in possibly winning a revolver in a raffle. The British had not yet imposed a sense of terror in the public mind about being caught in possession of firearms. Looking back, there was no doubt in Brigid's mind that the activities of the Volunteers and Cumann na mBan in Galway, as elsewhere, were in preparation for a rebellion to drive the British out of Ireland. It was as simple as that. Nobody knew when that rebellion might come, but everybody seemed convinced that when it came, it would succeed. In early 1916, she sensed that things were gaining momentum. People were more outspoken. There was a new tension. Those who took things seriously argued that the Great War couldn't last much longer, and the rebellion could not be delayed if England's difficulty was still to be Ireland's opportunity.

On Holy Thursday, while she was out in the Longford countryside — still selling tickets — somebody produced that morning's *Freeman's Journal*. It contained a sensational revelation: a Dublin Castle document, captured by the Volunteers, outlined a scheme for the wholesale arrest of nationalists and the military occupation of Dublin. Although only a teenager, and the smallest of small fry in the nationalist movement, Brigid Lyons instantly saw the situation as a matter of who would strike first — the Volunteers or the British military machine. Her reaction was exactly as the publishers of that document had anticipated.

The origin of the so-called Dublin Castle Cypher, 'Secret Orders Issued to the Military', was at first something of a mystery. It was bogus, and its urgent publication at the time was decided for several reasons. The differences between the two rival groups within the Volunteer Executive had reached a climax: the one side planning the Rising and led by Pearse; the other, led by MacNeill and Hobson, advocating wiser counsels — namely, no premature aggressive action. Connolly had cynically described the latter group as 'the next War patriots.' Both sides, however, approved the publication of the document. Those who hoped to avert a conflict felt that it would prevent provocative action by Dublin Castle, while those preparing the Rising hoped that it would assure Volunteers everywhere of the need for immediate action. For Brigid, reading the *Freeman's Journal* on that Holy Thursday, 'it convinced me that something was brewing hotly in Dublin.' Thursday's newspapers kept Longford — and Ireland — talking. Tension increased. What was afoot? Rumour endeavoured to answer by inventing the wildest surmises. One was that Volunteers everywhere had been warned by the Executive to prepare to defend themselves against suppression by the British. Saturday's evening newspapers published a note to the effect that an unknown man had come ashore in a collapsible boat and been arrested. There was no mention of Casement by name, nor of the arms ship *Aud*. Nonetheless, the news, such as it was, only added to the spate of rumour and counter-rumour.

MacNeill's notice in the *Sunday Independent* countermanding the Volunteer parades and manoeuvres arranged for that day simply confounded confusion. Only history would acquaint the population of the high drama enacted in the previous three days and nights in Dublin with MacNeill and Pearse and Hobson, and others of the high command, playing out a sort of Greek tragedy adapted to Ireland.

The countermanding notice read:

Owing to the very critical position, all orders given to Irish Volunteers for to-morrow, Easter Sunday, are hereby rescinded, and no parades, marches, or other movements of Irish Volunteers will take place. Each individual Volunteer will obey this order strictly in every particular.

'The very critical position' — the words had a sinister ring. The flood of rumours in Longford swelled to a spate. People watched the members of the RIC with a new and suspicious interest as they came and went on their bicycles. The British Army remained out of sight, confined behind the high walls of the local barracks. Although nothing happened and no fresh news came, tension remained high throughout Easter Sunday.

Easter Monday began as a lovely sunny morning. An excursion train had left early for Dublin. Friends of Uncle Frank had gone — en route for Fairyhouse Races. There were no newspapers. The public's need of news stimulated the rumour-mongers to higher flights of fancy. The day wore on in an atmosphere of apprehension. The return of the excursion train would surely bring some definite news. At the hour, the station was crowded, with everyone anxious to hear the latest. But the train failed to arrive. Another rash of rumours broke out — or what were still taken to be rumours. The train hadn't returned because rebellion had broken out in Dublin; the city was in flames and all kinds of dire tragedies were happening. People's thoughts immediately turned to friends and relatives in Dublin, and they felt helpless.

At midnight, the train arrived with Uncle Frank's friends aboard. What Longford had already heard was no rumour: Sackville Street was indeed burning, and the air over it thick with flying bullets. The streets near the Parnell Monument were strewn with dead horses — they'd actually seen them. Dublin too was full of rumour, but, it seemed, the Volunteers had stormed the GPO that afternoon, and other key points had also been taken.

Brigid remembered how they talked late that night — Uncle and Aunt Frank and her three cousins, Maureen, Bríd and 15-year old Peg McGuinness. Maureen and Bríd were now working in the business and were members of Cumann na mBan. Brigid also remembered sleeping badly. Next morning, Uncle Frank seemed very worried about Joe and his wife in Dublin. Then Jimmie Farrell, a relative, arrived in near hysteria — there were no longer any trains and his wife was a patient in the Richmond Hospital, and he was convinced that she'd be shot, if she wasn't dead already. He appealed to Uncle Frank to do something to get him to Dublin.

This was probably the excuse Frank McGuinness was waiting for. He went to his desk and took out his warrant of appointment as a Justice of the Peace. 'I'm going up to the barracks with this,' he said. 'I'll tell them they want me in Dublin Castle.'

The police told him he was free to go. Immediately he hired Paddy Victory's car. The party was Jimmie, the patient's worried husband; Tom Bannon, local teacher and nationalist; Frank McGuinness; and Paddy, the driver. As they piled in, her uncle turned to Brigid.

'Would you like to come?' he asked.

She recollected the incident: 'I didn't have to be asked twice. I turned to my aunt for her approval.'

'Oh, no! No, you couldn't go,' Aunt Frank said with horror. And on the instant, a second thought struck her. 'Well… maybe your uncle would be safer if you were with him.'

Brigid squashed into the middle of the back seat, conscious of the disappointment of her cousins who were as anxious to go as she was. She rationalised her special position — she was the eldest and she was on holidays.

Leaving a helpless and worried Aunt Frank waving from the front door, Paddy Victory's open tourer took off along the Dublin Road in a cloud of dust, for tarmacadam was as yet unknown.

# 6

# A HOLIDAY TRIP

THE SUN SHONE brilliantly on Tuesday 25 April. In the midlands, the lambs took fright, fleeing from the noise of the passing car. Hedges were breaking out in a mist of delicate new green. Everywhere there were clumps of primroses. The five travellers might have been pleasure bent.

No one had packed any clothes. Nobody was clear how long they might stay in Dublin. There was no apprehension as to what might lie ahead — only an anxiety to get there as soon as possible. Their sympathy was with Jimmie Farrell and his worry about his wife.

The journey was uneventful until they reached the vicinity of Marlborough Barracks (now McKee Barracks). There the car was brought to a halt by barbed-wire barriers across the road. They were questioned by British soldiers with fixed bayonets. Mostly the soldiers were young and inclined to be frivolous: if these country folk thought they had come for a day out in the big city, they were in for a rude awakening. The car could proceed no further. They were ordered out. They must walk wherever they were going.

Uncle Frank produced his warrant as a Justice of the Peace. He was on his way to Dublin Castle, he assured them. The order was repeated: the car could proceed no further. During this parley, Brigid noticed a heavy pall of smoke hanging like a thundercloud over the city centre. Along the south quays there seemed to be sporadic shooting. Time proved her right. Tuesday was the day British artillery was brought into action, and outlying Republican posts were recovered by the Crown forces.

The party broke up. Setting out on foot, each was intent on his own business. Uncle Frank's principal concern was his brother, Joe, and Joe's wife. They no longer lived over their business in Lower Camden Street. They had opened another business in Dorset Street, and they now lived at 41 Upper Gardiner Street. With the city centre in a state of siege, their only option was to walk round the perimeter. They took the North Circular Road, eventually reaching Drumcondra Road. In the distance, there was continuous shooting. All business was at a standstill.

Brigid was horrified to see young people lying about on lawns sunning themselves. 'Why aren't they doing something about it?' she asked, and Uncle Frank explained. 'If a bunch of Bolshies started a revolution in Sackville Street,' he said, 'there would be people who would say, well sure let them. Wasn't it a grand excuse for another day off work to enjoy the bit of sunshine while it lasted? And wouldn't the Bolshies be run in anyway — the British Army would see to that.'

On Drumcondra Road they saw a hoarding with a huge poster, 'Why not JOIN THE ARMY for the period of the war? You will like it. Your pals will like it. The Kaiser will hate it!'

At Upper Gardiner Street, Brigid and her uncle found Aunt Joe with Sorcha McMahon. At last a picture began to emerge of what had happened in Dublin. Excited, tense, and a little distressed, Aunt Joe was just back from the Four Courts, where she had seen Joe. Sorcha McMahon had been on dispatch duty since the Rising had begun. She had been doing the rounds from post to post bringing messages as well as good cheer and great hope. Now the principal concern of the women was how long it would last and how it would end.

Joe was with 'O' Company, the First Volunteer Battalion, Dublin Brigade, under Commandant Ned Daly in the Four Courts garrison. The Second Battalion, under Thomas MacDonagh, was in Jacob's factory; the Third under Eamon de Valera in Boland's Mill; and the Fourth under Eamonn Ceannt in the South Dublin Union. The Citizen Army was in St Stephen's Green under Michael Mallin and Countess Markievicz; and in the GPO in Sackville Street was the

Headquarters Command under Pearse and Connolly.

Frank McGuinness wanted to know about his brother, Joe. Between them, Aunt Joe and Sorcha McMahon filled him in. MacNeill's countermanding order on Easter Sunday had nearly wrecked everything, but in the early hours of Easter Monday, Thomas MacDonagh had issued the final order to the Dublin battalions of the Volunteers: 'The four City battalions will parade for inspection and route march at 10 a.m. to-day. Commandants will arrange centres. Full arms and equipment and one day's rations.'

Lieutenant Joseph McGuinness of the First Battalion had received the order to assemble under Commandant Edward Daly at the Colmcille Hall in Blackhall Place. There he learned the battalion's true intent. The morning was spent in making preparations. At 11.45 a.m., Commandant Daly gave the command, 'Left turn, quick march.' The pathetically depleted First Battalion set out (as elsewhere, there was one man instead of three), its objective being the Four Courts, and any suitable outposts in its vicinity. Daly deployed twenty men under Joe McGuinness to the Four Courts building, the sprawling domed centre of Ireland's judiciary. He set up his headquarters round the corner in the Fr Mathew Hall in Church Street, and the remainder of his men he deployed in five outposts in the surrounding streets.

Like all Volunteers that day, Joe McGuinness was to marvel at the lack of resistance met with in taking over key positions. In full view of the Bridewell police station, at the rear of the Four Courts, he had led his men to the Chancery Place entrance. Lieutenant Thomas Allen having taken the keys from a policeman, they entered the back of the building. A bolt on the inner door gave some trouble. Directed by Commandant Frank Fahy, Joe shot the bolt off. Then there was a lot of heavy work: smashing the great windows that overlooked the river, and barricading them with leather-bound tomes from the library.

Barricades were thrown up in the surrounding streets: bedsteads, commandeered lorries and carts, an overturned tram, Guinness barrels, and cabs with their wheels removed. The First Battalion proved to be the first to see action. Hardly were the barricades up before a troop of Lancers returning from the North Wall with supplies blundered into the middle of this Volunteer activity. Taken by surprise, they were met with a fusillade. In a moment chaos reigned. British soldiers lay on the street, their horses plunging wildly. The remainder made for the side streets only to be met with another fusillade. Cut off in all directions, the main body took cover in the Medical Mission building in Chancery Place. Unhorsed troopers were taken prisoner by the Volunteers. At least one trooper was killed trying to escape through North Brunswick Street, as was a little girl. The First Battalion had had its baptism of fire.

As a member of Cumann na mBan, Aunt Joe had been mobilised and had gone to Blackhall Street from where she had conveyed various dispatches. She had been to the McGuinness shop in Dorset Street, and had brought supplies to the Four Courts. Before the week was out, the McGuinness shops were to be stripped to provide for the welfare of the Four Courts garrison.

While Aunt Joe was talking, Rose McGuinness arrived unexpectedly from the Four Courts. The daughter of another McGuinness brother, and a member of Cumann na mBan, Rose had been serving in the Four Courts until injured by flying glass. Her hands were bandaged and consequently she had been transferred to dispatch duties. She was excited and full of optimism: something had started, and the boys would see it through. Her enthusiasm communicated itself. Brigid wanted to become involved.

'I'll go down to see Joe,' Uncle Frank said. Aunt Joe gave him a route via the back streets. After a tedious two hours, he returned. 'Joe'd like to see you, Brigid, and I have the password — Antonio.'

Uncle Frank had not been wasting his time. He had arranged to stay with John O'Mahony, the owner of Fleming's Hotel in Gardiner Place. A commercial traveller, O'Mahony had done immense work for the Cause, under cover of his business. (In the years ahead, Fleming's Hotel was to be closely associated with Michael Collins.) Frank McGuinness and John O'Mahony had that afternoon organised a handcart and from Joe's place in Dorset Street had collected supplies of shirts, socks, towels, blankets, sheets and other essentials. They had pushed their loads by the back streets to the Four Courts.

Tom Bannon decided that he would like to join the First Battalion. He and Aunt Joe and Brigid set out together. It was dark, and there seemed less need to keep to the back streets. Taking cover in doorways when the shooting intensified, they went through North Frederick Street and Rutland (Parnell) Square. At the Rotunda corner, they saw the dead horses still lying in Sackville Street since the previous day when the Sixth Reserve Cavalry (the Lancers) had ridden into a withering encounter with the men of the Volunteer Headquarters in the GPO.

There was a lot of shooting in Sackville Street, and smoke was billowing from burning buildings. The few people to be seen were darting close to the walls or peeping from the cover of doorways. There was less shooting as they progressed along Parnell Street, past Moore Street and Dominick Street. In Bolton Street, they met the first barricade. Everything had gone into its building, including sofas, go-cars and Guinness barrels. Brigid was amazed, even frightened, that this was the best that could be done against the might of the British Empire. They gave the password, 'Antonio', and they went through the barricade by entering through one door of a disabled cab and going out by the other.

There were no street lights, and the only noise was the sound of sniping. Along North King Street, the shooting increased — they were nearing the Four Courts. Unfamiliar with the locality on this occasion, Brigid would soon come to know it better. Tom Bannon too was to become familiar with North King Street, Church Street and Charles Street — those narrow streets that ramified in the shadow of the great Four Courts dome. Both were now depending on Aunt Joe whose destination was the Fr Mathew Hall, the Headquarters of the First Battalion. The Four Courts building — like the Mendicity Institute across the river — was an outpost occupied by 'O' Company, First Battalion, under Commandant Frank Fahy (afterwards for many years Ceann Comhairle of Dáil Éireann) and Lieutenant Joe McGuinness. It was the most important outpost because of its size, and it was therefore occupied by the largest company of the Battalion.

The Headquarters Battalion staff comprised Commandant Ned Daly (brother of Mrs Tom Clarke), Vice-Commandant Piaras Béaslaí, the adjutant, Eamonn Duggan (otherwise a solicitor who was to be one of the signatories of the Treaty), and the quartermaster, Eamonn

Morkan. Working from the Fr Mathew Hall, the staff kept in constant touch with the men at the barricades. The hall was also used as a first-aid station.

It was almost as dark inside as in the streets outside. A few guttering candles stood on the floor between mattresses where the wounded lay. In the flickering light, Brigid saw a man lying on a pillow soaked with blood. For her, this was war — real war. Despite the gloom in the hall, there was a strange buoyancy, a cheerful optimism about everybody. They were welcomed by Eamonn Duggan and Martin Conlon, who were engaged in arranging the transport of wounded to the Richmond Hospital (later Saint Laurence's Hospital).

An old friend of the McGuinness family, Martin Conlon was the husband of Peg, with whom Brigid had marched in the O'Donovan Rossa funeral. Peg, it seemed, had been sent to Galway by Cumann na mBan, but whether to rally the Volunteers there or to cancel everything with MacNeill's countermand wasn't then clear. Dispatch carriers weren't necessarily aware of the nature of the messages they carried. At that time, Brigid was unaware of the eminence of Martin Conlon in the Irish Republican Brotherhood. He was a kind, happy man in whose house in Cabra Park she knew many happy times — that same house where Bulmer Hobson was detained after his mysterious kidnapping on Easter Saturday 1916, which in fact had been orchestrated to immobilise his activities in trying to prevent the Rising.

Earlier on that Tuesday of Easter Week, a new paper of four pages had appeared. It was entitled *Irish War News*, and it carried Pearse's first communiqué saluting the citizens of Dublin. It called on them to give 'their allegiance and their loyal help to the Irish Republic. There is work for everyone: for the men in the fighting line and for the women in the provision of food and first-aid. Every Irishman and Irishwoman worthy of the name will come forward to help their common country in this her supreme hour.'

Pearse could turn a phrase to make heady reading. And he never failed to invoke the women. Brigid badly wanted to help these wounded men. But first she must see Uncle Joe. With Tom Bannon, she went down Church Street, huddling close to the buildings to avoid the crossfire. They entered the Four Courts through a hole broken in the high surrounding wall, and then crossed an open yard, again keeping close to the shelter of the wall. They reached a big room which might have been a courtroom. The first person they met was Peadar Clancy — a tall, handsome, diffident young man destined to become an Irish martyr.

In the Four Courts, optimism was high. The only light came from candles, shaded on the floor beneath the tables. The noise was intense, with Volunteers firing from the shelter of the windows, and being fired at from across the river. There were shouted jokes about the effectiveness of their Howth rifles and what things might have been like without them.

When Uncle Joe appeared, tired and bedraggled, he was delighted to see that Brigid had arrived on active service. Then Commandant Edward Daly appeared. With his sister, Mrs Tom Clarke, Brigid had already met Ned Daly in the previous summer, and remembered him as a quiet, yet forceful man. Now, in his uniform, as Commanding Officer of the Four Courts, Ned Daly looked infinitely more impressive. 'He probably wouldn't care to have been told so,' Brigid recalled, 'but Ned Daly was the nearest approach to a British officer in appearance and manner.' He inspired all who were privileged to work with him.

In the basement of the Four Courts, there was even more noise and activity. In the huge tiled kitchen, large pieces of silver and plate reflected the small flickering light of the candles under the tables. Added to the gunfire was the noise of cooking. The place was crowded with Cumann na mBan women, all preparing food. Volunteers came and went furtively in the semi-darkness. And the place was alive with rumours and reports — all, it seemed, in favour of the Rising. Impending help from Germany was the favourite topic.

Stores were still being brought in: quantities of bread, butter, ham and tins of biscuits obtained from the hotels and shops in the area. In the dark, prison-like basement there were moments of hilarity — boys shouting for food and calling the girls Cumann na Monsters.

As a visitor, Brigid was invited to have tea. 'Never in my life,' she remembered, 'had I tasted anything like it, but I said nothing.'

Presently Commandant Frank Fahy came in, wearing a military cloak, like a Napoleonic general. He sat by the range and asked for tea. In her enthusiasm to oblige the commandant, and in the semi-darkness, a young woman lifted a candle to the table. From somewhere a man shouted, 'Do you want us all to be shot? Keep that candle covered.' Eventually Frank Fahy got his tea, but it was too dark to see his reaction. A young volunteer then arrived, demanding a cup of tea. (For the women, the Four Courts was like that — one long round-the-clock disbursement of cups of tea.) The young man tasted his tea and spluttered, 'Are the Cumann na Monsters trying to poison us? I never tasted tea like that before.'

Then Frank Fahy agreed. He even suggested that the matter might be looked into. It transpired that somebody had made the tea with water in which turnips had been boiled. But the Cumann na Monsters lived it down. When danger lurks round every corner, turnip-flavoured tea is a relatively minor inconvenience.

And danger was indeed just round the corner — in the Medical Mission, to be precise, where the main body of the Lancers under a Lieutenant Hunter had taken cover on Easter Monday. Intensive gunfire told its own story. A party of Daly's men, firing from the Chancery Place gate of the Four Courts, peppered the Mission in an effort to winkle out the British. Later, some volunteers tried to set the building ablaze. Their efforts were repulsed, and Volunteer Paddy Daly was wounded.

The British also suffered losses. Writing fifty years later of his experiences in the area commanded by Ned Daly, Henry McKean, a medical orderly in the 56th Field Ambulance, Royal Army Medical Corps, stated: 'We made many trips, in a horse-drawn ambulance, to collect wounded and dead from several parts of the City. On one of these trips we brought the bodies of two officers from the Medical Mission in Chancery Place and these were two of the five officers buried in the Castle garden.' (On the discovery of these five graves in 1962, the bodies of the officers were exhumed and re-interred in the British Military Cemetery at Blackhorse Avenue.)

Asked had she any fear, Brigid replied, 'None, although shooting was going on all the time. I remember standing for a long time at a window with Frank Fahy. He was using a Howth gun and trying to get a sniper on a roof across the river. I was fascinated. Peering through the darkness, I thought it was only clothes waving on a clothesline, but the accuracy of the replying fire eventually convinced me.'

As the night wore on, the lads came and went. A cup of tea, a drag at a cigarette and a few minutes of light-hearted banter, before they returned to their posts refreshed. Some of the young ones were very weary, and some of the older men a trifle crotchety. Apart from the strain of continual gunfire, many had been on duty since they first paraded on Easter Monday morning. Lieutenant Joe McGuinness made no secret of the joy he felt in having his niece there. He made her feel part of the great adventure. 'I wouldn't have it otherwise,' he assured her, his smile and his wink full of pride. Uncle Frank was there too, and Tom Bannon and Mrs Frank Fahy in her Cumann na mBan capacity. A conservative man, Tom Bannon was deeply concerned about the situation.

'I think it's highly dangerous,' Brigid heard him say. 'I think they'll be caught here like rats in a trap.' At a later stage, he became serious with Brigid. She had no right to stay on in a situation already so dangerous, he told her, and which must inevitably become suicidal when the British had time to mobilise. She consulted Uncle Joe. His look spoke volumes.

'I have an exam in June,' she tried to explain. 'The only reason I must go is the fear of not getting back to Galway in time for lectures — and that wouldn't do.'

The burning patriotism in Joe McGuinness flared, but he paused and then spoke quietly, sincerely. 'There's nothing left to us but this,' he said, indicating their blacked-out surroundings with a background accompaniment of shattering gunfire. 'We must see it through. If you'll stay with us, Brigid, you must forget everything else. Your exams can be done later on. But this is our greatest chance to free Ireland.'

He looked at her like a man prepared for a grave disappointment. His look was more than she could bear. 'I'm staying,' she said decisively. And Joe McGuinness, ordinarily undemonstrative, embraced his niece and kissed her affectionately.

'I'm proud of you, Brigid,' he said. 'And someday you'll be proud too.'

After that, for better or worse, Brigid Lyons threw in her lot with the Four Courts garrison. She got down to work though the place seemed darker than ever. No provision had been made for the night, and some of the girls were exhausted. As the most recent arrival, she elected to stay up and continue the tea-making while most of the others tried to get some rest.

Having helped, with Tom Bannon, to lay in supplies for Daly's men, Frank McGuinness remained in the Four Courts until the small hours of Wednesday morning. Before leaving, he gave Brigid thirty gold sovereigns for safe-keeping. 'From that moment, I carried them all the time. You had no handbags in those days, so I carried them next my heart.'

Frank McGuinness might have had a presentiment. The next they heard was a rumour that he had been shot. Endless hours of anxiety brought the further news that he had been wounded in Gardiner Place, and was now under arrest. Thus the first of the fighting McGuinness clan was effectively removed from the scene of battle.

# 7

# IN SIEGE

UNKNOWN TO THE Volunteers, the British had, on Tuesday night, decided to concentrate on liquidating the GPO and the Four Courts. That meant an initial onslaught on the outposts of the Four Courts: the Mendicity Institute across the river, Jameson's Distillery and Reilly's Fort, the pub (now The Tap Bar) at the corner of Church Street and North King Street.

Like most mornings of Easter Week, Wednesday dawned with a clear sky. The sun rose brilliantly, its spring warmth a mockery as it fell through the barred basement windows into the smoke-fogged Four Courts dungeons. The big range, its fires burning continuously, had to be cleared of accumulated ash and cinders. The tea-making and sandwich-cutting went on incessantly. The comings and goings of the lads had become routine. Only in the variety of the rumours they brought was there any novelty. Mostly the rumours were optimistic. Everything was going well. At any rate, their rumours, their geniality and their gratitude for food and drink gave the women heart to go on.

Sorcha McMahon arrived that morning with dispatches. The Cumann na mBan often carried these hidden in their hair-buns. Her news confirmed the rumours: there was a big battle going on in Dublin Bay and the Germans were marching on Dublin from the Naas Road. In later life, Brigid wondered why nobody stopped to question where the Germans might be coming from via the Naas Road. The collective subconscious, no doubt, accepted it simply: let's believe what we want to believe — that all is going well.

But Wednesday 26 April was to be a day of successes and failures for the men and women in the Four Courts. Apprehension grew when it became clear that the Mendicity Institute had come under siege. Once the barrage began, it was incessant. The thoughts of those in the Four Courts went out to Seán Heuston and his men. Twenty-year-old Heuston had been promoted commandant on Monday morning, only because of the shortage of officers. Although virtually cut off, even from food supplies, he had, on the instructions of James Connolly, held the Mendicity since midday on Monday. His purpose was to prevent British reinforcements, which might arrive from the Curragh via Kingsbridge Station or via the western roads, from attacking his commander's headquarters in the vicinity of the Four Courts.

Having posted snipers at various vantage points and barricaded all entrances to the Mendicity, Heuston's first engagement had been with a regiment of British marching out from the Royal Barracks (now Collins Barracks). On the third day of the siege, following constant attacks from rifles, bombs and machine guns, Heuston's men were still valiantly in defence. The fierce battles fought by his paltry few with their Howth rifles against the many well-armed British make Heuston's defence of the Mendicity one of the most valiant highlights of a week of valiant deeds.

It was only when the British — the Dublin Fusiliers, in fact — got close enough to throw grenades into the burning Mendicity Institute that Heuston surrendered. The British were amazed when eventually he marched out under a white flag with only twenty men to become prisoners. Four of his comrades were dead. British casualties in attacking this little garrison numbered one hundred and eighty.

Medical Orderly Henry Macken of the Royal Army Medical Corps had some experience of being under fire from Seán Heuston's men:

We were stationed in King George's [now St Bricin's] Hospital and on Easter Monday night we were sent with a horse-drawn ambulance to the Castle. At Queen Street Bridge we ran into some firing from the Mendicity Institute. I felt a blow in my back and shouted to Captain Stanley, our doctor, 'I'm hit'. Captain Stanley turned me around to examine me and then said I was not half as bad as he was. Bullets had hit the iron hoops which held up the canvas cover of the ambulance, and a piece of iron had flaked off and struck me in the back. Captain Stanley had lost half his pants from the same cause. It was a rough week for an ambulance man and we had some narrow shaves. As ambulance men we took no part in the fighting, but we were close to it and I can say that the Volunteers were a very plucky lot of men.

The loss of the Mendicity outpost left the Four Courts more vulnerable from the south of the river and from the western approaches. But whatever demoralising effect its loss may have had on those in the Four Courts garrison, it was quickly counteracted by Commandant Daly's next move. About noon, he ordered an attack on the Linenhall Military Barracks off North King Street where forty members of the British Army Pay Corps had been under siege since the outbreak of the Rising on Monday.

Erected in 1728, and covering four acres, the imposing and historical Linen Hall had once been the great distribution centre for Irish linen before that trade passed to Belfast. Its handsome façade was ornamented by a clock and a cupola, and its courtyard was surrounded by an arcade. A high surrounding wall protected the building when eventually it became a British military barracks.

The attacking party on the Linenhall, under Captain Denis O'Callaghan and Volunteer Garry Holohan, gained admission by blowing the surrounding wall. After some resistance, a white flag went up, and presently forty British prisoners were marched out of the Linenhall by the Volunteers and through the Church Street barricades to the shelter of the Fr Mathew Hall. The morale of the First Battalion was again in the ascendant.

At the end of that week, a document was found on the body of The O'Rahilly who had been shot dead in Henry Place leading an attack on a British barricade. The document recorded 'a tribute for Commandant Daly's splendid exploit in capturing Linenhall Barracks… The population of the district are united in his praise. (Signed) James Connolly, Commandant-General, Dublin Division, Army of the Irish Republic, Headquarters, April 28, 1916'.

Because of the shortage of Volunteers, the need to watch the Medical Mission, where the party of British Lancers was still cut off, and in case the British should recapture the Linenhall Barracks, Daly gave the order to burn it. Thus began one of the greatest and most terrifying conflagrations ever seen in Dublin. Having completely engulfed the barracks, the flames spread rapidly through adjacent business premises. Already far out of control, things worsened when Messrs McMaster Hodgeson in Henrietta Lane became involved. More stocks of oil and inflammable material took fire. There were loud explosions and the air was full of acrid fumes. Terror spread amongst the residents of North King Street and Henrietta Street who, faced with the alternative of death from flames or from bullets, fled, risking the bullets. Had they known it, they were to encounter even greater terror before the week was out.

Without a fire brigade service, and faced with a major disaster, Daly ordered his men out to fight the fire. Unprotected, and without equipment equal to the magnitude of the blaze, they found their task made more hazardous because the British kept up continuous fire. For days and nights, flames licked the skies, and a black pall of acrid smoke hung over the area. The Linenhall Barracks was a costly undertaking in men and material, but the British had been denied one of their strategic strongholds in the area of Daly's First Battalion, and at the time that was important.

In the meantime, more British prisoners had been captured. Captain, Lord Dunsany of the Inniskillings, while driving into Dublin with dispatches, refused the command to 'stop' at the Cabra barricades. Daly's men opened fire, bringing the car to a halt by puncturing the tyres. Lord Dunsany received a grazing wound of the cheek. Brigid Lyons had no recollection of being privileged to serve the prisoner, Lord Dunsany, with tea. She clearly remembered, however, a young Volunteer who for an extra sandwich bartered a valued souvenir — namely, a brass button from the military greatcoat of Lord Dunsany. As a sort of talisman, she pinned this war trophy on her bosom, and then forgot about it.

Colonel R. K. Brereton of the Royal Irish Regiment, while driving in from Athlone, was also taken prisoner by the Four Courts garrison.

Colonel Brereton was held until the Rising ended. His recollections are revealing:

> What impressed me most was the international tone adopted by the Sinn Féin officers. They were not out for massacre, for burning or for loot. They were out for war, observing all the rules of civilian warfare and fighting clean. So far as I saw, they fought like gentlemen. At first they were elated and evidently full of hope. As they were pressed by the troops, and no doubt receiving bad news from outside, they looked anxious and tired, but still bore themselves well and maintained discipline among their men. They had possession of the restaurant in the Four Courts stocked with spirits, champagne and other wines, and yet there was no sign of drinking. I was informed that they were all total abstainers. They treated their prisoners with the utmost courtesy and consideration. In fact they proved by their conduct that they were men of education and incapable of acts of brutality. The officers with whom I came in contact were Captain [sic] Daly, Captain [sic] Fahy, Lieutenant McGuinness, Lieutenant Duggan and their sergeant-major. To all of them I owe a deep debt of gratitude for their generous treatment of me and my fellow prisoners.

Also held as prisoners in the Four Courts were Colonel Lindsay, captured with Lord Dunsany, and Lieutenant Halpin, a Limerick man. Lindsay was friendly and was accepted by everybody. He was, however, to figure more prominently later on when the positions were reversed and his captors became the prisoners of his British Army.

All through Wednesday, morale wavered as often as the rumours. It was a setback, for instance, to be told that the booming noises heard earlier were coming not from an Anglo-German naval battle in Dublin Bay, but from a British gunboat, the *Helga*, which had come up the Liffey and was now bombarding the city from close range. Hand-to-hand fighting was one thing, but British artillery was quite another. It was chilling. Nonetheless, the lads remained as happy and as optimistic as Cumann na mBan could make them. Necessity was often the mother of invention. Seán Flood was an excellent quartermaster under impossible conditions, but he had provided no means of roasting legs of mutton. What was the use of being a medical student if one didn't adapt one's anatomical skill to the problem in hand? Brigid Lyons borrowed a bayonet and, somehow, the impossible legs of mutton were rendered into chops, or something of the kind, but at least they could be slapped on a pan and perhaps made edible. And that was the important thing — to provide food for a garrison which, with prisoners, was enlarging.

It might have been of greater interest to a medical student to have been posted to the Fr Mathew Hall where the casualties were. But as far as Brigid was concerned, one didn't ask for favours — one did as one was told. Besides, Uncle Joe was in the Four Courts and to be alongside Uncle Joe in Ireland's greatest bid for freedom was something which, even then, Brigid Lyons knew that she would always cherish amongst her proudest memories.

Meanwhile, dispatches were being exchanged with headquarters at the GPO in Sackville Street. Their contents were not revealed to the rank and file, who still had to rely on rumour. They had heard, for instance, that the whole country had risen, and that fighting was particularly intense in Galway and Wexford. Time proved such rumours to be wishful thinking on the part of their inventors.

The Capuchin friars from Church Street were frequent visitors. Sometimes under a hail of fire, they came and went, but always they brought a cheerful reassurance and a sense of the spiritual which transcended all man's earthly efforts — even the freeing of Ireland, much as the friars too desired it. Linked forever with the 1916 Four Courts garrison, and later with the events in Kilmainham Gaol, will be the names of Fr Augustine and Fr Albert. With his long, grey beard and his cheerful countenance, Fr Augustine was like a brown-clad Santa Claus ambling through the courts distributing spiritual gifts with a jovial benevolence. The nearness of the Capuchins to the operations of the First Battalion provided a tremendous source of comfort in Easter Week, and in the grim weeks that followed it.

It may have been the Capuchins who brought the news of the food shortages in the streets of the Four Courts area. The barricades set up between Beresford Street and Church Street had resulted in the closure of Monks' Bakery. Also in the area were situated the Corporation

Markets, normally full of fruit, fish and vegetables, but no supplies had arrived since before the Easter holiday. The few grocery shops in the locality had been cleared out by Tuesday evening. Food supplies for the local residents were hourly diminishing. Their plight was worsened by their fear of leaving the cover of their houses in the face of continual gunfire. Pressed though he was for men, Commandant Daly reopened Monks' Bakery and had bread rationed out daily to the public of the area.

Shortly afterwards came the news that looting had begun. Looting to satisfy hunger might have been understandable — even excusable — given the circumstances. But the looters of 1916 were of the get-rich-quick mentality. There were those who looted food and drink and sold it to beleaguered citizens for exorbitant profits. And there were others who, risking their lives, simply went on a rampage, their light fingers itching to acquire anything from diamonds and mink to armchairs and tricycles. The British Army made a virtue of shooting to kill such looters, but it was the Volunteers, at a much earlier stage, and after the issue of many warnings, who were forced to waste valuable ammunition shooting over their heads in their efforts to disperse them.

By late on Wednesday night, the loss of the Mendicity Institute became apparent. While optimism remained at a peak and good humour was everywhere (Daly's men were afterwards said to be as tough as any in the whole Volunteer force), it was clear that the British pressure was building up against the Four Courts. The length of Church Street had come under long-range fire from the Birmingham Tower in Dublin Castle. There was sniping too from the tower of Christ Church Cathedral, and machine gunfire had begun from the vicinity of Jervis Street Hospital to the east. And of course there was continual sniping from the Lancers, still holed up in the Medical Mission close-by.

For all its height, the Four Courts dome provided no protection for gunners. It was from the height of the water tower of Jameson's Distillery, and the roof of Patterson's match factory that Daly's men provided their best replying fire. Volunteer Frank Shouldice distinguished himself for the accuracy of his shooting from his lonely perch on the Jameson Tower. Aided by field glasses, he silenced many an unsuspecting sniper.

Brigid remembered something else of that day, something that was to add another little boost to the morale of the First Battalion: 'I was standing at a window at the back of the Four Courts. I saw Mark Wilson and some others crawling along a wall like cops and robbers. When they were shot at, they'd take cover for a few minutes and then move on another little bit.'

She was curious. Somebody told her that it was an attempt to capture the Bridewell where there was a posse of Dublin Metropolitan Policemen locked up since the previous Monday. Further, they had taken some Volunteer prisoners and these must be released. There was a grave shortage of men.

Brigid went on: 'Some time later, I saw downstairs what I thought was a bunch of Germans. In fact, they were the great big DMP men who had been captured in the Bridewell. They had enormous helmets with spikes on the top, and they wore cloaks. I felt they couldn't be anything but Germans — they looked so like pictures I'd seen of the Prussians.'

Uncle Joe explained that the poor devils had been locked up and had had no food since the Rising began. Now all twenty-four of them were prisoners of the Four Courts garrison, but the Volunteers did not know what to do with them. 'Shoot them!' somebody suggested and everybody laughed, including the DMP men, who were also Irishmen.

With the ever-growing demands on the catering services, it was the early hours of Thursday morning before Brigid and five other girls decided to try to get some rest. She had not slept since leaving Longford on Tuesday morning. Mattresses brought from the Four Courts Hotel had been thrown on the floor in the Judges' Chambers. But there were no covers and it was cold. Undaunted, the Cumann na mBan met the situation.

'We got into the judges' robes,' Brigid remembered. 'Ermine, velvet, mink, sable — everything that was warm and luxurious. It was my first chance to get myself into the plush.'

Not even a lullaby of stuttering Mausers could keep those girls from sleep.

# 8

# THE BATTLE FOR REILLY'S FORT

VERY SHORTLY AFTERWARDS — or so it seemed to Brigid Lyons — the door burst open and Barney Mellows rushed in, holding a candle. 'I'm looking for two Cumann na mBan volunteers for Church Street,' he said. 'Peadar Clancy's been promoted lieutenant and he's opening a new post out there. An extension of our defences.'

Peadar Clancy was the first person Brigid had met on her arrival in the Four Courts. She recalled that, since then, 'I had heard a lot about his courage, his capacity for decision making, his military bearing and all that, although he was only about twenty-one. I thought I'd like to go, but I couldn't be so cheeky as to suggest it.'

Another girl sat up sleepily. 'Let that fat girl from the country go,' she said. 'She's not been as long here and she's not as tired as we are.'

The fat girl, who was Brigid, leaped out of her judicial robes. Another volunteer called Katie Derham came from the North Circular Road. 'I'd like to go too,' Katie said. 'I think my brother is out there.' All through those terrible days and nights, Katie had been very concerned about her brother, Micky.

'We were escorted by Barney Mellows over to Church Street,' Brigid recounted. 'It was a hazardous journey because the yard of the Four Courts was full of broken glass from the shattered windows. We had to crawl on all fours, and stop every time there was a hail of bullets and then crawl again. It seemed a long distance until we reached that hole in the wall. Through it we got out into Church Street. It was some time before dawn, and the only light came from the flames of the Linenhall Barracks which was still blazing.'

'We were taken into a small artisan dwelling, Number 5 Church Street [now, alas, swept away in the interests of street widening], the home of Volunteer Michael Lennon. He was there himself and tried to welcome us as if times were normal. He explained that he had sent away his wife and family.'

The job of the two Cumann na mBan volunteers was to convert the place to a canteen and first-aid post. There was a little sitting-room downstairs, and a kitchen at the back, with two small bedrooms upstairs. At the rear was a small yard with high walls.

Michael Lennon made himself generally useful. He brought kindling and coal, and the girls got a fire going in the little range in the kitchen. He filled every container he could find with water in case the supply might be turned off. Seán Flood, always the great provider, was bringing in hams and bags of potatoes and sides of sheep and anything else that could be procured.

At some stage, Michael Lennon said, 'There's going to be heavy fighting here, and we haven't even a stretcher.' Thereupon he seized his own stepladder, and broke it up. Then he took a hearth-rug from the floor, nailing it to the shafts of the ladder. The result was a make-do stretcher. He folded it and put it in a corner, saying to Brigid: 'Now you know where that is if anybody gets shot.' Then he went off to the barricades.

'Within half an hour, the stretcher was called for. In a few minutes, it was carried in with our first casualty — Michael Lennon himself. He had a wound in the abdomen with a bullet lodged near the liver. I dressed his wound as best I could, and sent him off to the Richmond Hospital.'

Lennon survived. The First Battalion had an arrangement with the hospital. Resident doctors came from time to time to the casualty station in the Fr Mathew Hall. 'The one I remember seeing most often,' Brigid said, 'was Michael Burke, a house surgeon at the time, and afterwards a consultant surgeon at the Richmond.'

In due course, Brigid and Katie Derham got things organised. As in the Four Courts, they cut up the mutton with bayonets, and cooked it on the range. Bread was short so they made do with potatoes. They produced them boiled, fried and chipped to satisfy the relays of hungry men. As they came and went, it became apparent that they were all from the barricades in Church Street, North King Street, the Quays and, so far, the most dangerous barricades of all — those on the bridge opposite Church Street at the front of the Four Courts. It led across the river to Bridge Street.

On that Thursday, most of the activity seemed to be on the river side of the Four Courts. News came in that the British had placed artillery on the Quays near Capel Street Bridge. Shells began to hit the east side of the Four Courts building. The Volunteers replied with everything they had in the shape of rifle fire. Then the British were seen to have occupied a house in Bridge Street. This brought them considerably closer to the Four Courts. It placed the defenders of the bridge barricades in serious jeopardy. The position was critical.

It was the unique and splendid Peadar Clancy who was detailed to carry out a life-or-death exploit — an act of naked heroism. The late Volunteer Patrick O'Neill was on the bridge barricade at the time.

It was there that I witnessed one of the bravest acts of the Rising. Peadar Clancy called for covering fire, and with a tin of petrol in one hand and a revolver in the other he dashed across the bridge. There was a derelict tram car on the south side of the river. Clancy entered and removed the cushions which he doused with petrol. Then through heavy fire he ran to the window of the shop over which the enemy were entrenched. Smashing the glass, he lobbed in the cushions setting the last one alight. Inside a few seconds the building was blazing fiercely.

A threatening situation was thus relieved by a single Volunteer, and the tightening ring of British steel had been lessened, however temporarily.

The name of Peadar Clancy was heard often on that day. It was spoken as if its owner were a god. Tired and hungry as they were, the exhausted men found in Clancy's exploit an effective inspiration as they went out in relays to man the puny barricades. During their brief breaks for food, they talked incessantly of the fight and of its progress, and of the sites of recent action: the Mendicity Institute, Bridge Street, and Ganly's across the river. While Brigid Lyons heard a lot about them at the time, she had no idea where or what these buildings and streets were. She was an innocent lost in the centre of a blazing city in revolt, the geography of which city she knew very little.

Of one thing she was certain on that Thursday: gunfire had greatly increased in its intensity or, in their new outpost in Church Street, they had moved nearer to it. The noise was deafening, unceasing, and sometimes terrifying. It seemed that the British military were closing in in force, and were being heavily engaged by the Volunteers. However, the two Cumann na mBan volunteers had more to do than there was time in which to do it. They tried to organise short breaks from duty, but it never worked — what with the boom of artillery and the rattle of machine guns and rifle-fire, it was impossible to rest. And besides, there would always be someone looking for the simple consolation of a quick cup of tea.

On one such occasion, Brigid was in a great hurry. From a teapot she tossed the tea leaves in the grate. Katie Derham smacked a spoon on her wrist saying, 'I told you not to do that.'

'What harm will it do?' Brigid asked.

'Don't you know it'll bring crickets?' Katie admonished.

Over sixty years later, Brigid said of that incident: 'Katie Derham was a good friend, and very sympathetic, and patient with my domestic incompetence, but with the Germans on the Naas Road, and a naval battle in Dublin Bay, and the might of the British Empire outside the door, I couldn't see what harm a few crickets could do.'

Disconcerting news kept coming in that evening. The British had made another attempt to cross Grattan Bridge in the direction of the Four Courts. They'd been repulsed by concentrated Volunteer fire. Eventually, with armoured cars, they had crossed the bridge and had begun barricading on the Four Courts side. Inevitably, they were closing in. Next, they rescued the Lancers impounded in the Medical Mission. Then they removed the dead bodies of soldiers which had been lying all week in Charles Street, an area continually raked by crossfire.

Commandant Daly valued the exchange of information with the other fighting battalions, and particularly with Headquarters at the

GPO. As well as the Cumann na mBan dispatch carriers, there was Charlie Lyons (no relation to Brigid) a small-sized Volunteer for whose fine work Joe McGuinness retained a special admiration. Charlie had broken into the Bluecoat School in Blackhall Place and got himself a boy's uniform. Dressed thus, he had repeatedly got through the enemy lines with messages. There was another good messenger, a boy called Fox, nicknamed 'Reynard'. On Thursday evening, increased enemy action prevented all such further communication. The Four Courts had been effectively cut off from HQ.

Daly held a staff conference in the Fr Mathew Hall. Would they counterattack eastwards, and attempt to re-establish communications with the GPO? On the information coming in from the advanced barricades, enemy movement was such that the decision was against counterattack. It was agreed that grim defensive measures must be undertaken. Fiercely and desperately, they must now contest every inch of ground.

Around midnight, the clamour became terrifying. The flames from the Linenhall Barracks had reached McMaster Hodgson, the wholesale drug firm. Chemicals and oil drums were exploding like thunder. The inferno round Henrietta Lane was reflected by dull red clouds of evil-smelling smoke over the night sky. It was as if the entrails of Dublin were burning.

There was no sleep for anyone throughout that night, and least of all in Peadar Clancy's little outpost at 5 Church Street. By dawn, everybody was very weary. But everyone was still game to fight on to the end. In fact, optimism seemed to grow with each passing hour. Fear was unknown — apart from one recorded incident where the nerve of a young volunteer broke on the barricades. He went berserk, and, for his own safety, had to be restrained.

It was on Friday that the British first entered North King Street — from the Capel Street end — that is, the furthest point from the Volunteers' barricades at the Church Street end. They had first occupied Bolton Street Technical School, commanding the Capel Street area. William Feeney, a schoolboy resident of North King Street witnessed the scene:

On that Friday evening just after 'Tom the clerk' at Anne Street [now Halston Street] Church had rung the Angelus bell, I saw an armoured car for the first time in my life, nosing around Capel Street into North King Street. There was a traffic island at the junction, with a fire alarm and a coffee shop on it. The armoured car stopped when it got round the corner and the officers got out. I watched them from the drawing-room window. They took out maps and studied them and then re-entered the vehicle and drove back around the corner into Capel Street.

Almost immediately a number of British soldiers emerged around the corner in extended formation, that is in single file and advancing on both sides of King Street towards the barricades. There was no firing and a deadly silence pervaded that entire street, until the troops arrived at Lurgan Street and near North Anne Street. Then a fusillade met them from snipers on the roofs of the houses of both sides of King Street. Pandemonium broke out among the soldiers, who now retreated back to their original starting point at Capel Street. From that onwards the firing never stopped.

The British flies had walked into the parlour of Daly's Fighting First. Prisoners were taken. In the Fr Mathew Hall they proved to be from the South Staffordshire Regiment and provided the news that Sir John Maxwell had arrived from England and had taken over command from Brigadier-General Friend. Maxwell — 'Conky' to his friends, 'Butcher' to his enemies — had once halted the Turks, had attempted to relieve Gordon at Khartoum, and had now come to deal with the rebellious Irish.

Clearly England meant business. So did Ireland. The battle of North King Street had begun. But the British were not to make the same mistake when they re-entered the street. Using mocked-up armoured cars (the boilers of railway engines mounted on lorries), they ferried their troops to forward positions. Backing the lorries up to the houses, the troops were able to enter despite a withering fire from the Volunteers. Thus began the nightmare and savage house-to-house battle of North King Street. The fiercest battle of Easter Week, it was to rage throughout that night.

Meanwhile, the First Battalion headquarters in the Fr Mathew Hall had become exposed. Vice-Commandant Piaras Béaslaí explained:

I urged Ned Daly to seek the greater security of the Four Courts, as commandant, and leave me to carry on in the field of action. He saw the force of my argument and took his departure accompanied by Eamonn Duggan, our adjutant… Ned Morkan, the quartermaster, stayed with me. The attackers were repulsed with considerable slaughter, but resumed the attack later and I could not spare a man from the barricades to reinforce our gallant defenders.

The Father Mathew Hall was occupied by ladies of Cumann na mBan and a number of our wounded men. I decided it was impossible to defend it, if attacked. I proceeded to remove all arms and explosives from the place and bring them down to the Four Courts. As there were about half-a-dozen barricades across the road, which must be climbed over, the journey for heavily burdened men was laborious, though the darkness was lit up like daylight by the fires.

Throughout Friday night and Saturday morning, the battle of North King Street raged. Maxwell had ordered his troops swiftly to drive their way through Daly's outposts so as to throw a cordon round the Four Courts. Already the eighteen-pounders of the Royal Artillery were scoring hits on the great dome of the building. But progress proved to be anything but swift for the North Staffordshire Infantry. They had been trained for trench warfare, not for this desperate inching through a warren of narrow streets overlooked by snipers.

Crude as they were, Daly's defensive barricades were highly effective in greatly delaying the British advance, making every approaching soldier an open target for the Volunteers. Behind those barricades, sniping posts had been established from which riflemen could command the street from roofs and upper windows. At this stage, the most important outpost of the First Battalion was Reilly's Fort pub (now 'The Tap Bar') at the intersection of North King Street and Church Street. It had been used as a Red Cross centre. Now the Volunteers used its windows to pour a concentrated and withering hail of fire into the attacking South Staffordshires in North King Street. Alternately crouching against walls and zigzagging forward over the bullet-swept cobblestones, the British slogged on laboriously in conditions so confusing and so trying that the strain eventually proved unbearable.

Around the corner, in 5 Church Street, Katie Derham and Brigid Lyons continued their ministrations to the near-exhausted Volunteers. Sometime on that Friday, Brigid returned to the Four Courts on a message. Again she saw the DMP prisoners, and again she mistook them for the promised Germans from the Naas Road. She wasn't alone in her optimism. Despite the withdrawal of some of the outposts, the boys were adamant that they would finish the job they had begun. Even the eighteen-pounders hitting the Four Courts had had no effect on their morale. She found Joe McGuinness still busy, still full of cheer, still the same jovial Uncle Joe. His thoughts had turned to the unfortunate residents of the area. They had been without food and light for eight days. Now their water supply had failed, and there were risks of gas leaks and further spread of the fires.

The prisoners from the South Staffordshires stated that, on embarking in England, they had thought that they were bound for France. The belief had prevailed until they paused at Ballsbridge on their march from Kingstown (now Dún Laoghaire) to Mount Street Bridge (to relieve the Sherwood Foresters). They were amazed when English-speaking housewives had come out of their houses to offer them sandwiches and tea. Close-shaven, tired and confused, the young soldiers also said that fighting conditions in France could hardly be worse than in Dublin.

Some time during the hours of darkness, the patience of the South Staffordshires in North King Street gave out. To them, Reilly's Fort seemed impregnable, and every attempt to storm it from the narrow street resulted in a litter of casualties. Finally, frustrated by these bloody rebel Shinners, they turned on the hapless civilians, smashing into the small houses, wrecking all before them. Men and boys were beaten into the cellars, leaving women and children cowed and screaming in terror. Wholesale murders followed. Riddled bodies were to be recovered for weeks afterwards from the rubble of the cellars.

This British military action became known as the massacre of North King Street.

However, the terrorisation of the civilians did not affect the fighting spirit of the Volunteers. At nine o'clock on Saturday morning, the battle was still at full pitch, with Reilly's Fort still impregnable. Outside the building, all week had flown a tricolour fastened to a lance captured from the Lancers on Monday. Fluttering in the Saturday-morning sunshine, it was still there to tantalise the pinned-down British.

For another three hours, the battle raged, the Volunteers holding off the British. About noon, the ammunition in Reilly's Fort was finally exhausted. After fourteen hours of fighting, the occupants made a dash from the house and got safely away to the cover of their own barricades. The British lost no time in occupying the evacuated building, from which they were then able to pour a hail of fire on the Volunteers at the Church Street barricades. The late Volunteer Patrick O'Neill recorded the scene:

> It was at this point that Lieutenant Joe McGuinness came on the scene. He immediately sized up the situation. If the men in the Father Mathew Hall were not evacuated immediately, this new British force would cut them off. McGuinness ordered volley fire at the windows of the 'Red Cross House' [Reilly's Fort] and under this covering fire he calmly walked up the left-hand sidewalk towards the hall. He was almost comical in appearance. His feet were encased in a pair of carpet slippers; in his right hand he carried a Webly revolver and in his left hand a lead at the end of which was a large dog! Finally the British fire slackened and Joe disappeared into the Father Mathew Hall.
>
> More British troops had meanwhile reinforced those already in the 'Red Cross House', and a murderous fire was directed into the street. In the midst of this, Joe McGuinness re-appeared accompanied by the garrison of the Father Mathew Hall. Miraculously, none of this party was hit.

They moved into Battalion HQ in the Four Courts.

In the meantime, apart from the barricades, 5 Church Street had become the last of the Four Courts outposts. Truly deafened by the continuous din, Katie Derham and Brigid Lyons were still catering and performing first-aid, as and when their services were required. It was probably when the Fr Mathew garrison was passing the door with Joe McGuinness that they heard anguished shouting. Volunteer Patrick O'Neill explained:

> O'Flanagan of C Company was one of them. He staggered along naked to the waist. His Rosary hung around his neck. He was shouting, 'My brother — they have killed my brother'. He carried a rifle with fixed bayonet. He looked demented. The rifle was swinging in wild circles in the air. He was trying to get back up the street and would have done so but for those around him. His cries continued as he was passed through our position and back into the Four Courts.

In the early afternoon, Commandant Ned Daly summoned a conference of his officers to consider the situation. Although only a lieutenant, because of the exceptional courage and capacity he had displayed, Joe McGuinness was invited. Daly received a report the points of which included:

(a) The occupation of 'Reilly's Fort' by the British had cut the Volunteer line in two.

(b) A considerable number of Volunteers under Volunteer Patrick Holohan had thus been cut off in North Brunswick Street.

(c) The British now had the whole length of Church Street under fire, the only protection left to Volunteers being their crudely constructed barricades.

(d) An attempt to recapture 'Reilly's Fort' had been repulsed with Volunteer losses.

Piaras Béaslaí summarised the situation:

> Communication with our General Headquarters in the GPO had been cut off since Thursday. We were only too well aware of the fires which had been raging in Sackville Street, which lit up all Church Street and made night as bright as day, but we were not aware that the GPO had been evacuated and was now a smoking ruin.

It was decided to make an effort to get into communication with General Headquarters and ask for instructions. Tommy O'Connor who had brought so many important messages between Liverpool and New York prior to the Rising, was with us and undertook to try to make his way to the GPO and return with a message. If held up by the British military he had a plausible tale to tell them. He carried no written message.

We decided if no word came, to wait till nightfall and then make a sortie in full strength and endeavour to recapture the lost position. While we were speaking Denis O'Callaghan called attention to the unusual silence outside.

In 5 Church Street, Brigid Lyons was trying to sharpen a knife on the edge of Volunteer Michael Lennon's range. There was a pile of stale loaves waiting to be sliced in anticipation of the afternoon's rush for teas. Katie Derham was drying spoons — the same half-dozen teaspoons that had done duty thousands of times that week.

It had been happening for a little while before Brigid Lyons noticed. What was it? She looked out the little back window. You could see a bit of blue sky over the high wall surrounding the yard. Funny, she thought, how the smoke of burning buildings can darken even the glorious sunshine. And then it suddenly occurred to her what had happened. She turned to Katie Derham.

'Have you noticed anything?' she asked.

Katie paused for a moment, listening. 'The shooting's stopped,' she said in amazement.

The moment impressed itself on Brigid's memory.

Suddenly the most extraordinary and inexplicable silence seemed to descend on the whole place. The shooting had died down, but it wasn't that — not just that. There was an extraordinary sensation of something terrible having happened.'

# 9

# THE SURRENDER

THERE WERE OTHERS too who had noticed the silence. Nonetheless, Volunteer Patrick O'Neill, on the instructions of Lieutenant Peadar Clancy was given a new assignment. It was on the roof of Patterson's match factory.

'I want you to go up there,' Clancy said, pointing to the water tower on the roof. 'The fire seems to have died down and you should be up before they have time to have a crack at you. There is a deep lip on the tank and once you get under that you'll be all right. I was already up there myself this morning. When you get there, watch the photographer's shop at the angle of Exchange Street and the Quays. If the British try to leave by the front, open fire and keep at it. I'll have you relieved in an hour. Good luck.'

When he reached the appointed place, Volunteer O'Neill noted that the photographer's shop was there all right, but there was no sign of life. Nor was there a soul to be seen on the Quays. As he kept watch, he noticed that the last of the firing had died away. In fact, an almost unearthly silence reigned.

In the last of the Four Courts outposts Brigid Lyons was chopping wood with a hatchet when a young Volunteer burst in and grabbed the hatchet. He began to hack the butt of his rifle. 'What are you doing?' she shouted.

'There's talk of a surrender,' he wailed. 'I'll never surrender my rifle. Nobody will ever use my gun again.'

Out in the back yard there was a group of Volunteers with axes and shovels frantically trying to tear a hole in the high brick wall.

'What are they doing?' Brigid asked.

'We'll never surrender,' the lad said. 'They're trying to escape. We'll carry on the fight some other place.'

Brigid Lyons looked out the window again at the frustrated little group that swore and stormed as they assailed the wall. Some were crying. She remembered the moment with these words: 'It was terribly touching and terribly moving.'

In a few minutes, the post was full of Volunteers, some in civvies, some in uniform. The talk was of the let-down of surrender and of how they could evade it. The lads couldn't let themselves believe it was true. Things were still confused.

Volunteer Tom Bevan handed his revolver to Brigid. 'If you can, get that home to my mother,' he said. 'Bring it when you're going.' She promised she would, and took the revolver. Then two others did the same. Her spoils of war were increasing: Uncle Frank's thirty gold sovereigns, Lord Dunsany's brass button and now three Volunteers' revolvers.

Back in the Four Courts, the exhausted Vice-Commandant, Piaras Béaslaí, had nodded asleep when Captain Eamonn Duggan rushed in and shook him violently shouting, 'Connolly has surrendered unconditionally.'

In retrospect, Béaslaí stated that though he naturally speculated much at the time on the outcome of the fight, the possibility of a general surrender had never occurred to him. He claimed that his outlook was not exceptional. The attitude of the rank and file, on hearing the news in 5 Church Street, bears out Béaslaí's contention.

'Knowing Connolly's point of view,' Béaslaí said, 'his desperate courage and belief in the necessity for a "blood sacrifice", I thought that the defenders of each position would be expected to fight on as long as fighting was possible. I found myself confronted with a wholly unexpected contingency.'

The order to surrender had been brought to the Four Courts by a member of Cumann na mBan, Nurse Elizabeth O'Farrell, assisted by Fr Columba, a Capuchin from Church Street who carried the handmade white flag for her. The surrender was received with astonished disbelief. There was an obvious reluctance to surrender unconditionally. The British used these moments of indecision to bring up artillery with a threat to shell the Fr Mathew Hall where some Volunteer wounded still lay. Preceded by a Volunteer with a white flag, Frs Augustine and Aloysius, of the Capuchins, emerged from the Hall into the no-man's-land of Church Street, and made contact with Colonel Taylor, British officer in charge of the sector and now commanding the Church Street barricades.

Colonel Taylor informed the priests that a truce had been arranged, but the Four Courts garrison was reluctant to cease fire, suspecting the 'truce' to be another British trick. He would spare the Fr Mathew Hall until they had had an opportunity to go into the Four Courts and convince the leaders that a truce had in fact been called.

Béaslaí said, 'As I accompanied Duggan from the room to the open space at the rear of the building, he told me that the order to surrender had been brought to us by a Capuchin Father from the Franciscan Friary who had received it from a British officer and that Daly had gone out to the gate to interview the officer.' Here Béaslaí was obviously referring to the ultimatum from Colonel Taylor.

Meanwhile, two hours had passed since Volunteer O'Neill had positioned himself high under Patterson's water tower. The silence had continued. Eventually he assumed that Peadar Clancy had forgotten him.

I got to my feet and climbed down the ladder. As I emerged from the factory window I saw a British officer approach along Church Street. He walked slowly over to Commandant Daly and Captain Duggan, both of whom were bare-headed. I could hear the officer say, 'That is so, the rebel chief has surrendered'. Suddenly the British officer asked for a drink and a glass of water was brought. He gulped it down and returned the glass with a bow. Commandant Daly saluted, saying, 'Very well. It is the fortune of war.'

Still dazed, Béaslaí emerged from the back of the Four Courts. He saw Daly talking to a British officer at the back gate, which opened into Church Street. The officer was surrounded by armed soldiers, their rifles at the ready. Holding their own rifles, groups of Volunteers stood about the yard looking on sullenly.

'Look, they have him covered,' a Volunteer suddenly called out. 'They're taking him prisoner.' Immediately, British soldiers appeared on roofs and other vantage points, all pointing their rifles at Daly.

'Let's keep them covered and fire if they fire,' another Volunteer called, and they lifted their rifles to their shoulders. A Capuchin priest ran amongst them, calling, 'Put down your rifles. There's a truce.'

'Then let them put down theirs,' Volunteer Frank Shouldice replied defiantly.

Having handed his sword to the British officer, Commandant Daly beckoned his officers to his side and led them indoors to the battalion staff room in the Four Courts. He produced a small typed document, bearing Pearse's signature:

> In order to prevent the further slaughter of Dublin citizens, and in the hope of saving the lives of our followers now surrounded and hopelessly out-numbered, the members of the Provisional Government present at Headquarters have agreed to an unconditional surrender, and the Commandants of the various districts in the City and country will order their commands to lay down arms.
>
> (Signed) P.H. Pearse
> 29th April, 1916 3.45 p.m.

Having read Pearse's instrument of surrender, Béaslaí looked up. He saw that Ned Daly's head was buried in his hands. He was weeping.

Béaslaí was

> … still in a daze, unable to assess the situation. It should be remembered that we had no knowledge of what had happened in the other parts of the country, or even, in the last few days, of what was happening in other parts of Dublin. We hoped, and persuaded ourselves, that Cork, Kerry, Limerick, Galway and the other centres were fighting as we were fighting. The wildest rumours were circulated and eagerly believed. There was a mutiny of the Irish regiments in the British Army! The Germans had landed troops in England! All Ireland was 'up in arms.' The news

of a general surrender after only six days came as a shock, and I found myself wondering what the effect of the Rising on public opinion would be.

Lieutenant Peadar Clancy called into his outpost at 5 Church Street. He seemed to be in a hurry. He had come to collect the remnants of his men. Brigid Lyons offered him tea.

'I can't stay now,' he said. 'But I'll be back.'

All of a sudden, 5 Church Street became as quiet as a vault. The two Cumann na Monsters looked at one another as if to say, 'What now?' On the instant, Katie Derham made her own decision. 'I'll try to get home to my mother,' she said. 'She'll be in a frightful panic.' Then she left.

Now alone, Brigid Lyons answered a knock at the door. Two old men from the locality came in. 'We hadn't a bite o' food for days,' one explained. Brigid remembered the incident clearly:

They and their families were hungry. They were very poor people. There were piles of stores still in the house, so I gave them as much bread and butter and ham as they could carry. Soon there were more callers and I did the same, until the stores began to run low. Then I remember distinctly taking back a loaf, a piece of butter and some ham. I shall never know why I did that, excepting that maybe somebody else from the battalion would come along feeling hungry. But no one came.

Alone again, 'the fat girl from the country' looked around Michael Lennon's little kitchen where she'd toiled continuously for over sixty hours. She wondered how poor Michael was progressing in the Richmond Hospital, and where his wife and children were. She wondered too what was about to happen to all those fearless boys who, so earnestly, didn't want to give up the fight. Never afraid of bombs or bullets, Brigid Lyons was suddenly afraid of her own company.

I took up an oil cape that was lying there, went out and pulled the door to. I walked down Church Street towards the Four Courts. Nearing the hole in the wall, I saw Peadar Clancy coming through it.

'We've had to surrender,' he said. 'Now we're to be marched away to the Rotunda.'

'You never came back for your tea,' she said.

'No, I couldn't.'

Silently, in the gathering dusk, they walked back to 5 Church Street. Dejectedly, he sat down in the kitchen.

'Will you have tea now?' Brigid asked him.

'No', he replied. 'I couldn't.' Peadar Clancy was like a man whose heart was broken.

She remembered sitting silently in the dusk with him for about fifteen minutes.

Then I said, 'Will I make you some sandwiches?' I don't think he replied. I wouldn't say they were very elegant, but I made the sandwiches and wrapped them in newspaper. I think he ate one sitting there. He was very, very broken, naturally. When I met him after his release from prison in 1917, he told me those sandwiches had saved his life and those of some of his comrades who had spent that night in the open in the grounds of the Rotunda. I was profoundly impressed by Peadar Clancy's chivalry. On our way back to the Four Courts, I was deeply touched that in all the stress of his grief in that terrible moment, in helping me through the hole in the wall he was as thoughtful and courteous as a knight leading his lady through a minute in a stately drawing room.

They found the main hall of the Four Courts in confusion. It was crowded with Volunteers and there seemed to be hundreds of British soldiers. Lights of some kind had been rigged up. Frank Fahy and Eamonn Duggan had addressed the Volunteers, telling them of the order to surrender. Waving automatics, many reacted furiously, vowing they would never give up their guns. Commandant Daly faced them: 'If you fire a shot, you must fire at me. I have my orders from the Commander-in-Chief. I have given my sword and my word to the British officer and nobody shall go back on it.'

Then a Capuchin priest appealed to the Volunteers: 'Boys, I know you find it hard to surrender, but it must be done. Think of your fathers and mothers, your wives and children. It's no use resisting. You will all be killed. You will be wiped out.'

'We don't give a damn about that, Father,' Daly said. 'But we must surrender. We have the order from our Commander-in-Chief.'

Presently a British officer stepped forward. 'Gentlemen,' he said politely, 'would you be good enough to fall in? You will march out that gate. As a mark of honour, your officers will be allowed to march at the head of the men.' This proved to be the ruse by which the British were enabled to identify the leaders of the Rising.

Joe McGuinness was with Ned Daly. Colonel Lindsay was beside them. At the last minute, Joe embraced his niece. 'Get home as quick as you can, Brigid, and tell Katie I'll be all right.'

Ned Daly overheard him. 'No, the city's under martial law,' he said. 'I don't advise you to go home or anywhere else. Colonel Lindsay here has given me his word of honour all you girls will be taken home in the morning.'

Brigid thanked him and said goodbye, never to see him again. Peadar Clancy also said goodbye as he was moving out with his men. When they had gone, Brigid had no idea what to do or where to go. The other girls seemed just as lost. Their number had been increased by arrivals from the GPO who had left after the surrender there. A Capuchin friar eventually arrived with instructions: 'You girls will all have to come upstairs and I'm to stay with you.' His name was Fr Columba.

Brigid recalled the situation thus:

> With fixed bayonets, the Tommies swarmed round us and marched us up the stairs. While they weren't objectionable to us, they were very firm and looked terrifying. Later on, under escort, some girls were allowed to the basement kitchen to make tea. We were escorted even to the doors of the toilets. All we had for food was some chocolate and cream crackers.

Presently they lay on the mattresses on the floor of the Judges' Chambers. For the second and last time in her life, Brigid Lyons sought slumber wrapped in judicial sables and minks.

By 10 p.m. on that Saturday, four hundred Volunteers had been herded together to spend the night standing on a small plot of grass in front of the Rotunda Hospital. Among them were Daly's Fighting First, or at least those who had so far surrendered. The detachment, under Volunteer Patrick Holohan, which had been cut off on Friday, was still fighting in North Brunswick Street, and would go on fighting well into Sunday. The Volunteers were still demanding to see Pearse's order before they would believe that he had surrendered. Even the Capuchins had failed to convince them. On that Sunday, Fr Augustine had to see Brigadier Lowe, the British General, in order to see Pearse, now a prisoner in Arbour Hill, to get a written note from him to take to Holohan before the latter would surrender. That saved the South Staffordshires from having to shoot it out. Thus Ned Daly's Fighting First Battalion was the first to see action on Easter Monday and was the last still in action on the following Sunday.

Writing fifty years later, Colonel P. J. Hally gave a professional soldier's assessment of Commandant Ned Daly's achievement in the Four Courts:

> From a military point of view the occupation of this area was sound. The movements of British troops from the Royal Barracks was seriously interfered with and large forces were tied down in the area all week. House-to-house fighting, strong barricade defences and intelligent use of snipers inflicted serious losses on the British and imposed a serious delay to their overall attack plans. A big British military effort was put into clearing this area and they had not succeeded when Daly, obeying higher orders, surrendered, marched his troops in perfect order to O'Connell Street and laid down his arms. In my opinion Daly showed excellent military skill by concentrating his force when he knew his small mobilisation strength by organising local attacks to retake ground lost by establishing strong points such as Reilly's pub at the corner of North King Street, naturally supported by fire from other posts such as Jameson's Malt House. To sum up, an excellent area, well-held, well-defended and well-led.

As Easter Week wore on, the various garrisons had become pinned down as British fire power and encircling movements had increased. But as Calton Younger wrote, 'Only the Four Courts garrison under

Edward Daly was able to maintain a series of outposts which gave flexibility to their operations.'

The immediate effect of Easter Week was the number of casualties. Including British military, Irish Volunteers and Dublin civilians, the number killed and wounded was approximately 1,300. *The Irish Times Handbook*, published in 1916 shortly after the Rising, gives the figure as 1,306. Max Caulfield records it as 1,351.

# 10

# THE REWARDS

AN OUTSTANDING MEMORY of all associated with the Rising was the prevailing June-like weather. Sunday morning, 30 April, dawned as brightly as the historic days that had gone before. Its sunlight threw into high relief the savage battle scars suffered by Gandon's graceful Four Courts.

Those who occupied the Judges' Chambers awoke early, not because they were rested, but because they were bodily weary and sore from lying on the floor. The remnants of the once-sprightly Cumann na mBan felt as wrecked as the building around them. Not a girl possessed as much as a sponge or a comb or anything which might assist their affronted femininity. They all eagerly looked forward to getting home to hot baths and a civilised breakfast.

The faithful Capuchin, Fr Columba, was still there by way of protection. His presence held some reassurance. At least the British would have to deal with them decently while a priest was around. In their innocence, they made no allowance for British Army suspicion of monkish men on the enemy side in times of war.

Meanwhile, Fr Columba informed them of what had happened elsewhere in Dublin. Half-awake, the girls heard about the dreadful looting, the appalling damage to the city centre, the burnings, the destruction and, worst of all, the terrible loss of life.

Presently British soldiers appeared. Again, under escort, the girls were allowed to make tea. Everything was strictly stiff-upper-lip: no conversation; silence in fact. When the Tommies looked at them, they appeared shocked — something that the girls felt must reflect the frights they themselves looked. Stuffed in her clothes, Brigid Lyons was still carrying those three revolvers, all of which were bulging inappropriately. Lord Dunsany's button was still fastened in her lapel, while Uncle Frank's thirty sovereigns she had sewn into the hem of her skirt. She had become so familiar with revolvers that, for the moment at least, her naivety had overlooked them as the most incriminating of her possessions. 'I was determined to keep those revolvers,' she said. 'Hoping to be able to deliver them as I had promised.'

A British officer came up the stairs. Sullenly, he surveyed the array of dishevelled women sitting on mattresses on the floor. 'You girls are under arrest,' he snapped. 'You're to assemble in the yard. You're going to Richmond Barracks (later Keogh Barracks in Inchicore).'

'That was a bit of a shock,' Brigid remembered. 'But the Capuchin insisted he'd try to come with us.'

They were about to move off when a girl nudged Brigid. 'Those revolvers — for God's sake, get rid of them. If we're under arrest, we'll be searched.' Many, many years later, Brigid lamented, 'It turned out I was never searched and I was very sorry I had left them behind.'

Transport of the women prisoners was coldly efficient.

We were trundled into a lorry. We had to sit on the floor on straw. I found that drive quite interesting. It was lovely and sunny and we seemed to go off into the country, though how that could be on a journey from the Four Courts to Inchicore I can't explain. In the distance you could see smoke over the city, and there was still spasmodic shooting. The few people who were on the streets looked frightened. They were huddled in gossiping groups. At Inchicore we were marched into Richmond Barracks, and lined up on the square. There were crowds of Volunteers. The first man I recognised was Colonel Lindsay. 'You broke your word,' I told him. 'I thought I was getting home today.' He looked tense. He was now a different man. He didn't reply, and the other girls told me for God's sake shut up.

Colonel Lindsay had lost the bonhomie he had shown as a British prisoner in the Four Courts. Now the boot was on the other foot. He was a British officer again, helping the 'G' Division to prepare the way for General Maxwell's bloodbath. The rebel leaders must be identified for the mockery of Maxwell's courts martial, and for all that was to follow.

Brigid Lyons watched the drama unfold:

The Volunteers were lined up on the barrack square, and there seemed to be hundreds of British soldiers about. The Dublin girls recognised various Volunteers, including Seán McDermott. Most of them were only names to me. Countess Markievicz was there too, still looking defiant in her uniform. Presently we were marched into the barracks, and up countless stairs. I thought it the highest building I'd ever climbed. We were packed into a little room where we found Winifred Carney. She had been secretary to James Connolly in the GPO. She had come in earlier with the men who'd spent the night standing in front of the Rotunda Hospital.

Through a little window the soldiers teased us as to what we'd been up to. The sentries threw in a ration of dog biscuits. Then we were brought out one by one for interrogation by British officers — names, addresses, who we knew, our policies. We acted up stupid and the interrogations ended with a self-righteous British lecture on our naughtiness — you know, 'It hurts us more than it hurts you.'

Back in the overcrowded room, the women were given tins of cocoa, but no food. Later, they were ordered to the square again, where they were lined up 'like the prisoners we were'. Meanwhile, Dublin Metropolitan Policemen had joined in the identification exercise. Countess Markievicz was directed to join the women. Brigid recalled:

In her green breeches and tunic, and a hat with a green cockade, she expressed a flamboyant defiance of British military might. A member of Connolly's Citizen Army, she had fought all week as an officer at the Royal College of Surgeons. Now she was being demoted to the ranks of Cumann na mBan. Just then it was hard to equate her with Yeats' description: 'What voice more sweet than hers when, young and beautiful, she rode to harriers.'

An officer informed the women that they were going to Kilmainham Gaol. The Countess was ordered to the head of the contingent. Brigid continued:

> We were marched across the square towards the gate, leaving the men to their various fates. I'll never forget the moment that gate was opened. All hell broke loose in the street. The British infantry closed in around us for our protection. They marched two abreast all round us, we marching three abreast in the centre. Otherwise, we'd have been lynched by the women outside. They were loyalists, and British Army wives. The hostility, the abuse, the shrieking and shouting was terrifying. I think it was mainly directed at Countess Markievicz, probably because of her breeches and tunic and her defiant attitude at the head of the march. In the circumstances, it seemed quite a journey from Keogh Square to Kilmainham.

The old jail was frightening for the women. It had not been occupied for years, and was damp and dark and dreary. Brigid remembered it vividly:

> We were brought into an evil-smelling circular room where, ranting and raving at us, a fearful-looking old man held up a lantern to peer at each of us. He was like the terrifying jailers one had read about. A British officer went through the usual drill: names, addresses, occupations, etc. When he'd finished, he said, 'Beatty, bring them down that way.' Beatty was the old jailer. He replied, 'I'll bring them down this way first', and he marched us down a dark, dank corridor. Suddenly he swung his lantern above his head and shouted, 'Read that.' Written up over a window was: 'Sin no more lest a worse thing come unto thee.'
>
> 'But we haven't sinned,' I protested.
>
> 'Shut up,' he shouted. 'It's to the long drop you should be taken — every one of you.'
>
> I didn't know what that meant, but I was warned again by the other girls to keep quiet. I was the fat girl from the country, talking out of my turn as usual.

The young women were brought upstairs and put five in each cell. It was afterwards established that about one hundred women were held in B Wing, above and below the cells occupied by the men who were executed. There was nothing whatever in the cells.

> The doors were locked on us. We just flopped down on the stone floor, and lay there dead beat. Thirsty, we knocked on the cell door and called for water. That seemed to be the funniest thing they'd heard for a long time — and we got no water.
>
> Sometime towards morning, we were wakened by two nurses, as I thought, but in fact they were wardresses sent from Mountjoy Prison. They were taken aback. We weren't the kind of women they'd expected. One was pleasant and human. The other was a formidable official, though I met her afterwards and found her a nice person.
>
> Presently the cell door was unlocked. Outside there were two soldiers, one with a fixed bayonet. The other pushed in tins of slimy cocoa — fearful stuff — with hunks of dry bread. By then we were very glad to get it, such as it was. Around noon we were given a tin of stew. No forks, spoons or anything — all you had to do was put it on your head! Meantime, although I'd lost my revolvers, I still had my gold, and my button, and somewhere I'd acquired a penknife. With this I fished out any edible bits floating in the stew.

There was no ventilation, and as the day wore on, the prisoners all got fearful headaches. A doctor came. He arranged for them to have bed-boards and a blanket and said that there was to be no more than two in a cell. Some of the girls were moved out. Brigid spent that night with May Lennon.

The following day, they were allowed ten minutes' exercise, pacing around a yard. They were not allowed to speak. Brigid takes up the story:

> We saw some we recognised — Countess Plunkett, for instance, mother of Joseph Plunkett. There were others the Dublin girls knew, but who were only names to me. We never saw Countess Markievicz again. She was kept in solitary confinement.

We were brought down for interrogation. This was where my Dunsany button caught up with me. I was wearing a voluminous showerproof coat my aunt had lent me going into the Four Courts. In the meantime, somebody had given me a long, warm tweed skirt — somebody's cast-off I suppose — because I'd come up from the country wearing only a light costume. I was very glad of that tweed skirt in Kilmainham. The Dunsany button was in my lapel. It was a British Army button, and was recognised by my British interrogator. From my occupation — medical student — he came to cynical conclusions: was it a decoration for medical services to Lord Dunsany?

The interview included another lecture, and ended with a warning that I'd have to give an undertaking never to get mixed up in this sort of thing again. I was alone so there was no one to tell me to shut up. 'I'm hoping to be a doctor,' I told the officer. 'I expect to be always where there's trouble and where my services may be needed, so I couldn't give you that sort of undertaking.'

Then he resumed his questions: who did I know in the Movement? What rank was so-and-so? At that, I acted up like the fat girl from the country. I knew nothing. I was in it by accident. I don't know how much he believed me, but eventually he let me go.

Brigid remembered one of the prison guards, 'a bouncy sort, always seeking popularity', who took sympathy on her:

He visited me occasionally. He told the others he had great sympathy for 'the student', as he called me. Every time he came, he said the same thing: 'I think you'll be let home soon, don't be worrying.' And every time I said the same thing, 'It doesn't worry me. I want to be here with my friends and I want no special treatment, thank you.' I think I disappointed him.

On the Tuesday, May Lennon was moved to another cell and Brigid was left alone. No reason was given. On her return from the exercise yard, she found 'an undesirable person' huddled in the corner of her cell.

She was a drunk street-walker and I refused to go in with her. So they put me into another cell, alone. That afternoon, a lovely tea-tray was brought in. It seemed I was next door to Countess Plunkett, who was having her meals sent in. She had sent her tea-tray to the lonely waif next door. It was the first cup of civilised tea I'd seen in a whole fortnight.

Brigid didn't mind being alone during the day, but she was frightened at night.

The wardress had said, 'We can't lock your door on the outside, so don't touch it and don't go out.' There was a sentry walking up and down all night. As I lay shivering, I could hear the sound of sniping in the distance. It came at odd times from far away in the city. It was around 3 a.m. I heard a sudden fearful barrage of savage shooting near at hand. In fact, it was just outside. Alone in that freezing cold cell, I was stiff with fear. This shooting was unlike anything I'd heard at the Four Courts.

In the morning, Brigid asked the wardress about that terrible shooting. She looked bothered. Then in a frightened whisper she said, 'I think they were shooting some of the men.' That was terrifying. Fortunately I wasn't to know the whole truth for some time: that what I'd heard at dawn that morning was a British firing party shooting Pearse, MacDonagh and poor Tom Clarke.

In the exercise yard that day, any sly word we could exchange was of course about the shooting. Bríd Foley said, 'No, they daren't shoot them. They'd be too afraid of American opinion. Nobody'll be shot, you needn't worry.' Bríd had an air of authority, and what she said was comforting.

Later that day, Brigid was moved to another cell where there was a Miss Mulhall, a town councillor. Outside the door, there was a flight of iron stairs.

Early on Thursday morning I heard somebody stumbling down the stairs, and then the sound of feet stamping along the corridor and then down more iron stairs. In a few minutes there was that awful concentrated shooting again.

LIMERICK COUNTY LIBRARY

Time was to tell that Joe Plunkett, Ned Daly, Willie Pearse and Michael O'Hanrahan were shot dead in Kilmainham Gaol on Thursday 4 May 1916.

The following morning the prisoners heard the sound again. That was John MacBride. Brigid recalled:

For months afterwards, I wakened at that hour. I could always hear the awful shooting again. It never left my mind.

On Sunday morning, the prisoners were brought to Mass in the prison chapel. Seated on the balcony, the women were heavily guarded. The ground floor was full of male prisoners.

I got a whack of a bayonet and was told 'Sit down and keep quiet.' I had recognised three Volunteers who went to communion, two still in their uniforms: Eamonn Ceannt, Con Colbert and Seán Heuston. With Michael Mallin from the College of Surgeons, they were shot the following morning — the last time I was to hear that terrible death rattle of concerted fire.

The greatest comfort for Brigid and the other women was the frequent visits of the good Capuchins from Church Street: Fr Albert and Fr Aloysius. However, they gave them no news as to who had been shot.

My greatest concern was poor Tom Clarke because I knew him best. The priests knew all about it because, as we learned afterwards, they had attended to all the men shot in Kilmainham. They were just trying to spare our feelings.

On Monday night, 8 May, Brigid and the other women were brought out of the cells and lined up in the main hall.

We were told the British Government in its generosity had decided to release us. But first we must give an undertaking to give up being wicked rebels. We were given a solemn warning that if ever again we were suspected of such activities (and they now knew our names, addresses and descriptions), we would be yanked in for the duration. The duration of what wasn't specified. The officer concluded, 'You're free to go now, or you can stay until morning.'

'We were told that story before,' I said. 'We were told at the Four Courts we could go home in the morning, but it didn't happen — so I think we'd better go now.'

Groups of girls went into discussion. The Sullivan sisters, Pauline Morkan, Flossie Meade and May Lennon agreed with me we'd go immediately. Pauline's people had a pub on the Quays at the corner of Queen Street, so she invited us to make for there. It was the nearest refuge, and there was martial law.

By the time the women got out, it was dark. There were no street lights, but there was a moon, and the city was dead silent. There were British sentries every hundred yards or so along the streets. Brigid remembered being halted by every one. When they had explained themselves, a soldier would escort them to the next post. They could hear the occasional sound of snipers.

At Pauline Morkan's place, the women were refused entry by a group of soldiers. Brigid recalled Pauline begging to go into her home and to bring her friends.

They said no, the house was occupied. She asked to go in to collect some belongings. She was allowed while we waited on the quays outside. She returned crying. 'They're all over the place,' she said. 'And everything's torn to bits. There's no hope of staying there.' I didn't know how things were with Aunt Joe, but I suggested we try there. It was quite a step to Upper Gardiner Street, and there were risks because of the curfew. Apart from soldiers, there wasn't a soul to be seen.

Finally, a soldier offered to escort us. Happily, he was of the better type. He tried to cheer us up. 'If you can't get in anywhere,' he said, 'I have an aunt who has a nursing home in Mountjoy Square and I'll get you in there.' He was probably a Dublin boy in the British forces. He came all the way to Gardiner Street. It was now 1 a.m. Mrs Farrell came down and opened the door. When she saw the soldier, she tried to close the door again. 'No, you can't come in here,' she cried. 'We know nothing about anything.' The population was demoralised.

Eventually she got tea for us all, with real bread and butter, and we had a wash and went to bed, and slept like logs. Looking back at that night, it was rather a terrifying experience, particularly as we were so innocently oblivious of all the risks involved. But fair is fair, the British soldiers were very helpful.

In the following days, there was nothing else talked about but 'The Rising'. Everybody coming into Aunt Joe's shop in Dorset Street had a story, each more tragic, more thrilling, more exciting than the last.

We were beginning to piece things together: who had been executed, who wounded, and the jail sentences. After court martial, Uncle Joe got deportation to England and five years' penal servitude, reduced to three. Uncle Frank had gone home wounded and was promptly arrested on arrival in Longford. Tom Bannon was arrested and detained in Richmond Barracks.

The wholesale deportations to English prisons were depressing. Under heavy escort, the Volunteers were marched through the city to the cross-channel boats. But it was Maxwell's vindictive executions of the leaders which cast the deepest gloom. In those sad days, Mrs Tom Clarke was a frequent visitor to Aunt Joe's house. She had made two tragic journeys to Kilmainham Gaol, the first to take leave of her husband and twenty-four hours later, now a widow, to take her last leave of her only brother, Ned Daly. Yet there was no bitterness, no recrimination. In spite of her sacrifices, she remained a dignified, serene woman.

Aunt Joe was a source of comfort to Kathleen Clarke. At least Joe McGuinness had not been executed. From various sources, his fate, and the fate of the Four Courts garrison, gradually emerged — from that Saturday evening when the First Battalion had been marched away under British escort with Ned Daly at their head, followed by Duggan, Morkan, Béaslaí and Joe McGuinness. Along the quays and in Sackville Street, they were spat at, screamed at and had hostile fists shaken at them by furious women — again principally the wives of British soldiers.

As they marched through the ruined Sackville Street, some of the young volunteers wept, not at the destruction — that was the price of war — but at their own sense of frustration. Frequently a defiant shout went up: 'We'll rise again!' But the stolid British escort took no notice. Every humiliation was piled on them. At the Parnell Monument they were stopped, a British officer ordering their leader, Ned Daly: 'Go back among the other prisoners — at the double!'

In the grounds at the front of the Rotunda Hospital, the men joined the GPO garrison. All were made to stand — for want of space, sitting was impossible — on a small lawn in the centre of the forecourt. There they remained standing all night, without even the opportunity to relieve themselves. There were only insults and taunts of 'bloody Shinner rebels', particularly for those who gave their names in Irish. It seemed the British were only itching to turn their guns on the lot of them.

On Sunday morning, the men had been marched to Richmond Barracks. Brigid Lyons and her colleagues had arrived there at about the same time — in the comparative comfort of a lorry. Unknown to her, Uncle Joe was somewhere in that crowd of Volunteers on the barrack square. Indeed, in the stages through which they passed, uncle and niece had curiously similar experiences. All day, the identification process had continued segregating those for deportation from those for court martial.

At the preliminary investigations, the British interrogating officers were ably assisted by two officers who had been the most pampered officers in the Four Courts: Colonel Lindsay (captured with Lord Dunsany) and a Lieutenant Halpin. Following the taking of 'evidence', Duggan, Béaslaí and McGuinness were informed that they were for court martial. In fact, they were among the first six prisoners to be 'tried'. The other three, the first to be executed, were Pearse, Clarke and MacDonagh.

On that Sunday night in Richmond Barracks, four prisoners found themselves sitting listlessly on the floor of a cell devoid of furniture. They were Ned Daly, Peadar Clancy, Liam Ó Broin (afterwards Professor of Romance Languages at University College, Galway) and Joe McGuinness. Bored by inactivity and anti-climax, the effervescent Joe enquired, 'What about a song, lads?'

There were no objections and Joe obliged with 'The Darlin' Girl from Clare'. Clancy followed with another song. Then it came Ned Daly's turn. Ned was the least likely man to sing at any time, but he surprised the little company. He suddenly broke into a sentimental love song, giving it everything he had in volume. There was a sudden interruption. Peremptorily, the door opened. A British officer, brandishing a revolver, burst in. Glowering at the prisoners, he bellowed, 'If there's another sound from you lot, you'll all be taken out and disposed of.' He departed, leaving them to consider his threat. After ten minutes of bored sighs and yawns, Joe enquired, 'Eh, lads, isn't it time we were going home?'

With such flashes of humour are lit man's darkest hours. Not surprisingly, Joe McGuinness was to gain the reputation of being the happiest prisoner with whom to share a cell. The incident was related to Dr Brigid Lyons Thornton, and to the author of this book, by Professor Ó Broin some sixty years later.

Early on Monday, Duggan, Béaslaí and McGuinness were escorted to another building in Richmond Barracks and there made to sit on the floor. Presently a second escort arrived, bringing Pearse, Clarke and MacDonagh. The six were conducted to another building, three into one room and three into another, in each of which a mockery of British judicial processes was enacted. On its conclusion, Duggan, Béaslaí and McGuinness were escorted to the original room and again made to sit on the floor. Eventually, Pearse, Clarke and MacDonagh, their 'trials' concluded, were brought in. All six were then escorted to a gymnasium and there left together.

Piaras Béaslaí recorded these moving moments:

Pearse sat on the floor apparently in deep thought. He did not once address any of us. Clarke seemed in a mood of quiet, deep satisfaction that he had lived to see what he had seen. He said confidently, as he had said on the Sunday in the same place, 'This insurrection will have a great effect on the country. It will be a different Ireland.'

As for MacDonagh, he chatted freely and seemed in the highest spirits. He declared that a German force had landed in England and seemed to think that the British Empire was tottering to its fall. Years afterwards, I found out that Yarmouth and Lowestoft were bombarded by vessels of the German Navy in Easter Week, 1916, and concluded that some rumour of this had reached Tomás and was responsible for his story of a German landing.

At length towards nightfall, we were all marched together under a heavy escort to Kilmainham Prison. A little sergeant with a strong Cockney accent showed me into a cell and surprised me by telling me he was Irish.

Together in the same cell, Duggan, Béaslaí and McGuinness, were wakened on that Wednesday dawn by a fusillade in the yard below. It was no less chilling for Joe McGuinness than for his niece incarcerated elsewhere in that ancient prison, but he had to wait some time to learn of its significance. The little sergeant ran into their cell congratulating them. 'I thought you were going to be shot — I did, honest. Didn't you hear that shooting at daybreak? I'll say no more.' There was no need. They guessed the worst and, like Brigid Lyons, they were to hear the sound of more executions before they left Kilmainham Gaol.

The friendship of Mrs Tom Clarke and Mrs Joe McGuinness was of long standing. The events of Easter Week, and their awful aftermath, brought to their friendship a new and tragic dimension.

# 11

# PICKING UP THE PIECES

BRIGID LYONS WAS unsure exactly when, but at some stage after Easter 1916, somebody suggested that it was time Miss Lyons thought well of getting back to her studies in Galway. Then she made a discovery. Police enquiries had been made in Longford concerning her activities. That had made her something of a marked woman. In fact, she was not free to travel to Galway until she had first reported to the British Military authorities at Trinity College and obtained a permit.

There was martial law in Galway. The city seemed to be under a dark cloud of apprehension. There had been an attempted rising under Liam Mellows. It had achieved nothing, beyond making things very much worse for the people. The British authorities were behaving like vicious watchdogs.

Mellows had been under open arrest in England. Having evaded the police, he had got back to Galway in time for the commencement of the general Rising. He had alerted the local Volunteers and, on the Tuesday of Easter Week, they had mobilised from all over the county. They attacked barracks, destroyed bridges and cut telegraph wires. They seized the town of Athenry where, by Thursday, one thousand men had mobilised. Encounters with the British forces followed with loss of life on both sides. The British began an encircling manoeuvre at Moyvore and a deadly battle became imminent. Mellows was determined to see it through, until a local priest intervened, persuading the men to disband. Whether they wished to or not, hundreds of them were rounded up and deported. Mellows escaped to the hills.

In aborting the Rising in Co Galway, as in other areas in the provinces, the British had been ably assisted by the work of the Royal Irish Constabulary with their local knowledge. The gloom now hanging over Galway city was also largely a result of the watchfulness of the local RIC — that infamous body of Irishmen in the pay of Britain, for which pay many believe they served her both too loyally and too well.

Brigid Lyons found Miss Kyne quite unprepared to believe that her return to college had been delayed because of her participation in the Rising. Miss Kyne knew only that Miss Lyons had been missing her lectures, but to pretend that she had been in the Dublin Rising — now that was too much! It was a reaction Brigid was to meet with repeatedly amongst her contemporaries. That Lyons one dramatising herself! She found them reticent, uncommunicative and not at all as friendly as they had been.

Brigid believed that the coolness of her contemporaries was caused by their shock at the way 'the Lyons one' had become such a blatant liar during her Easter holidays. Her reputation was in doubt until *The Irish Times Handbook* arrived in the newsagents. There it was, in cold print, in the lists — the name of Brigid Lyons, imprisoned in Kilmainham Gaol for her part as a rebel in the First Battalion in the Four Courts. Overnight, she became rebel Galway's darling!

Sent for by the Dean, the Reverend Hynes, Brigid was gripped with terrible misgivings. What had he heard? And the punishment? Would she be sent down, expelled, disgraced — and her dearest ambition be destroyed? But — praises be! — it was not that way at all. The benevolent Dean sat expansively in his office, nursing an intense curiosity and desire for first-hand news from Dublin.

Dean Hynes put his student though her paces. Her experiences with British interrogators paled by comparison. He wanted the fullest account. He wanted all she knew. And he wanted an awful lot she didn't know. Because she'd been in the Rising, he believed that she had actually been more involved than was the case. In her confusion, she forgot to explain the coincidence that had bought her to Dublin, and ultimately to the heart of Commandant Edward Daly's First Battalion in the Four Courts.

Nonetheless, she had obviously acquitted herself satisfactorily. With Mary Quigley, another student, the Dean invited her to luncheon with Canon Farragher, parish priest of the Aran Islands, at the Railway Hotel (now the Great Southern Hotel). Something of an ordeal, the lunch was also an occasion of some delight for one who had eaten sparsely in recent times. The details of the Rising, as much as she could give, were mulled over again. The priests discussed it very seriously. They had a long, learned argument as to whether Pearse and his followers were morally right in going out when they were virtually certain they hadn't a hope of success. On one thing they agreed: their courage was never in doubt.

Clearly, public opinion was shifting and changing, the consensus quite distinctly coming around to Pearse's way of thinking: a blood sacrifice had been necessary. The swing of opinion was accelerated by the sickened revulsion at the horrors of Maxwell's summary executions. The arrival in Ireland on 12 May of Prime Minister Asquith, on a visit of enquiry, and his assurance to General Maxwell of the approval of the British Government of all he had done, in no way helped to change the direction which public opinion was taking. Asquith's assurance to Maxwell was all the more arrogant, coming as it did on the very day in the dawn of which the general had completed his task with the execution of the crippled Seán McDermott and the gravely wounded James Connolly who was carried to the yard, then strapped in a chair to be shot. The shooting of Connolly was the culminating British error that alienated Irish public opinion for generations to come.

The story is told that while Connolly lay dangerously ill in Dublin Castle, the late Dr Alfred Parsons of Baggot Street Hospital was called in consultation, not for the benefit of the patient, but to answer the question: 'Is Connolly fit to be shot?' Dr Parsons' reply — 'A man is never fit to be shot' — made no difference to General Maxwell's intentions which had to be put into effect before the arrival of his Prime Minister later that day.

For Brigid Lyons, the transition from the excitement of rebellion to the confusions of chemical formulae was not easy. Short as the term was, it was even shorter because of her late return. She tried to take up where she had left off, but things were depressing. Nothing in Galway was like before. Nationalist activity had gone underground, and everybody seemed frightened. As she said, 'There was nothing that gave hope of our ever being able to start all over again. We were like waifs without guidance.'

Although reasonably clear as to its outcome, she presented in June for her examination. She passed physics but failed chemistry, a not discreditable performance considering the nature of her recent distractions.

Things were quiet in Longford when she returned. People were not in fear as they were in Galway. Everybody was sporting a tricolour badge, but as in Galway, the leaders were all gone. She went to Aunt Joe for the summer, and found that as in Galway and Longford, there was something wanting in Dublin too. Those who mattered were not there any more. All that was left were the empty ruins, the ashes, and, not least, the human tragedies thrown up by the receding tide of war.

That summer, she spent much time with Mrs Tom Clarke and Aunt Joe in the Clarkes' garden in Richmond Road. The three small Clarke boys were there: Daly, Tom and Emmett. It was a comfort to the widow to have them and her friends in those desolate months. She accepted what had happened as part of the price of Ireland's freedom. But often she went over her grim experiences when she was brought to Kilmainham Gaol twice within twenty-four hours for her last words — first with her husband, and then with her only brother, aged twenty-five. Before that month of June 1916 was out, she suffered still another bereavement — the death of her uncle, John Daly, the famous Limerick Fenian who, in 1881, had been sentenced to penal servitude for life.

As a practical protest against his imprisonment, and an act of faith in his principles, John Daly was elected MP for his native city of Limerick, but as a serving prisoner, he was disqualified from taking his seat. It was in Portland Prison that he first met Tom Clarke and formed a lifelong friendship, Clarke eventually marrying Daly's niece. Sometimes Mrs Clarke talked about her life in America, when she had gone there to marry Tom Clarke. She had lost her trousseau on the journey out. That had marked the beginning of a life which was never easy. It was a relief to return to Ireland, and to see her husband settled in his tobacconist's shop in Parnell Street, Dublin. Now, all that was gone — burnt out during the Rising.

Despite her bereavements, Mrs Clarke had already begun to organise to respond to the destitution of the dependents of the dead and wounded and the prisoners of Easter Week. She founded the Volunteers' Dependents Fund to give immediate aid. Then came the National Aid Fund. The two bodies amalgamated to become the Irish National Aid and Volunteers' Dependents' Fund. As well as its charitable purposes, the National Aid Fund also welded together the remnants of the forces that might otherwise have scattered. It rallied the nationalists and, from it, the new Sinn Féin movement was nourished. Young people became interested, and Sinn Féin ideas began to get through to the prisoners in British jails where they provided a new impetus for resistance against British rule.

General revulsion towards Maxwell's executions was first shown in the massive support given to the dependents' funds. It came from all levels of Irish society. A gift sale at the Mansion House brought in everything from family heirlooms to prized book collections. Artists John Lavery and William Orpen gave blank canvasses, the purchaser to pay £600 for his or her portrait. The majority that had so recently denigrated the rebels of Easter Week was now shaping and reshaping its opinion, as if at last it comprehended Ireland's passion for freedom and Britain's for domination. Increasing activity in the work of the National Aid office soon demanded more attention than voluntary workers could give it. Mrs Clarke looked around for a full-time secretary to take on a heavy responsibility.

Having spent her summer largely occupied in collecting for National Aid, Brigid Lyons returned to Galway in October. She passed her chemistry exam and began her second-year lectures. Study was harder, but the course was becoming more interesting. Nationalist activity in Galway was at a low ebb. A highlight was the picketing of prisons when prisoners were coming or going. Brigid recalled:

You cheered them as hard as you could, and you booed their jailers even harder. If you went back to your books with a sore throat, well at least you'd let off a head of steam that compensated for your sense of deprived retaliation.

Also, there were parcels to be organised for the prisoners — and letters to keep them cheered. When a prisoner was released, his arrival at Galway railway station would be the occasion for a hurriedly organised nationalist turnout, displaying sufficient defiance to keep the British authorities aware that Ireland's spirit was not yet broken.

The biggest excitement came in Christmas week, 1916. John Dillon had put down a motion for discussion at Westminster on 'the Irish prisoners of war'. On 21 December, Henry Duke, Chief Secretary for Ireland in Lloyd George's new Government, stated that 'the time had come when the risk of liberating the internees would be less than the risks which might follow detaining them longer.' On 22 December, six hundred untried prisoners were released from Frongoch internment camp and reached Ireland in time for Christmas. Bonfires and torches blazed in welcome wherever they went. But the jubilations were marred by the remembrance of those under sentence and who still languished in British prisons. In particular, Brigid Lyons remembered her Uncle Joe McGuinness in Lewes Jail.

Amongst the prisoners just returned was that young man called Michael Collins. His contemporaries had praised his rare qualities of leadership shown in Frongoch. Somebody recommended him to Mrs Clarke as a possible organiser for her National Aid Fund. She interviewed him. His resemblance to Seán McDermott impressed her. With feminine intuition she concluded that he must possess something of McDermott's organising ability. She appointed him. That day, Mrs Tom Clarke performed a task for Ireland more momentous than she could possibly have realised.

# 12

# IRELAND'S FIRST REPUBLICAN MP

GENERAL TOM BARRY called 1917 'the year of the shadowed gloom after military defeat'. The Allies fighting Germany also had reason to be downcast. In answer to their refusal to cease their blockade, the German Government had just announced a renewal of submarine warfare against merchant shipping. As American commerce would be affected, British hopes brightened in the belief that at last the United States must enter the war.

Irish hopes were brightening too — if perhaps less glowingly. British methods of demoralisation had reached a new low. Men and boys were arrested for singing 'disloyal' songs, flying tricolours, wearing badges — for any trivial reason that might be interpreted as an expression of political feeling. A man was even arrested for reciting 'The Ballad of Reading Gaol'! He was acquitted, however, the bench pointing out that, though Irish himself, Oscar Wilde was not particularly interested in Irish sedition.

Like most of Ireland, Galway had caught the blizzards of January 1917. The cold notwithstanding, hearts beat warmly wherever nationalists gathered. Brigid Lyons was elected honorary secretary of the local branch of Cumann na mBan. An entertainment group began fundraising for the National Aid Fund. For their first programme they decided to produce Lady Gregory's play, *The Rising of the Moon*. The honorary secretary informed Michael Collins, secretary of the National Aid Fund, of their plans. His reply welcomed their help but warned them to comply with the Defence of the Realm Regulations, by first obtaining the permission of the local District Inspector, Royal Irish Constabulary.

The D.I. in Galway, before issuing a permit, requested a guarantee that there would be no disturbance and nothing would be expressed derogatory to the police or the Empire. He was very nice about it, explaining that, as a duty, the police would attend on the night, but of course they would pay for their tickets. He issued the permit and he was so charming that Miss Lyons ventured to explain that there were three policemen in the play and suggested that he might lend RIC uniforms for the actors. At that, the District Inspector drew the line.

A great success, the entertainment brought a profit of £50, a considerable sum in those days. A cheque was sent to Dublin and Collins sent an effusive letter of thanks. Many times in the subsequent months, Brigid received messages through Uncle Frank: Michael Collins wanted to know when there was to be another profitable entertainment organised in Galway. He was unaware of the inroads anatomy and physiology made on a girl's time.

February brought more foul weather. It also brought some excitement. It was in North Roscommon, but, in Galway, Brigid followed it in the newspapers. A by-election was pending. The Nationalists entered the fight as a political party to contest the seat against the Redmondites, the Irish Parliamentary Party. Count Plunkett, father of the executed Joseph, was chosen as the candidate. Crowds, both Sinn Féin and Volunteers, flocked to North Roscommon to give their help. There was a new upsurge of feeling. The election result confirmed that feeling: the Redmondite candidate got 1,708 votes, while Plunkett got 3,022.

Despite the awful weather, Roscommon erupted in jubilation. This was the first indication of a nationalist resurgence. While it was the first Sinn Féin election success, Count Plunkett had not stood as a Republican. He had never stated during the campaign that he would not attend Westminster Parliament if elected. As it turned out, he never took his seat.

In Galway, swotting over Gray's *Anatomy*, Brigid Lyons yearned to be out there, plodding through the Roscommon snowdrifts. She would have liked to have helped, for often she had met Count and Countess Plunkett with Aunt Joe, and had visited them at home in Upper Fitzwilliam Street. Nor could she ever forget the Countess' tea-tray in Kilmainham Gaol — sent in to the anonymous prisoner next door. Of the Count, she remembered:

> He was a charming and retiring man and was very intellectual. Perhaps because of his beard, he was always thought to be older than he was. In February 1917, being the father of the executed Joe, he aroused tremendous emotional sympathy. To waken the Nation again to the Cause, Count Plunkett was just the right man for the job at the time.

Shortly, she was to meet the Plunketts again in even more exciting circumstances.

Another by-election was pending, this time in South Longford, a stronghold of the Parliamentary Party. An emissary arrived from Dublin for a discussion with Frank McGuinness. He brought a proposal — namely, to nominate Joe McGuinness as a candidate in the South Longford by-election. Brigid thought that her uncle, with his boundless energy, would make a marvellous MP. But there were difficulties. She recalled:

> Uncle Frank didn't take to the idea. There were old inter-country jealousies and Roscommon men were never popular in Longford. A native of Tarmonbarry, Co Roscommon, Uncle Joe was therefore a foreigner in Longford. And as well as being a garrison town, Longford supported the Parliamentary Party. And also, as Joe was in prison, Uncle Frank thought it might be illegal and he mightn't even be accepted as a candidate. After much argument, Uncle Frank finally said all right, go ahead, and he'd give it all the support he could.

Time proved that the emissary had come from Michael Collins whose influence in the nationalist movement was increasing rapidly. Collins had also sent an emissary to Lewes Jail to seek the approval of Joe McGuinness to his candidature. McGuinness was absolutely opposed to the idea. As Dorothy Macardle recorded: 'Joseph McGuinness [was] a man so uncompromising in his separatist principles that the suggestion of standing for election under the machinery of the British Administration was repugnant to him.'

Joe's prison colleagues held discussions. All supported outright rejection of the idea, excepting Collins' friends, Thomas Ashe and Harry Boland. The letter refusing the nomination was drafted by de Valera, signed by Joe McGuinness and dispatched to Dublin. Suspecting its source, Collins carefully examined the letter. 'That's the long hoor,' he concluded, targeting de Valera with a colourful missile.

Collins, the young pragmatist, was furious. What the patriots in Lewes Jail did not seem to understand was the virtue of McGuinness' determined separatism in the current context. It was the weapon of greatest value to him now, for with it, and membership of the British Parliament, he could flout on Irish ground that parliament's most cherished traditions and institutions. Without further communication with the men in Lewes, Collins decided on Joe McGuinness' candidature.

Shortly afterwards, Dan McCarthy and Joe McGrath arrived in Longford. Dan McCarthy proved a noted director of elections, all victorious for Sinn Féin in the 1917–18 period. In later life, he became secretary to President W. T. Cosgrave. Joe McGrath, after a successful political career, became a world figure as head of the Irish Hospitals' Sweepstakes. Brigid noticed that the tension associated with the original emissary was now gone. Joe McGuinness was to be the Sinn Féin candidate in South Longford. Michael Collins had decided, and Dan McCarthy and Joe McGrath relaxed and played ragtime on the piano while everybody sang, 'Felix Kept on Walking'. They seemed to bring a new spirit into the McGuinness household and indeed into the town of Longford.

Frank McGuinness had not been alone in his doubts about his brother as a parliamentary candidate. For other reasons, the men in Lewes were angry with Collins and did not spare him in their messages. In reply, a letter from Collins to his friend Thomas Ashe, also in Lewes, stated: You can tell Con Collins, Seán McGarry and any other highbrows that I've been getting all their scathing messages and am not a little annoyed, or at least was, but one gets so used to being called bad names and being misunderstood.'

Frank McGuinness placed 5 Main Street, Longford, at the disposal of the Sinn Féin Committee. An enthusiastic electioneering campaign began on behalf of the unwilling candidate lodged in a British prison. Brigid Lyons was appointed full-time secretary to Dan McCarthy, the director of the campaign.

A vivid poster was printed. It was to become historic. Orange-coloured, it showed a prisoner in black, wearing the black arrows and the little prison cap. The slogan read: 'Put him in to get him out!' Brigid joined the bill-posters:

> We used tons of flour in making paste and nearly broke our backs over open fires in the country kitchens. As quickly as we put them up, they were torn down because the opposition was getting active. Then we tore down the British Army recruiting posters, pasting my uncle's in their place. I kept some copies of that famous poster, but they disappeared with my copy of the Easter Week Proclamation and my Dunsany button and all my souvenirs — all stolen by the Black and Tans in a raid in 1920.

The opposition was the Parliamentary Party as represented by Paddy McKenna, a farmer from south Co Longford. Brigid recalled:

> He was a fine type, but he *was* a parliamentarian, so that was that! The local MP was J. P. Farrell, also of the Parliamentary Party. He became very hostile to us. This was hurtful for Uncle Frank, for although he had broken away from the Parliamentary Party in 1916, he and J. P. Farrell had remained good friends. This was the first evidence of in-fighting between Farrell and himself.

Brigid's job was to find speakers and arrange areas for them.

> I wrote to everybody in Dublin who might respond. And then it happened — letters, money and support came pouring in. The first cheque was for £20 and came from Madge Daly, sister of Mrs Tom Clarke and of the late Ned Daly. And so it went on. Then I got letters from Uncle Joe in Lewes. As he'd been given no option, he'd finally decided we might need some advice. He sent bits for speeches, and things he'd like said. We saw to all his requests. It was the least we could do in the circumstances.

The pace quickened. Meetings increased and there was a galaxy of splendid speakers and noted names. Michael Collins spoke. Brigid recalled:

> That was the first time I had met him. Also Seán Milroy, Alec McCabe, Darrell Figgis, Larry Ginnell, Arthur Griffith, Seán McMahon [afterwards Chief of Staff of the Army], Rory O'Connor [later to be executed], Herbert Moore Pim from Belfast, Alex Lynn, Mrs Pearse, Mrs Tom Clarke, Mrs Desmond FitzGerald, Joe Stanley [the publisher of *Nationality*], Lily O'Hanrahan, John O'Mahony and James O'Mara. It was a real resurgence. Even some of my student friends from Galway turned up: John A. Madden and Phelim and Corny O'Leary, who undertook fundraising. One morning, there was a knock on our door at 3 a.m. I went down to find Pádraig Ó Conaire with his bundle on his shoulder. He had come to help in whatever way he could.

Seán Nunan (afterwards Irish Ambassador to Washington and Secretary of the Department of External Affairs) came as a sub-organiser with his brother, Ernan. The Nunan brothers were famous just then through the publicity given to their fight in England against being conscripted. Although born in England, they considered themselves Irishmen with Irish ideals. They refused to fight Germany for small nations, preferring to fight Britain for their own small nation. After imprisonment, they eventually got back to Ireland and threw themselves heart and soul into the Movement.

Accommodation in Longford became impossible and the overflow went to surrounding towns. People opened their houses and many went to the Greville Arms Hotel in Granard. This was owned by the Kiernan family: Kitty, Helen, Maud and Chris who ran the place with their brother, Larry. They were a charming family who sacrificed much for Ireland's sake. Kitty was to become engaged to Collins — but all that was in the future. Brigid recalled:

> Meantime, we met plenty of opposition: stones flew, particularly in Longford town, and there was many a fight and many a window shattered. Most of this trouble came from the 'separation women', the wives of Irishmen away in the British Army, and a

tough lot they were. From our advance publicity they'd know who was expected, so they'd gather at the railway station and boo and scream at our distinguished speakers.

Eilís Ní Chorra of Cumann na mBan came from Belfast to help. She recorded her impression of the rowdies:

> On our way to and from the committee rooms we had to run the gauntlet of what one of the boys called 'the scatteration allowance women' who howled abuse at everyone wearing the tricolour. This happened all the time we were in Longford, their favourite slogan being 'To hell with the jail-bird! Up McKenna and the Union Jack! Three cheers for khaki and the boys in the trenches.' Our slogan was 'Put him in to get him out' for our candidate was in prison.

Oddly, there was no opposition from the RIC. They tried to keep the peace when the rows got too bad. Privately, some members of the force were sympathetic, but they daren't show it. After all, they were Irishmen and, no more than the nationalists, they did not want to see their country partitioned — and this could result from supporting the Parliamentary Party which had once consented to partition.

'We also had other kinds of opposition,' Brigid remembered. 'The bishop, for instance, was frankly hostile. The young priests were with us, but like the policemen, they daren't admit it. The hierarchy had outlawed us because of 1916, but still they were just as much against the partition of Ireland as we were.'

On 8 May 1917, the eve of the election, a manifesto against partition was published, signed by three Catholic archbishops, fifteen bishops and three Protestant bishops, as well as many men in public life. On the same day, Dr Walsh, the Catholic Archbishop of Dublin, made a despairing statement that he believed the partition mischief had already been done. He said: 'The country is practically sold.' This was grist for the South Longford election mill. It was such a tremendous boost that stacks of the bishops' manifesto were brought from Dublin, arriving in Longford in the small hours of the polling day. The organisers worked like demons to distribute it all through the constituency. It did immense psychological good.

Transport of every kind was organised for the polling day on 9 May. As farm work was in full swing, many were in the fields and had to be encouraged to vote. 'On our way', remembered Brigid, 'we sang, "The Soldier's Song" and waved tricolours and bellowed "Up McGuinness". Mostly it was reciprocated from the fields, but occasionally we got back a defiant "Up McKenna! Down with Sinn Féin".'

Eilís Ní Chorra remembered too.

On election day we helped to bring in voters from outlying districts. It was exciting to spin along behind a big tricolour, to be saluted by the driver of practically every car we met. A group of people on a cart would stand up and cheer. Children climbed ditches to greet us. Men working in the fields waved to us with their spades, and women rushed to their doors to call out 'Up McGuinness every time!' All this I thought very encouraging until one of our men said, 'I wonder how many of them have a vote.

In fact, many did not have a vote because the register was out of date. Principally this hit the young people — all staunch Republicans who found themselves disenfranchised through British-controlled local Government maladministration. Sinn Féin was well aware of this loss of potential voters. Herself disenfranchised, Brigid remembered her personal concern that day:

When all this is over, I thought, and we lose, it'll be the end of everything. It would be a catastrophe and one just couldn't be sure. Some people, even former friends of Uncle Frank, were blatantly for McKenna, some were wavering. Some would put out the green flag with the gold harp, the flag of the Parliamentary Party, but only a few had the courage to put out the tricolour, the Republican flag. There was a shop in the town owned by the wife of an ex-policeman. Her proudest boast was, 'Well himself may be an RIC pensioner, but I've got the shop in my name, so I can put out any flag I like.' And she did!

The excitement of polling day was eclipsed by the count which began next morning in the Courthouse. Eilís Ní Chorra remembered the tension:

Leaving our bean-a-tighe saying the Rosary that our man would win, Máire [her friend from Belfast] and I accepted an invitation to sit in the drawing room window over a shop facing the Courthouse. Sharing the view with us were Count and Countess Plunkett, Mrs Clarke and several local people including an enthusiastic Frenchman and a German with his Irish wife. How the time crawled! Inside the Courthouse we could see figures passing and re-passing the windows. Cheers and counter-cheers kept us guessing. Then a Party man threw open the Courthouse window and flung down a card with 'McKenna' on it. McKenna's supporters produced a big green flag [a Union Jack would have been more in keeping with their policy] and waved it while they cheered. For a moment our people remained silent, then seemingly with one voice, they broke into 'A Soldier's Song' and the opposition cheering died away. A man from the centre of our crowd made a speech: 'No matter what the result of this election is,' he declared, 'we have the youth of Ireland with us. We have the Ireland of the future.'

Brigid Lyons never forgot those same anxious hours.

We were outside the Courthouse all day. Eventually, in the afternoon, Uncle Frank came to a window. His face was sorrowful and he gave us a thumbs-down sign. First there was a sigh of grief from the supporters and then a terrible hush. Then people began to show their sympathies: the green flag of the Parliamentary Party came out at the windows — many from houses who'd been pretending to be our supporters. Sure now that victory had gone the other way, they showed the Party flag. Then suddenly there was pandemonium — a mistake was discovered. There would have to be a re-count. Uncle Frank shut the window and withdrew and we had to face more tension.

Eilís Ní Chorra picks up her memories from the window opposite the courthouse:

We heard a deep, rousing cheer from outside which sent us running to the window, to see a big Republican flag being waved from the Courthouse window by Frank McGuinness, brother of our candidate. I looked down. The street was a heaving, swaying mass of green, white and orange. Beside me Máire was hanging out of the window waving a tricolour, so was the daughter of the shop-keeper who had told me regretfully, an hour earlier that she could not put out a flag, such being forbidden on licensed premises.

Brigid Lyons was numb when Uncle Frank threw that window open for the second time. Between waving and trying to hold a tricolour, he all but fell. He could not be heard, but his facial message was clear enough. What had happened was eventually explained. A packet of fifty vital voting-papers had been pushed aside. It meant winning the seat for Republican Joseph McGuinness with a majority of 37 votes. Asked if sabotage were suspected, Brigid replied:

> We'll leave that to history. All I know is that Seán Nunan and myself ran all the way to the Post Office and sent a telegram to Lloyd George saying, 'Longford has given you the answer'. What good it ever did I wouldn't know, but it satisfied us at the time.

Longford went wild with excitement. British journalists sought interviews, but the man of the moment was not there to be interviewed. It was like a wedding without the bridegroom. The journalists were told that the new MP was in a British prison. Next day, *The Manchester Guardian* declared South Longford to be 'the equivalent of a serious British defeat in the field'.

For Eilís Ní Chorra:

> The rest of that day is a jumble of memories as half-crying, half-laughing, we paraded the long street of the town. Tricolours erupted from many windows. There were cries of 'Up Longford! Up Kerry! Up Dublin!' even 'Up Belfast!' It was some time before we learned that our majority was 37. Not a big one, but in face of all the odds against us, it was a glorious victory for 'the jailbird!' And it was the beginning of the landslide which swept the Irish Parliamentary Party out of existence.

For Brigid, the end was something of an anticlimax.

We all went off to celebrate at the Greville Arms in Granard. There was a huge bonfire that night on the hill behind the hotel. From there, you could see dozens of others over miles of the flat countryside. Then we had a sing-song. That was the night I first heard 'Danny Boy'. Looking ravishing as usual, it was Kitty Kiernan who sang it to a room full of admirers.

Despite the successful outcome of the campaign, the unilateral decision taken by Collins on the candidature of Joe McGuinness was never forgotten for him. Collins, the man of action, was a natural decision-maker. He had no time for doctrinaire politicians or, in his own words to Tom Ashe, 'any other highbrows'.

In referring to the South Longford election, the Longford-O'Neill biography of de Valera, written over fifty years later, states:

The men outside had calculated rightly the chance of success. The appeal which they had made to the public had, however, not stated any clearly defined aim. 'Put him in to get him out' was a slogan which won sympathy for the prisoner, but it did not necessarily keep the Republican flag flying.

Without doubt, the success of Joe McGuinness in May 1917 initiated the resurgence of Irish Republicanism.

# 13

# A MAN CALLED DE VALERA

BRIGID LYONS KEPT an autograph book during her uncle's famous campaign. Today it possesses a strange interest, not alone for the historic signatures, but particularly for the love–hate sentiments written by many of those famous people. A random selection reveals the spirit of resurgence that was abroad at the time.

England! Damn your concessions
We'll have our country!
Rory O'Connor, 8th May, 1917 — second year of the Irish Republic.

Their spirit lives amongst us.
Margaret Pearse, 8th May, 1917.

Annseo! Longport dom ag an dtogd mór
Pádraig Ó Conaire 8/5/17.

Political freedom may be recovered in twenty four hours but nationality once destroyed may take generations to recover.
Paul de Nagy to the Hungarians.
Seán Milroy 9-5-17

Joseph S. McGrath, I.R.A., Lieutennt.

Easter Week vindicated, Eve of the Poll, Longford, 1917.
That we'll avenge their deaths we swear
No matter tho' we're few
And Erin's colours shall replace
The red, the white and blue.
Eamon O'Fleming, 8th May, 2nd year of the Irish Republic.

Joe McGuinness assisted to create Easter Week 1916 and brought
victory to Ireland and Longford, 1917
John O'Mahony 10/5/17

'Do not say Hungary WAS? Say with me Hungary shall be!' —
Szcheny to the oppressed Hungarians 1838
Arthur Griffith, Longford, 10/5/17

'Freedom is a goodly thing' (James Barber circa 1493)
John F. McEntee, Dartmoor, Lewes, Portland, Belfast.

Kathleen Ní Houlihan, your way's a glorious way.
Thomas Ashe

South Longford Election, May 1917
Some trouble and crosses of course we had
Brigid and I
But, bless you, we never found time to be sad
And a very good reason why
We were busy as bees and we weren't so mad
As to stop in our work to cry.
Dan McCarthy [Director of the Election]

Austin Stack, Tralee
Tralee Gaol
Spike Island
Richmond
Kilmainham
Mountjoy

Dartmoor
Lewes
Portland
Pentonville

We are digging the grave of British Constitutionalism in Ireland in
South Longford.
Up McGuinness!
J. M. Stanley 8/5/17

Today shall be as yesterday
The red blood burns in Eire still
H. J. Cahill Wilson, Honorary Secretary,
Election Committee 8.5.17

As in the summer term of 1916, Brigid Lyons returned to her
university lectures very late in May 1917. As usual, she found Galway
an anticlimax, principally for its sheer lack of nationalism. But at least
they had heard of the South Longford election. Some even enquired,
'Who is this Republican McGuinness? And what does it all mean?

Galway still had not caught up with the rising tide of resurgence.
Many gave the impression that they would prefer to remain aloof.
Even the university students were disinterested. Brigid recalled, 'The
Rebellion, they'd tell you, was a social hangover from the 1913 Strike.'
It seemed to her almost as if Galway were permeated by a pro-British
feeling.

Examination time arrived all too quickly. She could only hope and
pray — and try. During the physiology paper, on a hot June afternoon,
she noticed the superintendent taking a peculiar interest — as if he
suspected her of something. Towards the end of the three-hour stint,
he finally approached her, producing a telegram.

'I suppose I shouldn't — not during an exam. Better read it
quickly,' he said, as if he expected her to faint at the contents. The
telegram had come from Longford. It read:

Prisoners released. Will arrive Dublin to-night. Uncle.

Joe McGuinness released! The moment was imprinted on Brigid's memory. 'I felt like abandoning the exam. I'm sure if I'd had the fare to Dublin, nothing would have stopped me.'

She failed that exam. The result could hardly have been otherwise. Still buoyant, she rushed home to Longford and then to Dublin. Everywhere there were celebrations and parties for the released prisoners. As the man who had gone into prison as an Irish rebel and come out a Member of the British Parliament, Joe was in particular demand. Although looking ill and half-starved, he retained his sense of humour. As an MP, he had been put on the Westminster guest lists. For the amusement of his comrades, he used to stick up on his cell door in Lewes Jail his invitations to Londonderry House and to Ascot.

Brigid returned to Longford to help organise Uncle Joe's triumphal entry to his constituency. A letter awaited her. It was from Dan McCarthy, the Sinn Féin Director of Elections, at the Old Ground Hotel, Ennis:

Here I am in another stiff fight for Sinn Féin. However, with hard work we hope to win. Any chance of you coming here? Milroy is the only one with me at present. 90% of the priests of East Clare are supporting our man. Congratulations on your uncle Joe's release. I hope you are in the best of form and having a good holiday. I would like to have a line from you at your convenience.

Excitement was piling on excitement. Another by-election! This time in East Clare, with the newly released de Valera as the Sinn Féin candidate against Paddy Lynch, the local Parliamentary Party man. But East Clare was another day's work. Meanwhile, Uncle Joe's reception had to be planned.

The big day was a glorious Sunday in June, one of the most exciting Longford ever witnessed. The town was festooned with flowers and banners and flags. The sense of occasion was tremendous. That afternoon, a cavalcade of motor cars came into view on the Dublin Road. From side streets, contingents of Volunteers and Cumann na mBan, led by bands, joined the parade. Uncle Joe sat in the back seat of an open touring car accompanied by Eamon de Valera — he who had disapproved of McGuinness as a candidate. Thomas

Ashe and Michael Collins were there too, and a host of other supporters.

From a platform in the Market Square, there were speeches. Brigid was surprised and delighted at Uncle Joe's clarity and composure in both the Irish and English languages. Not that she ever doubted his ability, but this was the most awe-inspiring occasion he had ever faced. That night, there was a banquet at Stoker's Hotel in Longford.

Joe stayed on to meet and to thank his new constituents. Everywhere he was given a hero's welcome. He addressed many meetings, at all of which he spoke in Irish and in English. Brigid assessed her Uncle Joe more searchingly than ever before:

He was a complete idealist — never had his feet on the ground. His money, his business, his life, everything was forgotten for the Movement. He was a soldier rather than a politician; he was jolly, full of fun and a good prisoner. Joe was such a good prisoner everybody wanted to share his cell. He kept their spirits up!

The Church frowned on this new breed of Irish politician, as Brigid noted:

Someone advised Joe that, as the new MP, he should call on the bishop. His Lordship had still not forgiven us for 1916. Anyway, Joe went to the palace, and we all waited anxiously to see what kind of a reception he'd get. Somebody said, 'Never mind now — the bishop will give him a large cheque, you'll see', and somebody else said: 'Ah no! There'll be no fear of that!' An amusing character called Tom Kelly said to my uncle when he came back, 'Well, and what did you get, Joe?' 'Well,' Joe replied. 'He gave me his blessing.' To which Tom retorted, 'Well there's neither head nor harp on that [a reference to the coinage of the time]!'

Like most of the elderly priesthood, the bishop was to mellow with time. Meanwhile however, it was disillusioning for those who had sacrificed so much for the freedom of their country, that a highly influential section of Irish society, the educated Christian priesthood, should display such outright animosity, indeed such lack of charity. This attitude created a wave of anti-clericalism.

Pressure was such in Longford that, with her Uncle Frank, Brigid drove at night to reach Ennis to join Dan McCarthy in the famous de Valera East Clare campaign of July 1917. An entry in her autograph album marks the occasion:

In remembrance of the South Longford, Brigid, and your arrival in the 'wee sma' hours of Sunday morning for East Clare election. Cathal O'Shannon, 1 July , 1917.

Ex-Wandsworth, Frongoch, Reading and Belfast Jails.

At the election headquarters, the Old Ground Hotel, Ennis, she first met the Sinn Féin candidate, Eamon de Valera. Although his name was everywhere in Clare, and he had a magic appeal for the people, she was disappointed.

I knew his name as a 1916 leader, but when I met him, he wasn't at all the man I'd expected. He was just out of jail and was very thin and gaunt. I was shocked at the haggard, aged man he appeared to be. I didn't think he had long to live, but I was wrong.

She also met Peadar Clancy again — the young officer whose gallantry in the Four Courts she had admired: 'He had been ill in prison. He had lost his hair, and looked very poorly.' It was not difficult to distinguish those who had just been released from prison. Their faces reflected their experiences. In fact, the East Clare campaign was Longford all over again, only in a more exciting way because the prisoners were out. The bridegroom was present on this occasion.

In another way, East Clare lacked the challenge of South Longford. There was now more money, the campaigners were more experienced, the political situation was less tense, the clergy were not so resentful, the local bishop was actually in favour, and there was a bigger election committee and many more workers. The presence of the candidate had the greatest rallying effect.

As in Longford, the British press turned up, only in greater strength. On polling day the *Daily Telegraph* announced that East Clare was 'the most important election that had ever taken place, or ever will take place, in Irish history.' Countess Markievicz, fresh from her sentence of death, had arrived. 'Madam' could not stop herself from cutting a dash in the streets of Ennis. Her flamboyance was part of her, and recent events made her more than ever attractive to the press, particularly the British press. A Countess, once presented at Court and who had proudly shot British soldiers — she was irresistible!

Cathal O'Shannon recorded an amusing incident about the Countess and the press:

One day when Dan McCarthy, the Director of the election, was sending me out in a car along with Miss Brigid Lyons, as she then was, niece of Joe McGuinness, victor in South Longford, to look up personation agents, I saw him pestered by a London press photographer who wanted a photo of Countess Markiewicz when she should arrive. Dan sent the photographer over to our car and Miss Lyons and I duly had our picture taken. On our return we found that Dan had persuaded the Londoner that Miss Lyons was the Countess and that I was a convert from Orangeism to Republicanism and that I had helped to land the rifles at Larne for Carson's Volunteers! Luckily for the photographer the arrival of the Countess that night enabled him to cancel by telegraph the publication of our photo and substitute for it one of the Countess.

As Director of Elections, Dan McCarthy's qualities were remarkable. He was a natural administrator. Without seeming to pressurise them, he got the most from his workers. Without his training, Brigid Lyons doubted if throughout her life she would so often have found herself saddled with honorary secretaryships. Also, without McCarthy's influence, Cathal O'Shannon might never have become a distinguished journalist — as the following story, recorded by O'Shannon, illustrates.

We had so many meetings and speakers from all over Ireland that the local press hadn't near enough reporters to cover them. Dan attended to that as he did to innumerable other needs. When he and I could snatch an odd hour of peace, and a few were in the hotel bar, he set me composing for the local editor's use summaries of speeches which he and I thought speakers out at meetings in the constituency ought to be making whether they were or not! And if any orator dared to complain of the result, Dan laughingly brushed him off with 'Well, if you didn't say that, you damned well should have. That's what's wanted in this election', and with that he turned to some more pressing task.

Cathal O'Shannon used the word 'orator'. However, Brigid was sure there were none! Most of the speakers made their points, but they all lacked oratorical finesse. The candidate, de Valera, was colourless and disappointing and without platform personality, she believed. She found his fascination for the people hard to explain, beyond the fact that he was the one leader who had survived 1916. His speeches had sincerity, but were poorly delivered. It was only when people turned to the newspapers that they realised the challenging things he had said — provided that the reports had not been invented by Dan McCarthy and Cathal O'Shannon!

An aesthete, an ascetic, and for all that, a member of the Kildare Street Club, Edward Martyn of Tullira Castle, Co Galway, had founded the Palastrina Choir at Dublin's Pro-Cathedral, was a founder member of Sinn Féin and a one-time enthusiast for the Gaelic League. He also founded the Hardwick Street Theatre. Offering what he considered some good advice to the East Clare candidate, he said, 'You will get on all right as long as you hold to Griffith', which advice brought only a de Valeraian scowl.

There was never any doubt about the issues before the Clare electors. De Valera was clear-cut: 'We want an Irish Republic,' he said. 'Because if Ireland had her freedom, it is, I believe, the most likely form of government.'

A former Crown Prosecutor, and a member of a prominent Co Clare family, Paddy Lynch KC, the Redmondite candidate, was equally specific: 'Clare voters do not want to see their sons shot down in a futile and insane attempt to establish an Irish Republic,' he said. Dorothy Macardle concluded:

> The people of Clare knew that they were putting forward a pioneer candidate for the Republic and knew what dangers they were confronting. They knew also that the making of Irish history was in their hands. Old men and women who had never before ventured to a polling booth came down from the remote cabins in

the mountains on July 10th to vote.

It was an exaggerated claim. Greater courage on behalf of an Irish Republic had been shown against far greater opposition by the South Longford electors three months earlier. The success of South Longford had resulted in the release of all Irish prisoners from British jails.

The result of the Clare election was an overwhelming victory for Sinn Féin: de Valera, 5,010, against Lynch's 2,035. When the result was declared, hectic rejoicing broke out in Ennis, in Co Clare, in all of Ireland. Sinn Féin, it seemed, could no longer be stopped. The Parliamentary Party had been dealt another stultifying blow. Sadly, a victory celebration in Ballybunion was fired on by the police and a man was killed. A verdict of wilful murder was returned by a jury against the constable responsible, but he was not arrested. Instead, Republicans were arrested for flying tricolours during the election campaign. The British authorities adamantly refused to recognise the swing of Irish public opinion.

In Ennis, Brigid added to her collection of autographs. A selection shows the spirit of the time:

Constance de Markiewicz, IRA, Easter Week, 1916. Kilmainham, 174 Mountjoy, Q12 Aylesbury. Ennis, 8th July, 1917

Seamus de Burca
Q 163 Late Portland, Lewes, Maidstone and Pentonville.
Sentenced to death
But still alive and kicking
And if the Clare girls wish to try
I'm ready for some kissing
Ennis, 8.7.17

Liam Ó Briain, Dublin, P.C. 1st Batt. Stephens' Green, Richmond Barracks, Wandsworth, Frongoch, Wormwood Scrubs.
The compensation — East Clare. 8.7.17

The highest distinction my country can bestow:
A free citizen in a free state.
Seán de Brún 9.7.17

De Valera's signature stands in isolation over the date 11.7.17, without frippery, jingles or catch-cries with which to make history. In contrast, Collins filled a page with a poem:

The night shall brighten to a noontide blazing
Over hill and glen
And the days to come on Freedom's fullness gazing
Shall recall the men
Who though weary soul'd with war and dreams proved hollow
Met the foe with scorn
Keeping the old flag flying that their sons might follow
On the road to Morn

Micheál Ó Coileáin
Capt., I.R.A., Easter, 1916

Had the British only paused to consider the ethos of the Irish people then, or ever, how differently British and Irish history might have been written.

# 14

## BOOSTING MORALE

ANOTHER ELECTION WAS scheduled for August 1917, this one in Kilkenny. The Sinn Féin candidate was William Cosgrave who had been sentenced to death and reprieved in 1916, and who was to become the country's first Prime Minister when the Irish Free State was founded in 1922. The Sinn Féin election machine went into action again. And again, Brigid became a cog in that machine. She rallied workers and support. Having met him in Ennis, she included Peadar Clancy. He replied:

Cranny,
6.8.17

Dear Miss Lyons,

I got your letter some days ago and would have replied before now but I have got very lazy since coming home. I fear my letter to your Uncle was written at the wrong time but the fact is I had written portion of the letter before reading of his visit to Longford. Now, about Kilkenny, I do not think I will go there. I'm sure they have more helpers than they need. The constituency is such a small one and more or less conveniently got at from Dublin, everyone who can give any assistance will surely be there. I am going to Dublin some day of this week and I may yet go down for the last days. Are you going?

When speaking to you at Ennis you gave me some particulars about that man Tierney and I have been thinking since that the poor fellow may be the victim of neglect and ill treatment. If you remember what he told us about his father it is only reasonable to assume that his family may not take a very keen interest in his welfare. Under the circumstances I think we should take some steps to find out what his condition is. While in Dublin I may have an opportunity of finding out something about him. Will you kindly give me the particulars? You can address your letter to me at 70A, New Street, Dublin. Pollard and this man are the only people whom I know of who are yet in trouble. They both proved good men and it would be very poor gratitude if we failed to do our very utmost for them.

Hoping you are quite well and enjoying your holidays.

Mise do chara fíor buan,

Peadar MacFianneada.

Despite illness, Peadar Clancy had worked as hard as anybody in the Clare election. When there was time, he had tried to educate people like Brigid Lyons who were unquestioning activists without also being analysts on the differences then existing between the Irish Republican Brotherhood and Sinn Féin. She had no interest in these finer political differences:

> It was only the Movement for me. The Movement was anti-British and that was all that mattered, but I never forgot the earnest way he would talk about it all. Peadar Clancy had been deeply involved from boyhood, and his life afterwards — and his death — proved the depth of his involvement. He was a completely dedicated man.

Ever after, for Brigid Lyons, the word bravery was synonymous with the name of Peadar Clancy. Once, during Easter Week in the Four Courts, when Clancy passed by, her Uncle Joe had said, 'That's the bravest man we have. He's shown such courage, he's been promoted.' That was why 'the fat girl from the country' so willingly volunteered when Barney Mellows looked for Cumann na mBan girls for Peadar Clancy's outpost in Church Street.

The laziness, mentioned in his letter, was excusable — if indeed it was mere laziness. Tuberculosis was the plague of Ireland at the time. So many young men and women were falling ill as a result of the privations of active service and imprisonment that concern for them was growing. Rather than for himself, Clancy's concern was for the welfare of others, as the letter shows.

Brigid's cousin, Rose McGuinness, who had also been in the Four Courts, had fallen victim to tuberculosis. She had been in hospital for months. Visiting her through the summer of 1917, Brigid was saddened by what she saw. Rose was very ill, yet she was very cheerful and hopeful — as were all of the patients. The euphoria of tuberculosis was a new experience for the fledgling doctor — one with which, in time, she would become all too familiar. Perhaps it was then that the realisation came: when the fight for freedom was over, there were other enemies in Ireland to be defeated — enemies as threatening as the muzzles of British guns.

Sinn Féin won the Kilkenny election. The poster used in that campaign was a variation of that 'invented' for the Joe McGuinness campaign in South Longford. Cosgrave had been released so the poster read: 'We got him out to put him in.' During the general election of 1918, Arthur Griffith was in prison, so his poster reverted to the Longford version: 'Put him in to get him out.'

Cosgrave's Kilkenny victory was 772 against 392. The celebrations were marked by British revenge. For making 'speeches calculated to cause disaffection', eighty-four Republicans were arrested during the month of August. Amongst them was Thomas Ashe, the tall blonde Kerry Adonis who had accompanied Uncle Joe when he arrived in Longford as the new MP. That night, after the banquet at Stoker's Hotel, Mick Collins and Tom Ashe had seen Brigid and her cousins home. They dallied, their talk concerned with the fate of Ireland.

In 1916, Ashe had been sentenced to death and then to life

imprisonment. In August 1917, after court martial, he was sentenced to one year's imprisonment with hard labour amongst the criminals in Mountjoy Prison. In protest, he went on hunger strike and, on 25 September, during attempts at forcible feeding, he collapsed and died. His funeral provided another parade of Ireland's defiant resurgence. Thirty thousand followed in the cortege, as countless thousands watched it pass. Volunteers in uniform carried rifles, two hundred priests marched, and there was the *Last Post* and three volleys over the grave.

Of Thomas Ashe and his treatment, Brigid said:

Normally a quiet man, but a man of tremendous character — there's no doubt Tom Ashe was driven to the action he took in Mountjoy. His cruel death turned hordes of people in favour of the Republican Movement. Public opinion was taken by the fact that a man of his type would give his life so cheerfully for a cause. It made people feel there was something in Republicanism worth examining and possibly worth supporting.

On her return to Galway in October 1917, Brigid again stayed with George Nicholls and his wife, Peggie, at University Road. Being close to college, it was convenient, as well as being a home from home. In all, she spent four happy years there. A solicitor, George was deeply involved in the Movement, for which he was in jail oftener than he was out. The boredom of life in prison often turned strong men to unlikely pursuits. It was about this time that George Nicholls, solicitor, turned poet. His 'poem' is untitled, but he makes no attempt to hide the source of his inspiration:

Come listen awhile to a mournful tale
Concerning a cailín renowned as a Gael
Who loved all young men with devotion so deep
That their faces used come between her and her sleep
Her name was Brigid Lyons, a student was she
Who for a profession a doctor would be
And she learned dissecting but alas and alack
Her knowledge caused nothing but ruin and wrack.

For, though to relate it doth give me much pain,
Poor Brigid got a fit of dissection on the brain
And all she did see and whatever she'd feel
She wanted to treat with a dose of cold steel,
Now this was so sad that my readers must weep
At the young maiden's trouble so dire and so deep
For in her wild frenzy, her shrieks and her groans
Were awful to hear as she studied her bones.
At last she got better or so 'twould appear
She certainly was not so wild or so queer
And as sure as the sun shines in heaven above.
She with a fair youth did fall deeply in love.
And the poor fellow wed her one bright summer day
And that wedding brings me near the end of my lay
For though when I tell it my heart grieves and groans
Poor Brigid found she wanted a new set of bones.
She retired with husband one dark night to bed
And next day poor husband was found cold and dead
For of him a subject his fond wife had made
So of females beware or you'll sleep in the shade.

Brigid passed her outstanding exam. That stimulated some more serious study. Not that her ambition to be a doctor had weakened. It was just that life was so full of so many demands — and none greater than those of Ireland. But she made a new resolution: while she could serve Ireland politically, she might serve her even better medically. It helped, at least for that term, to keep her mind on human rather than national pathology.

One Sunday evening, in Longford during Christmas, her Uncle Frank announced, 'They want you in the Committee Room.' The 'Committee Room' was where electioneering work was done. She wondered what was afoot, but Uncle Frank would say no more. She recalled:

After the Rosary in the Cathedral, I went up to the Committee Room. A group of men there began making speeches about the work I'd done for them. I was most embarrassed. Then they presented me with a gold wristlet watch inscribed 'From the Longford Sinn Féin Club.' My initials were engraved on the back. I have kept that watch all these years. Once it was in for cleaning and the jeweller said, 'You know there's an inscription on this watch?' and I said, 'Oh yes, that was a presentation watch. I'm very proud of that inscription.'

'But,' he said, 'there's another inscription. Have you not read the other one?' I said, 'No, I never saw any but the one inscription.' So he fixed his magnifying glass in my eye. There, engraved in the most minute letters were the words: 'To hell with Ireland. God save the King.' I have no idea when or where or how that sick joke was perpetrated, but it never diminished my pride in that watch.

The year 1918 has been called the year of the rising morale, but its early months gave no cause for rejoicing. After their successes in 1917, Sinn Féin lost three by-elections, two in Ulster (South Armagh and East Tyrone) and the third in Waterford, the seat of the Parliamentary Party leader, John Redmond, who had died on 6 March. Prominent Republicans were still being arrested on almost any pretext, but principally for making 'speeches calculated to cause disaffection'. Uncle Frank was 'taken' for such a speech, his crime being considered all the more enormous because he was an ex-Justice of the Peace. During his trial he expressed his defiance with the words, 'For Ireland I consider it a privilege to be promoted from the Bench to the Dock.' He was lodged in Sligo jail with a six-month sentence.

Shortly afterwards, Michael Collins came to Granard and made an anti-conscription speech at nearby Legga. On his return to Dublin, he was arrested for preaching 'disaffection'. At the time, there was grave public concern at the continual threats by the Government to introduce conscription in Ireland. Anti-conscription speeches were outlawed.

Under escort, Collins was brought to Longford Court. With her cousins, Brigid got permission to see him.

He was delighted, and because he'd had nothing to eat we arranged to have breakfast brought in. His 'trial', of course, had been a matter of form. He was sentenced to three months in Sligo Jail. He was taken to the railway station. Ignoring his police escort, he talked happily from the carriage window, making jokes loudly, about Sir 'Johnnie' French, Lloyd George's dictator, appointed to impose conscription on the Irish. As the train moved off, Collins waved as cheerfully as if he were off on a three-month holiday.

Imprisonment did not cause his sense of humour to desert him, as his letter to Brigid shows:

Sligo Jail
18th April 1918

A Chara Dhil,

It's nearly twelve months since I saw your writing, but I recognised it. I happened to learn accidentally about half an hour before I got your letter that your uncle was here. Really it seems too funny that he of all people from Longford should be 'tuk'. I mean of course that it wouldn't strike one as being likely that the police would interfere with him. I am looking forward to getting a glimpse of him at Mass on Sunday. It will be only his back though — they put the 'sentenced men' nearer the altar than those on remand. Saw Michael Drumm yesterday but only for a moment as he was passing from one part of the 'House' to another so had no converse with him. Whitney from Drumlesh I have not seen. O'Neill was transferred to Belfast a few days ago.

The situation is most awfully interesting. Conscription especially. I wonder what some of our friends say now. I'm sure the Longford ladies must feel very triumphant — how was this they had the refrain

'Soon conscription will be got
And McGuinness will be shot'.

Well they've got it — I wonder will they carry out Poor Joe's execution? But it's all the good stalwarts I'm interested in — the people who used to say — No! The Irish Party stopped it. The poor devils. J. P. Farrell at Edenmore was very good on the conscription question. Says he 'Of course they're introducing conscription' and says he 'Why wouldn't they?' says he. 'When they see all the marching and drilling of them Volunteers' says he. 'But' says he 'When it does come' says he 'They'll be under their beds' says he. So now we know why 'twas done. As for the Western Front — well I'm looking forward to seeing records broken in Channel swimming during the next few weeks. It is to be feared though that by having to make the journey to the water too quickly they won't get a chance of doing their best. Query — which is gaining the greater number of recruits — conscription or the hammering on the Western Front?

I believe Paddy McKenna gave up his commission of the Peace. He'll be under the 'yellow streak' next.

With all good wishes and kind regards to yourself and the others.

Micheál Ó Coileáin

Collins was preoccupied with the subject of conscription because the country was similarly occupied at the time. German pressure on the Western Front called for more British manpower and, urged strongly by Sir Henry Wilson (a native of County Longford!), Lloyd George looked enviously at the youth of Ireland. Excuses were sought to conscript these idle rebels as British cannon fodder. On 12 April 1918, a German submarine put ashore in Galway an Irish prisoner of war — namely, Joseph Dowling of the Connaught Rangers and C.O. of Casement's Irish Brigade. Like Casement, Dowling was arrested. Lloyd George alleged 'a German plot' and pressed on with conscription to remove troublesome Irishmen to more useful work on the Western Front. Lord Wimbourne, the Lord Lieutenant in Dublin, denied the plot and questioned the wisdom of conscription of the Irish. He was summarily replaced and, within a week, his successor had issued a proclamation that 'a German plot' *had* been uncovered in Ireland.

On 16 April, the Conscription of Ireland Bill was passed and, two days later, united in common cause, all political parties in Ireland held a conference at the Mansion House in Dublin. That evening, the Catholic hierarchy issued a manifesto:

> We consider that conscription forced in this way upon Ireland is an oppressive and inhuman law which the Irish people have a right to resist by every means that are consonant with the law of God.

On 23 April, there was a general strike in protest against conscription. Sinn Féin Headquarters decided that Collins could no longer be spared. Men were rallying in thousands to the ranks of the Volunteers. There was work to be done. Therefore, against all their principles, it was decided that Collins should seek bail. Collins himself was always against the idea that men with important work outside should remain in prison, rather than pay bail money. Accordingly, two Longford businessmen, Michael Cox (a cousin of Brigid Lyons') and Michael Doyle, went bail, and Michael Collins was released from Sligo Jail. He drove straight to Granard. The local Volunteers gave him a royal reception before he left for Dublin.

A month later, on 17 May 1918, helped by his contacts in Dublin Castle, Collins warned members of the Sinn Féin Executive of their imminent arrest. By the next day, on the pretext of 'the German plot', seventy-three members of Sinn Féin were arrested and deported, including Griffith, de Valera, Count Plunkett and Joe McGuinness. Maud Gonne MacBride, Mrs Tom Clarke and Countess Markievicz were among the women arrested. Thus nearly every candidate returned to parliament by Sinn Féin was now in prison. Collins evaded the swoop and immediately became a wanted man. Now he began to build up his famous intelligence service.

Brigid stayed with her Aunt Joe in Dublin for the summer of 1918. Gloom prevailed in the Longford and Dublin McGuinness households. Uncle Frank had been transferred from Sligo to Belfast Jail, and Uncle Joe was now in Gloucester Jail. Nor was Rose McGuinness any better. After a brief period at home, she was back in hospital. The gloom wasn't helped by the rumours about the treatment of prisoners. Their efforts to be classified as political prisoners, rather than as criminals, sometimes resulted in penal therapy: solitary confinement in handcuffs or muffs for days on end. A letter from Uncle Frank was, however, characteristically cheerful, despite the irritations of his Aunt Dora (The Defence of the Realm Act):

> Number 512, Frank McGuinness,
> Belfast Prison
> After Mass, Ascension Thursday
> May 9th, 1918
>
> Dear Bridgie,
>
> I suppose you think I have forgotten you altogether. Well I have not. I was glad to hear of you going back and trust you are not feeling worried about Mr. Lloyd George's new trouble.
>
> I would have written sooner but for being changed from Sligo to here so suddenly, that I have missed two days in the excitement. Fleming wishes to be remembered to you. Joe McDonagh is feeling good and so is Austin and in fact all the others are in the pink. Now my Aunt Dora is such a cranky old dame that she hardly allows me time to write and then when she does I'm not allowed to write what I would like to! Hard lines, isn't it? Well as to the change, it's like leaving a poor lodging house and going to a swell hotel, to leave Sligo and to come here. I mean in style and appearance, but not exactly so in regard to food. Of course, I'm not getting my food from outside like in Sligo, but depending on the prison fare augmented by parcels (which is not very satisfactory for me at any rate) from all those who are charitable enough to think of a poor devil in jail who is hourly expecting the parcel post to bring him something.
>
> We are all doing the novena here! Devotions at 4 o'c. each evening in the chapel, so if you are writing to your Aunt you can inform her that we are well looked after from the spiritual side anyhow. We get the daily papers which is a great matter.
>
> Bye bye now. With kind regards from
>
> Uncle

This letter is crowded on the back of a 'Form 21|A.D.|2988|1902.' The front is entirely taken up with regulations. Some are worth quotation:

> The permission to write and receive letters is given to prisoners for the purpose of enabling them to keep up a connection with their respectable friends and not that they may be kept informed of public events.
>
> All letters are read by the Prison Authorities. They must be legibly written and not crossed. Any which are of an objectionable tendency, either to or from prisoners, or containing slang, or improper expressions will be suppressed.
>
> Prisoners are permitted to receive and to write a letter at intervals, which depend on the rules of the stage they attain by industry and good conduct, etc.

It was hardly surprising that crowds of spirited men cooped up for months should rebel periodically against their conditions. Paddy Fleming from Athy, mentioned in the above letter, was just such a man. He strongly objected to being classified as a criminal. His conflict with the prison authorities, particularly at Maryborough (now Portlaoise) Prison, and the vicious punishment meted out became something of a cause célèbre even among those well used to the British prison system as applied in Ireland. A pamphlet published on Fleming's case shocked all shades of public opinion.

In June 1918, Kate McGuinness of Longford received notice that her husband, Frank, was about to be released. Overwhelmed with delight, she journeyed to Belfast to meet him. On arrival, she was casually informed that he had just been transferred to Reading Gaol for an indefinite period. She was not to see her husband for a further seven months and then only for a brief parole allowed him on the occasion of a family funeral.

# 15

# THE KILLING PANDEMIC

DURING THE SUMMER of 1918, Brigid occasionally met Michael Collins socially, despite the fact that he was now a marked man. Nobody liked a party more than he did, and he liked visiting, however briefly, the houses of sympathisers — people who didn't stand on ceremony; people he could call on unexpectedly and, when he left, as unexpectedly, they understood and weren't offended and never asked awkward questions. In Dublin, Mick Collins had a list of such friendly households, with a spare bed always waiting. Some were close to his heart — especially those with children. The home of Batt O'Connor in Brendan Road, Donnybrook, was such a one.

Another was that of Denis Lynch in Jones' Road near the DWD whiskey distillery where Denis was a chemist. The Lynches gave musical evenings. Their sitting room had a particularly luxurious settee with some beautifully embroidered cushions, Mrs Lynch's pride and glory. Anyone who found it really necessary to sit there first moved the cushions to a safe distance. On getting up, they would feel it a duty to replace them to restore the impeccable look of that settee. Brigid recalled a typical soirée at the house:

Somebody was in the middle of a sentimental song when suddenly there was a bouncing, heavy-booted step on the stairs. Everything stopped and Mick Collins charged into these sophisticated surroundings like an actor playing an unsophisticated countryman. The hero of the hour! Everybody shifted to offer him a seat, but it was the settee that attracted him. He plonked himself down regardless, stretching his great legs. He wore the biggest, clumsiest boots ever seen outside a farmyard. Known as Bluchers, he explained, they were his climbing boots, very suitable for tramping and traipsing, but indispensable for getting over walls and roofs and anything else that impeded a man in his escapes from the Forces of the Crown.

Far from worrying about her cushions, or the footwear he favoured, Mrs Lynch was only too thrilled to see Mick Collins still in one piece and still a free man. His usual scintillating self, Mick contributed a song and a recitation before dashing away into the night. With capture or death courting his every movement, it was a typical Collins social call.

Always when they met, Brigid evoked for Michael Collins something of the little town of Granard, something of the Kiernan family — in particular, something of her friend, Helen Kiernan. Anxiously, he'd enquire when she'd last seen them and how they were. In fact, he was in love with Helen Kiernan. And that wasn't surprising. Apart from their patriotism, the generosity of the Kiernan family was a tradition in the Movement , and many an Irish rebel had already lost his heart to one or other of the charming Kiernan sisters.

With a strong Irish-Ireland background, the younger Kiernans, following the early deaths of both parents, were left in charge of the Greville Arms Hotel. Larry and his four sisters, Chris, Kitty, Helen and Maud, measured up to their responsibilities. Nothing was too much for them if it was for the men and women of the Movement. They kept open house, they entertained, and they accommodated the crowds on Longford's great occasions. It was during the South Longford election that Mick Collins came under the spell of the Kiernan sisters. Helen was his special interest. Whenever he could escape from Dublin, it was not to Cork he went, but to Granard.

With Collins, every day was a working day, and every night too. An occasional snatched weekend was the most he allowed himself, for by 1918 things were hotting up. His trips out of Dublin were fewer. Nor did Helen Kiernan get to Dublin very often. The friendship suffered as a consequence. Even when Helen came to Dublin, Mick was too often preoccupied.

The habitual meeting place for Brigid and Helen was Mitchell's, the most fashionable café in Grafton Street, where Helen Kiernan's elegance stood out. Brigid recalled:

> Inevitably we talked about current romances. I heard Mick's name less and less. Then she mentioned a new romance. She was very much in love. He was a solicitor called Paul McGovern from Cavan. Eventually they married. With Mick Collins, Uncle Joe and my aunt I attended their wedding reception held in Walter Cole's Georgian house, number 3 Mountjoy Square, which, in the future, was to be the scene of much nationalist activity, including the secret meetings of the Dáil and meetings on the Treaty negotiations.

Michael Collins was very upset about losing Helen Kiernan. While he did not have the time to devote to her, he was genuinely affectionate and serious in his feelings. His free time had become non-existent, but the odd weekend he left Dublin, it was back to Granard he went, sometimes with his great friend, Harry Boland, who was courting Kitty Kiernan. According to Brigid:

> Everybody who went to Granard fell in love with the Kiernan girls. Dan McCarthy used to joke about it when we were arranging speakers. 'No, we can't send him,' he'd say. 'He got to Granard last week.' Granard became the prize rendezvous. The Greville Arms flourished until it was burnt out in the sacking of Granard by the Black and Tans in November 1920.

In October 1918, when she was due to return to University College Galway, Brigid collapsed one morning at Mass. A new disease called influenza was about to reach pandemic proportions. An outbreak of this virulent infection occurred in Maynooth College. Unwisely, the authorities closed the college, distributing both the students and the infection throughout the country.

The 1918 flu did not necessarily hit the debilitated or the elderly. It mostly hit the strongest, the young — those least likely to die in normal times. The Republican Movement lost many fine young men. Lacking resistance, they did not take the opportunity to take to bed in time, and many were dead within twenty-four hours. Brigid remembered:

> At one stage, my three cousins and myself were hit at the same time. Then Aunt Frank's staff went ill. Finally, she had to give in and close the business. This was the general picture everywhere, and the doctors were so busy it took two days before they could visit you.

Having spent the month of October in bed, Brigid realised that her academic year in Galway was wrecked. Preparations were beginning for the general election in December, so she joined the helpers in the Longford election rooms. While electioneering had now become almost routine, she felt unequal to it. She collapsed again. But the will to survive is strong. What was happening in the political world still mattered — that and the regrettable loss of a year in her medical course.

On 10 October, the mail boat *Leinster* was sunk by a German submarine shortly after leaving Kingstown (now Dún Laoghaire). Over five hundred people perished, and there were stories of pyramids of bodies piled on the piers at Kingstown. A month later, on 11 November, came the Armistice. But some 50,000 Irishmen would never come back. Brigid's cousins had dashed into her bedroom with the news 'The War's over!'

> I was feeling very ill, but I remember thinking the war is over and we still haven't got our freedom. I could feel no joy. In the street outside, there was a lot of noise from the pig fair. When the news of the Armistice broke, the British soldiers went berserk. They came up through the Main Street and began climbing on the creels of the pig carts. People pushed them in on top of the pigs. Between the squeals of the pigs and the bellowing of the soldiers, the place was like a bedlam. I was too ill to look out, but my cousins gave me a running commentary.

Influenza had hit hard in England, too, and nowhere harder than in the prisons. Pierce McCann, a Sinn Féin MP and a fine young man, had died in Gloucester Prison. He was said to have been neglected, so the authorities had tried to make amends. Uncle Joe had written reassuringly:

Gloucester Prison
Wednesday morning 9 0'c.

Dear Bridgie,

This will reach you by B. posting it outside for me on his way home. I wrote to you yesterday and told all about our boys. There's nothing new since, only Desmond FitzGerald was taken to the nursing home last night. I suppose his wife's coming made them afraid to have him here when she'd come. He was in good form going. We are delighted to be able to get them to a nursing home as they cannot take them back here when they recover and of course they're better looked after there too.

Tell Katie not to be uneasy about me. I get a chop every day for dinner now and rice pudding. All of us now get these extras since the others got ill… The doctor is extra kind and only for him we'd get very little.

I hope there will be no trouble with Labour in Longford about selection of candidates. It's likely and almost certain that the Proportional Representation Bill will be passed before June and that will simplify things and give everyone a chance. So let them stick together as well as they can. I am of course in favour of giving them their full due but no more and we must be firm on principle.

You might write to John Cawley and tell him I'd be glad if he allowed his name to go forward for C.C. We will want the very best men. Paul Cusack too should be put forward and Larry Kiernan and Jim Flood if they will go. All our work of the future will depend largely on local representatives and every effort should be made to select the very best men.

We are surprised here that there seems to be a feeling of disappointment at how things are going amongst you all in

Ireland. Griffith and all of us here think they are going as well as can be expected and that everything will come alright for us still.

Write me now fully about Katie and how she is. I'm expecting a letter from her today tell her. I'm praying constantly for her and you all to be saved from sickness and feel very grateful to God who has saved myself amidst all the dangers of the past week. Be of good cheer. I will be home early next month.

Joe

As the general election campaign got underway, Brigid began to recover. She exchanged one fever for another. She was appointed Honorary Secretary of the McGuinness Election Committee. They all felt a duty to Joe, locked up as he was in a foreign prison. His letters helped to guide them. The one that follows was used as a pamphlet and was 'issued for the candidate by his election agent, P. J. Hannan, Solicitor , Longford'.

Gloucester Prison.
Nov. 25th 1918

Dear Bridgie,

I expected a reply from you to my last two letters before this but none came so far. I sent from here last Wednesday Nov. 20th my address to the electors addressed to you. Have it published if it reached you. All candidates selected from this prison sent a general statement to Harcourt St. about two weeks ago signed by Arthur Griffith and myself.
[At this point the published pamphlet contains an insert in heavy type: 'People of Longford, you have not got the address because the Government suppressed it. Did they suppress that of J. P. Farrell? Not they… Let them see that the Irish people are aiders and abettors in the 'CRIME' of Joe McGuinness]
I read with pleasure in the *Herald* an account of the first meeting in Ballinalee. A magnificent start under good auspices in

that place sacred to the memory of … [Here there is another insert in the pamphlet: 'We know the name he could not write. It is a name that will live in the heart of Ireland when the LONGFORD LEADER is forgotten.' It was Michael Collins who addressed that meeting in Ballinalee and the reference to the *Longford Leader* means the newspaper of which J. P. Farrell, the rival candidate, was proprietor.]

I suppose you have heard all the rumours of our release? Looks as if they were only rumours. So the work must be harder than ever on all. Make it such a victory now that the effect will be felt throughout the world. I'm confident of the result, but every vote will count, every vote on our side must be polled. This will require very careful organisation owing to the size of the register, SO EVERY MAN AND WOMAN MUST HELP.

Katie is improving slowly. She will be upset that I'm not home this week. Write her cheerful letters from time to time if you are able. I trust all my friends are nearly recovered from their illness. Let those who were ill be careful of venturing too much until they are fully recovered. I was awfully shocked to see the death of my very dear good friend Michael Whelan. I wrote his wife a letter of sympathy, the best I could. I feel his loss personally very much apart from politics. He was so true as steel in his own quiet way.

I got the LEADER yesterday. It's very poor and looks as if they thought the fight a hopeless one. Let this not lull our people. The figures must be huge this time. Let me know of anything I can do from here. I am going to try, even if they are suppressed, to get in touch with my supporters. Write me as often as you can. Any word of Frank lately?

Best love to you all.

Your Uncle Joseph

As polling day approached, Brigid forgot her convalescence. She found new strength. It came partly from her own sense of nationalism, but mainly from the frustration expressed in Joe's letters. She *must* try to allay the helplessness of a candidate engaged in electioneering from a foreign prison cell. Knowing that the British authorities were delaying and suppressing prisoners' correspondence, it was in her official capacity that Uncle Joe next wrote to her.

Gloucester Prison.
1st December, 1918.
Honorary Secretary
McGuinness Election Committee
2, Main St.
Longford

A Chara,

Your letter of November 25th only reached me this morning. You will note therefore how all correspondence is delayed of late. Apparently none of my letters of the past fortnight have reached you. I wrote you enclosing form of authorisation to act as my agent, to be handed to Mr. Hannan, Solicitor. I wrote my address to the electors on Nov. 20th. It was returned seven days later with a note stating that reference to politics were not allowed to a prisoner. I then wired Mr. Hannan acquainting him of this fact. Myself and all the selected candidates here on the same day sent a joint wire to the INDEPENDENT. I have had no intimation so far that any of these communications have been received. I again wrote another letter yesterday to my agent, Mr. Hannan. Would you find out if he has received any of my letters?

I answered Maggie's letter two days ago and also wrote Father Markey and Mr. Connolly on 26th Nov. I wrote to Father Ryan yesterday and addressed it to Aughavas, Bornscoole, but was not certain if this was correct. In one of my letters to you I asked you to send me a list of the clergy to whom I should write. I trust you have already done so as I only know a few of their addresses owing to the late changes which I understand took place since I left.

Indeed I feel Michael Whelan's death more than I can tell you and feel I have lost a good friend from every point of view. I wrote to his wife the day I saw an account of his death. I know it will leave them in a bad way there. I am dropping a line to Mr. Flynn today asking him to do the best they can under the circumstances.

I was delighted to hear of P. McGarry and other likely supporters. I feel I will get a good number of those who last time were against me. However, let every man and woman roll up their sleeves and not turn them down until the night of Dec. 14th. Get in touch with Tarmon, Ruskey and Kilglass, Beramogue and Curraghroe for whatever vehicles they can spare on your side on that day.

I mentioned in my letter to Mr. Connolly that I expected all the members of the club's men and women who were young enough could march to the polls early, stepping to the measure of Joe - Joe - Joe - McGuinness, in order to give the older people a chance of voting before darkness sets in by bringing cars for them. NO JOY-RIDING for anyone under 45.

Owing to many being laid up with flu, or likely to be during the vital days, it would be advisable to have substitutes appointed and trained for polling booths in every district. Each person's duties in a townland or district ought to be given to him in writing and a note taken of who is to be held responsible in a case of failure.

I am glad Tom was able to get things going while you were still weak. Let all of you be careful not to overwork or take too much risk with your health even if a vote were to be gained by so doing. For though I'm anxious to have the majority a huge one, I would be sorry that any worker of mine suffered in health.

I am glad Mr. Regan is doing so well on the hustings. I hope P. Fanning will throw in his weight also in that direction. I hope Harry is well by this. Give my regards to William Moore, Tom B. McCoy and all the other boys and girls. I'm glad you wrote Katie. I had no letter from her for over a week now. I hope your Aunt Frank will not over-worry. God is directing all our actions and we are going to win.

Love to self, Maureen, Maggie, Bridgie and everybody who has a vote.

Joe Up McGuinness

Polling day was 14 December 1918. There had been no need for all Uncle Joe's advice and frustration. He may have been an MP but there was little he had to teach his election organisers in Longford. In May 1917, they had learned the hard way, taught by Dan McCarthy. In December 1918, the public mood was more reliable. It had been largely a matter of getting the people out to vote in defiance of the intimidation of the British authorities — raids, arrests and seizures were still being directed against Republicans, and the polling booths on 14 December were watched by armed military and police.

Christmas intervened before the result became known. There was little to make Christmas 1918 a happy one. Shops were without festive fare. Many families were bereaved from recent deaths in the flu epidemic. True, the Great War was over, but in Longford that only revived bitter memories of local losses. Colonel, the Earl of Granard, had raised a regiment of volunteers in 1914. With the 10th Irish Division, they had gone to Gallipoli in 1915. At least a third of their force had been decimated by bullets, shells, drowning and dysentery. The memory of the futility of Gallipoli died hard.

Although still waiting for the election result, Uncle Joe wrote more cheerfully from Gloucester Prison on 20 December. One corner of this letter has unfortunately been torn off:

Dear Bridgie,

I was expecting a letter from you the last two days telling me of how you think things stand. I got your wire on Monday night. I was not a bit uneasy at newspaper reports of Monday or Tuesday. Wednesday was near my own estimate.

I hope you and all the rest in 2 and 4 [Main Street, Longford] are recovered after your great efforts of the past month. I'm glad everything went well, with the exception of the window smashing which I suppose [blank]. I am sure the [blank] upset over it all. [blank] all I know hoping [blank] be there for Xmas if not in the flesh we will in spirit. Even prison can be a palace in these days of good reports from Ireland. It's glorious to be alive. We are all here in high spirits and not a bit downhearted. I sing 'The Girl from

Clare' just as good as ever.

God guard you all.

Joe

Joe McGuinness' optimism was justified. On 28 December, the results of the general election were declared. Out of 105 candidates returned for Ireland, 75 were Republicans, 26 were Unionists, and the Parliamentary Party secured only 6 seats. The people had voted for Sinn Féin, and a Republic, by a majority of 70 per cent. Nationalist Ireland had finally forsaken constitutional Home Rule in favour of Sinn Féin, the party whose avowed policy was nothing less than an independent Irish Republic.

The result in Longford was a microcosm of that in the country at large. The Declaration is written in impeccable long hand:

County of Longford
Parliamentary Election 1918
I hereby give Public Notice that at the Parliamentary Election for the County of Longford held on the 14th of December 1918 Joseph McGuinness of Upper Gardiner St., Dublin was duly elected: and I hereby give further notice that the total number of votes given for each candidate was as follows:
James Patk. Farrell 4,173
Joseph McGuinness 11,122
Dated this 28th day of December 1918

J. Fitzgerald
Returning Officer

Nineteen months earlier, McGuinness had won the South Longford by-election with a majority of 37 votes. This time, his majority was 6,949. It reflected the intensity of the revulsion of Irish public opinion against Maxwell's executions of 1916. Sinn Féin had achieved this success although over one hundred of their leaders were in jail, including thirty-six of the candidates. It had been achieved largely by political novices, and despite the censorship of the Post Office and the press. It had been achieved by dedicated people like young Brigid Lyons who gave their all, even risking their health in the great fight. And because she was a woman, and still far from being thirty, she did not even have the satisfaction of casting a vote.

# 16

# AN UNDERCOVER GIRL

TO MEET THE overwhelming will of the people, arrangements commenced immediately to convene Dáil Éireann as an Independent Constituent Assembly of the Irish Nation. On 21 January 1919, in Dublin's Mansion House, the first Parliament of the Republic of Ireland met for two historic hours. Thirty-six of the seventy-three elected Republicans, including Joe McGuinness, were absent, being still in prison. Ireland's Declaration of Independence was read and a democratic programme was adopted. An act had been performed from which the nation could never withdraw.

On the same day as the Dáil first met, an ambush took place at Soloheadbeg in Tipperary in which Seán Treacy, Dan Breen and others attacked an RIC party escorting gelignite to a quarry. Two RIC constables were shot dead. Faced with this audacity, and the meeting of the Dáil, Dublin Castle intensified its campaign of repression. With the establishment of Dáil Éireann, the Volunteers became the Irish Republican Army. The British prepared to suppress the Dáil, while the IRA prepared to defend it. Thus the stage was set for the opening of the Anglo-Irish War, the first shots of which had already been fired at Soloheadbeg.

The joy of the McGuinness family at Joe's success at the general election was short-lived. At the end of January 1919, the death of Rose McGuinness occurred. Three years earlier, she had been one of the first casualties in the Four Courts. Ever since, and despite chronic illness, she had never wavered in her devotion to the freedom of Ireland. There was no doubt her illness had been aggravated by her nationalist activities.

When Uncle Frank was notified at Reading Gaol, he applied for parole on compassionate grounds, and got home in time for the funeral. Joe did not apply because he himself was ill. Brigid remembered that day.

> The local Volunteers carried the coffin from the house to the chapel at Whitehall, Tarmonbarry — a journey of about three miles. It was sad to watch that procession winding its way along the country roads on that bleak January evening. In the cemetery, two young Volunteers mingled with the crowd. After the last prayers, they fired a volley. Quickly they passed their revolvers to somebody who was waiting. I saw the boys stooping as they escaped through the crowd. It would have been extremely serious for them if they were caught. The risk they took was the measure of their last tribute to Rose McGuinness, the girl who had fearlessly gone out in 1916.

Passing through Dublin on his return to Reading Gaol, Frank McGuinness called on Lord Mayor Larry O'Neill to deliver messages from his friends in prison. Sympathetic and helpful, Alderman O'Neill gave his replies to take back. He offered to try to get Frank's parole extended, but Frank declined, preferring to return on time. Frank's last request, before Brigid saw him off at the boat, was for any ointment she could prescribe for the itch that was rife in the prisons. She recognised it for what it was — scabies — but in the prisons of England, it had become known as 'The Republican Itch'.

Uncle Frank reported on his return journey to Reading Gaol in a letter dated 10 February 1919:

Dear Bridgie,

Just a line to say that, after some trouble, I arrived safely on Saturday evening. I had to put up in London on Friday night owing to the dislocation of railway traffic due to the fact that the men working in the tubes were all out on strike. I suppose you people over in Ireland will be saying that the Sinn Féiners are at the bottom of this trouble too, like what you are saying about the Belfast strike, but, from what I heard in the hotel where I stopped, the folks over here say it's due to some other cause and the Sinn Féiners had nothing to do with it.

I was very comfortably put up but felt very lonely in the midst of millions of people. I'm making no complaints, but simply stating a fact. I arrived in Reading at 3 pm and instead of going straight to His Majesty's hotel I went to the George for a change and had a good square meal after which I took a tram and went around to see the town and made my way at 6 pm to my old room in Wing E3, C15.

I found the boys all in good form but, expecting hourly to hear of their release. They wondered to see my coming back and immediately gave up the notion of their release for some days longer at any rate. I pitied the poor fellows in their disappointment and wished I had not come for longer. However, we are all on the alert, now that the Prime Minister is back in London, and expect to arrive in dirty Dublin by the end of the week without fail.

I do hope those hams and turkeys which are awaiting us will be in eatable condition when we arrive, for they will be very badly needed in this cold, frosty weather. I told the boys about them but am very sorry now I did so, as they can't talk or think of anything else since.

Snow lies two feet deep from Crewe to London and all along down to Reading and frost has followed which makes it, for the first time, so cold here that it's well nigh unbearable. I'm sorry now but I took the Lord Mayor's offer and take the seven days extra which he so kindly suggested getting for me. I was always unfortunate and will remain so I'm afraid.

Tell your Aunt Katie not to ask you work too hard as I'm afraid you will get knocked up again if you are not careful. Kindest regards to her and all the kind ones in No. 2.

Your fond Uncle Frank

February was ushered in with news of the escape of de Valera from Lincoln Prison, in company with Seán Milroy and Seán McGarry. The genius behind this escape is attributed variously. The many subsequent jail breaks known to have been masterminded by Collins earned him the title of 'director of escapes'.

With Harry Boland, Collins (now Minister for Home Affairs in the new Dáil cabinet) had been in England arranging every detail of the escape. De Valera was concerned that two such important men should be at risk. As a wanted man, Collins went to England risking his freedom and his life to rescue de Valera. In support, went his greatest friend, Harry Boland. They both loved Kitty Kiernan, but tragically they split on this and on the Treaty. At heart, they remained friends.

On a moonlit night, one month later, Collins managed to spirit Robert Barton over a twenty-foot wall out of Mountjoy Prison. Shortly afterwards, there was a mass breakout from the same prison. Brigid said of 1919 that it was a year in which 'one's life seemed to move in the shadow of prisons, Irish and English, with one's concern for those who languished within them.'

A medical student colleague, Paddy Mullins, had arrived in HM Prison, Galway, from whence he wrote to Brigid on 28 February:

A Chailín Dhil,

Well Bridgie I hope you are in the bloom of health and enjoying a fair amount of happiness. Exit February in sun and calm and peace of a sort. The only discordant note will probably crop up in the day's INDEPENDENT. Marvellous the effect of sunlight on the soul, is it not? No, I haven't turned street-preacher, but I've been reading Benson on spiritualism and a few more of the 'occult theories'. Table rapping appears to have a future when it can reduce the soul to a little bright splash of something phosphoric and then treat it in the ordinary chemical way with test-tubes and nitric acid and the evidence of the senses, it MUST needs get some respect. It reminds one of Pat Cusack looking for the formula for living protoplasm on the second day of his attending zoology lectures.

Please Bridgie forgive this ráiméis, but sure it's the only thing I can put in a letter. Seán T. O'Kelly seems to be busy over in Paris. Things look good lately, now that the world is made safe, etc. The next job will be to make democracy safe for the world, what with Fritz Adler becoming President of a republic and [?] Cottin 'refusing to recognise the court'. I would not like to be a monarch just at present. An individual has come into the convict regions lately who indulges in the soubriquet of 'Arab King' of Galway gutter fame. There seems to be a general conspiracy against crowned heads. In a paper the other day I saw a somewhat anatomical definition of a monarch: 'A monarch is a process on the distal end of a monarchy: it sometimes possesses a head which is a facet for articulation with the crown, etc.' It seems as though the general unrest were entering the medical faculty.

You must be tired of this effusion, but I have forgotten how to go a decent letter. One of our boys — Sheehy from Kiltimagh — has gone home on parole to see his mother. The Galway boys send their obeisances to 'Miss Lyons' who appears to stand on a high pinnacle of their estimation. But now I'm descending to the doggerel of flattery.

May the sun that is warm today shine kindly on you
Mise,

Paddy Mullins
P.S.
Latest news to the effect that College has closed for a fortnight. O'Brien, a new student from Limerick, died yesterday I heard. It appears to be a very virulent epidemic.
Paddy Mullins

The work done on behalf of prisoners by Brigid Lyons, and people like her, can never be calculated. With parcels, protests and letters, the women managed somehow to keep the male morale high. On 26 March, medical student Paddy Mullins wrote his gratitude. He was still '212 Mullins, Patrick, of H.M. Prison, Galway.' (The prison, incidentally, stood on the site now occupied by Galway Cathedral.)

A Chailín Dílis,

Thanks! A thousand thanks! and while I am still in the happy glow that follows the receipt of a 'welcome' letter, I set myself the task of penning an epistle that, after all, must pass the Censor. Yes! the crop of beards has been an overwhelming business. Personally, after three weeks beard-growing in the attempt to look like a Bolshevik, I succeeded in sporting the appearance of a well-to-do tramp with a tendency to drink. But those days have gone. The poor internees must have had to suffer an unmerciful amount of chaff on the question of facial adornment. I trust sincerely that your uncles will not be long in returning to their pre-jail status of health. About the reception, etc. — well I'll say nothing at present and at all events it cannot suffer heavily for want of my weighty opinions.

Well 'the day is not far distant' when we shall pack up our household goods, cast a longing, lingering look at our cells and windows and go forth with the trust of children into the big world beyond the Corrib. And for your congratulation intrinsically sweet, I send you my heart's thanks. But I begin to grow sentimental.

About returning to College — well Bridgie, a lot of that is in the lap of Fate. You see, I've been haunting colleges for some twelve years and for shame sake I doubt whether it would not be the more manly thing to apply for a passport. But I shall first drift homewards, kneel at the parental knee, taste the adipose calf and then think the matter over for a few days.

But this is all about 'I'. It is wonderful what an egoist one becomes when he gets 'cut off' for a few days. Yes, I shall throw all my influence on Dr. Dillon's pan of the balance. It should count. I have a plan made up — to write a threatening black-hand letter to Howley, hinting at death (capital D) if he SHOULD by any means vote for Mr. Dillon: then sign myself 'Sinn Féiner'. That should work it.

Of news I have none. But I shall write you when I get out. Our brief period of prison life has not been severe. We have fairly decent hours, and a wing of the prison to ourselves. But it is the 'spirit' of the treatment that counts more than the actual conditions.

All your friends, Kathleen, Annie, Eve, Daisy have been in 'flu-land' and are convalescent. Was it not sad about Bill Forde, V.S. [veterinary surgeon] (Tessie's brother)? It was certainly tragic. I trust you are in the best of health and spirits. For the present, Mise, le grádh mor,

Paddy Mullins.
P.S.
MacNamara, Shemus Ryan, Davenport, Ward and all the boys are well and send their best regards.
Paddy
P.P.S.
And you meet Jack Darcy please give him my love. I hear he is to be back again after Easter.
Paddy

Paddy Mullins' prison letters seem to carry more meaning than the written words convey. Yet they passed through the censor without so much as one erasure. A letter from Brigid's friend, Una Sharkey, in Sligo Prison, is in sharp contrast. One may conclude that the erased sections were not complimentary to His Majesty's Prison Service. Even the address was erased and the word Sligeach altered to Sligo.

10th March '19
A Chara Dílis,

X X X X X X X X X X X X X X X X X X X X X X X X X X X X X X X
X
X X X X X X X X X X X X X X X X X X X X X X X X X X X X X X
X X X X X X X We were indeed delighted to get your letter. I hope your aunt is now better. I know the homecoming of dear ones is

Brigid Lyons with her cousin Rose McGuinness taken in 1915 or 1916. Rose was one of the first casualties in the Four Courts in 1916. She died in 1919 and was given a military funeral.

Mrs Tom Clarke with her sons Daly, Tom and Emmett shortly after the execution of her husband in 1916. Mrs Clarke autographed the photograph for Brigid in April 1966 during the fiftieth anniversary celebration in Dublin Castle.

Caitlín bean uí Chléirigh
14· 4· 66

The Joe McGuinness election campaign in full swing in 1917.

The declaration of the poll in South Longford on 9 May 1917, which Joe McGuinness won by 37 votes, while still a prisoner in Lewes Jail for his part in the Easter Rising.

This photograph was taken in Sligo in 1917 and was given to Joe McGuinness by a Father Silke. The occasion was probably following the general release of prisoners. Included are Eamon de Valera, Mrs Mulcahy of Sligo, Countess Markievicz, Count Plunkett, Joseph McGuinness and Darrell Figgis.

A selection of the first Dáil, which met at the Mansion House, Dublin on 8 January 1919. Joe McGuinness (with beard) can be seen standing behind Eamon de Valera.

Frank McGuinness in 1919.

Seán Mac Eoin wearing the uniform of the new Free State Army in 1922.

a Cara Dom                 3/6/1921

The attached is for you
from Sean. Keep it carefully.
See note on back.
Phots very like him. You
can almost see the fiery energy
rushing from him.
Best wishes

                        M.

Enlarged (I believe you his small photo to corall by name)
9 myself
attached Photo taken in Mtjoy of Tom Traynor (executed / Sean McE
                                     + Tom Whelan)

On behalf of Seán Mac Eoin, this
photograph was sent to Brigid Lyons by
Michael Collins (see the letter above)
having been smuggled out of Mountjoy
Prison. It was taken by a friendly warder
and shows (l-r): Thomas Whelan
(hanged 14 March 1921), Sean Mac
Eoin who was then awaiting trial for
murder, and Thomas Traynor (hanged
26 April 1921).

Brigid Lyons with her resident student colleagues at Mercers Hospital, 1920.

Brigid Lyons worked for a period in 1922 in the Treaty Committee Office in College Street, Dublin (later to become the Cumann na nGaedhal office). She is seen here with Brinsley MacNamara, the playwright and novelist; Nellie McHugh and Bridie Breen. Centre front is Kay McGilligan who accompanied the Treaty delegation to London.

Receiving her Diploma in Public Health
from University College Dublin in 1927.

Brigid with Capt Eddie Thornton
in Nice, 1925.

At the ordination of Fr Pat McGuinness were back row l-r: George
McGuinness, Frank McGuinness, Fr Pat McGuinness, Edward Thornton and
Mrs Frank McGuinness. Front row l-r: Miss B. McGuinness, Mrs Joe
McGuinness, Mrs C. McGuinness, and Brigid Lyons Thornton.

Major-General Piaras Béaslaí lays a wreath on the grave of Michael Collins, 24 August 1958. Behind and to his right is Brigid Lyons Thornton with her nephew Barry Lyons.

James Dillon and Brigid Lyons Thornton on the occasion of the retirement from public life of Gen. Richard Mulcahy, Gen. Seán Mac Eoin, Prof, Michael Hayes and Prof. Patrick McGilligan on New Year's Day, 1966.

just the thing she needs. Well, at last John Bull has condescended X X X X to let out our men when he couldn't possibly do aught else — unless indeed he wanted to have 80 funeral marches from the British 'keeps' — not indeed that I imagine his softer feelin' got the better of him there. X X X X for how could X X X X to mingle with some honest men with such a dirty trail if Johnny knew his paper wall would still keep things dark he'd chance it — but now, dearly bought as the paper wall has been, it's insufficient to cover up the hypocrites and wily as they have been and so much engrossed in their inequities, they seem to have forgotten there is a King of Kings.

This letter goes on to discuss the death of Pierce McCann in Gloucester Jail and the need for Ireland to place her trust in God. It ends as follows:

I hope your uncles are O.K. Give them both a rebel's welcome and may God reward their sacrifices. I am sorry I won't be up for 15th, but I WON'T apply for parole. I applied here for parole to attend my brother's month's mind and reply came a week later the day I should be out. Hence one sample is enough for X X X X X X X X X X X X X X X X X X

P.S.
Give X X X X X X X X X

The signature on this letter has been erased and the name 'Una Sharkey' is written in a different hand.

In March 1919, despite the many protests, all those arrested after the fabricated 'German Plot' were still in English prisons. Influenza was rife amongst them, adding to the concern of relatives. On 6 March, Pierce McCann died in Gloucester Prison (Una Sharkey had referred to him in the above letter.) Officially he was an MP, having been elected for Sinn Féin in December 1918. The death of an MP in prison had an impact at Westminster. The House of Commons immediately decided to release all Irish internees and convicted prisoners. Once again, their arrival in Ireland was marked by wild scenes of jubilation. The question uppermost was how long it would be before they would be arrested again, for the reign of terror seemed to be intensifying.

In April, Brigid began clinic sessions at the Mater Hospital and Forensic Medicine lectures at University College Dublin. (Although she had begun her career at University College Galway, she eventually qualified at University College Dublin.) Hospital clinics began at 9 a.m. when a retinue of students walked the wards behind renowned teachers like Sir Arthur Chance, Mr P. J. Smyth, Dr Henry Barniville (a dashing young man and a friend of de Valera's), Dr Redmond, Dr Dempsey and Dr F. X. Callaghan.

The new student was rather timid. As a stranger from Galway, in a tightly knit Dublin group, Brigid felt intimidated by these knowledgeable Mater students. There were two young doctors, both called Matthew O'Connor. To differentiate them, they were known as Matthew Seán and Matthew Harris. The Doctors O'Connor seemed to know just about all there was to be known about medicine and surgery. With their apparent vast knowledge, they had a strangely mesmerising effect on 'the fat girl from the country'.

In June, Brigid passed her Forensic Medicine exam, and another hurdle was crossed on the road to qualification. The summer months she divided between study and political activity. Uncle Joe was now at home and the Dáil was meeting clandestinely at Walter Cole's house in Mountjoy Square. Like other girls with innocent faces, Brigid was performing duties, the importance of which became known only in later years. The transmission and storage of highly confidential documents associated with the activities of the Dáil became a heavy responsibility. Known rebels, as most TDs were, dared not carry these documents or retain them in their homes. This was where Collins' select little army of reliable women came in. Acting like innocents abroad, they included in their activities intelligence gathering, dispatch carrying, and the conveyance and concealment of cheques and secret documents. With her contacts in Longford and in Galway, Brigid Lyons made a particularly useful undercover girl. In the quiet of the Medical Library at University College Dublin, her textbooks were often interleaved more with Michael Collins' notes than with those of her professor of medicine. She remembered the period:

By now I knew nearly everybody who was directly or indirectly concerned in the Movement. Trusted by Michael Collins, I used to take messages for, and keep papers belonging to him. Intelligence papers would be left with me for a period and then transferred somewhere else in the hope the British wouldn't catch on. I was a sort of centre for people from Longford and from Galway.

Life was hectic and exciting, and sometimes distressingly sad, especially when the death of a Volunteer was announced. It's difficult to express one's feelings at the time. One just lived for the Movement. I had no other interest, beyond whatever time I could devote to medicine. The resurgence we saw in 1917 was rapidly gaining momentum in 1919. It strengthened our belief in a successful outcome to our efforts at some future stage. But we knew there were hard times ahead. Nobody had any doubts about that. From 1916 onwards, we knew an Anglo-Irish war was inevitable. There was never a moment when it was out of our minds. Our intention was always to continue the fight, however changed the circumstances. Our purpose had become so concentrated, we hardly any longer met anybody who wasn't actually part of the Movement.

On 7 September, in an arms raid in Fermoy, Liam Lynch and the Cork Number 2 Brigade of Volunteers attacked the King's Shropshire Light Infantry on their way to church. A British soldier was shot dead. At the inquest, the jury refused to bring in a verdict of murder. That night, two hundred British Regulars went on a rampage in Fermoy, looting and burning the jury men's houses. This incident established the pattern of attack and reprisal in what was to develop into a horrifying war.

Three days later, Dublin Castle suppressed Dáil Éireann. Griffith said, 'Britain has proclaimed the whole Irish nation as an illegal assembly.' The undercover work of volunteers like Brigid Lyons became even more hazardous. But they were not to be intimidated. On her return to Galway, in October, she was to carry more than secret papers. She became engaged in procuring arms for Volunteers, and in their distribution. The following letter sent to her by a Galway fellow student bears witness to her activities at the time:

> Royal Exchange Hotel,
> Parliament Street,
> Dublin
>
> A Chara Dílis,
>
> I would be exceedingly obliged if you would by some strategy with some G.H.Q. officers keep us in the foreground so as to let us have a Thompson machine gun for The Cause that is so dear to you.
> Sorry I could not call to see you.
> Le meas,
>
> Seán Ó Donncadha
> Engineer to East Connemara and Galway City Brigade

Arms were not easily procured, and a Thompson machine gun was rather a large order. The distribution of revolvers was easier. She carried them one at a time in fancy shopping bags to students' digs. About that time, she also became associated with Seamus Murphy, editor of the *Galway Express*, which had been acquired with Sinn Féin funds. She was still living with George and Peggy Nicholls whose house was constantly raided.

In the teeth of growing danger, defiance intensified with every new British outrage. Christmas 1919 was heralded by Lloyd George's announcement of Britain's intention to partition Ireland.

# 17

# HELL LET LOOSE

IN THE LOCAL authority elections, held on 15 January 1920, Sinn Féin swept the country. The party won control of all cities and boroughs, excepting Belfast. Subsequently, Sinn Féin instituted its own courts and began to collect the rates. The beginning of the end of British administration of Irish affairs had begun. Total breakdown was imminent.

The pattern of outrage and reprisal was now established. IRA attacks on RIC barracks increased in number and ferocity. By the end of May, 66 policemen had been shot dead and 75 wounded, 351 evacuated RIC barracks had been destroyed and 105 damaged, and 15 occupied barracks had been destroyed and 25 damaged. Those of the RIC who remained were ostracised locally.

De Valera was on a fundraising tour of the United States. If, as Arthur Griffith put it, the centre of gravity of the political situation was for the present fixed in the US, then the centre of gravity of the military situation was very much fixed in the capital city of his war-torn country. Under the direction of Collins, the Volunteer Force had become the Irish Republican Army, committed to the riddance from Ireland of every vestige of British influence. Masterminded by Collins, the capacity of the IRA as a guerrilla force was increasing powerfully — too powerfully for the liking of the British Government.

Assistant Commissioner Redmond, Dublin Metropolitan Police, of the Dublin Castle Detective Force, attempted to trap Collins in a raid on one of his offices. On 21 January, Redmond was shot dead in Grafton Street by the Collins 'Squad'. In reply, Dublin Castle offered £10,000 reward for the body of Collins, dead or alive. Already a homeless and lonely man, Collins had now become an outlaw, the prey of any money-grabbing malingerer who wished to turn informer.

After the marriage of Helen Kiernan, Collins continued to visit Granard on the odd occasion when he could leave Dublin. He was usually accompanied by Harry Boland whose concern was his girlfriend, Kitty Kiernan, Helen's attractive sister. During Boland's absence in America with de Valera, and still mourning his ill-fated affair with Helen, Collins became interested in Kitty. Their occasional meetings were to be even fewer, for much as he admired her, he had to weigh his duty to his friends against that to his country. Collins chose to remain in Dublin at the pulsating centre of his intelligence machine.

Goaded by the power of Dublin Castle, Collins began to menace the British forces with a dictatorial ruthlessness offset by the cocky touch of a pimpernel. His name and fame became headlines in the world's press. And Ireland being Ireland, he made bitter enemies amongst the begrudgers posing as his friends.

Facing her Third Medical, Brigid Lyons was, as usual, torn between her own special loyalties — medicine and Ireland. In the panic foreshadowing an exam, she always had regrets about the time devoted to Ireland. However, in the hope that God helps those who help Ireland, she presented in March 1920 — and passed her Third Medical. 'I pulled up for lost time by getting honours in that exam,' she recalled. 'I was very proud.'

The newspapers were full of stories of desperate deeds. As yet, the West was comparatively peaceful. The summer term of 1920 was Brigid's last at University College Galway. The weather was glorious, providing the opportunity to organise fêtes on the Corrib to raise funds for prisoners' dependants, and for families bereaved in the fight. These activities, together with a growing devotion to the study of medicine, occupied her until June. Then, with Annie Griffin (sister of Fr Michael Griffin, killed later that year by the Black and Tans), she left Galway to become a resident student at Mercers' Hospital, Dublin.

Meanwhile, the British had intensified their policy of suppression. To supplement the depleted ranks of the RIC, the first English recruits to that force arrived in Ireland on 25 March 1920. Thereafter, reinforcements continued to pour in. Hastily recruited (many, it was said, from the prisons of England), the men wore uniforms that were partly RIC (black pants and caps) and partly British Army (khaki tunics). Thus they became known as the 'Black and Tans', a name which for all time will be associated with their murderous thuggery rather than their bastard uniform. They were followed by yet another force, comprising British ex-officers, to serve as auxiliaries to the police. The Auxiliaries were commanded by General Sir Hugh Tudor, a friend of Winston Churchill's, and a rivalry sprang up between the Tans and the Auxies as each force sought to outdo the other in perpetrating ever greater savagery. What Brigid Lyons remembered of their activities in her home town typified the repressive gangsterism indulged in by these armed British bullyboys sent specifically to demoralise the Irish:

I remember the daily raids in Longford when the 'Auxies' set out in their Crossley tenders. After they'd been ambushed a few times, they decided they'd take hostages. Nobody knew who was going to be taken out next, or whether he'd come back alive. A story was told of a young man whose sympathies would not have been Republican. He was taken by the Auxies into a pub, and a glass of whiskey ordered for him. Then the Auxies spat in it and ordered him, at gunpoint, to drink it.

Shops in Longford were looted repeatedly. Both of Uncle Frank's shops were broken into and all the goods torn from the shelves and trampled on the floor. There was no reason. It was simply sheer vandalism. Nothing was taken away, but as much as possible was destroyed.

At this stage our house had been emptied of furniture because every other night burning was threatened. My aunt was sleeping in the Workhouse. My cousins, Maureen and Peg and Bríd, were sleeping in various friendly houses around the town. Hardly anyone was sleeping in their own house because the reign of terror was so fierce. The family returned each morning and tried to keep the business going. Then Peg, my youngest cousin, was arrested and kept overnight in the local barracks. Next day she was taken to Athlone and later transferred to Mountjoy Prison without any charge. She was aged seventeen. Horatio Bottomly raised the matter in the House of Commons — without any result. After three months, she was released.

Life was like that. Nobody knew when it might be their turn to be carted off. Business was at a standstill. People were afraid to come into town. There was curfew and life was a misery. Brigid's Uncle Frank also fell victim to the Black and Tans:

Once Uncle Frank was taken out of the house by the Tans. They hung a placard round his neck reading: 'To Hell with Sinn Féin. God save the King'. He was marched up and down the middle of Longford to humiliate him because he was known to be nationalist, and had been in jail, and helped the Cause, and was Joe McGuinness' brother. It helped to show off their power. The townspeople were shocked. Bríd McGuinness, my cousin, overcome with indignation, rushed among these thugs and tore the offensive placard from my uncle's neck. The tension was terrible because everybody was certain it would end with them putting a bullet through him, and maybe the girl too — they were often very drunk. However, the episode ended fortunately, a kindly local policeman having said something to calm the Tans.

Everybody feared them. Girls had some time for ordinary British soldiers, and even at the risk of having their hair shaved off, might go out with them occasionally, but never with the Auxies or the Tans. They were particularly wicked men sent to Ireland expressly to break the spirit of the people. The real heroes of the time were the old people who lived alone and who carried messages and baked and cooked and kept the boys of the Flying Columns who were on the run. The mere fact of ever having known a Republican was enough to have your house burned to the ground, and even your life taken. The Flying Column lived wherever they could, in dugouts in the hills and mountains, and in barns and haggards. Indeed, a lot of people from whom one might not have expected sympathy did in fact provide food and shelter for those on the run. Every man, woman and child in Ireland hated the Black and Tans. Even the dogs in the streets fled before them.

If Longford was bad, Dublin was worse. In June, when Brigid arrived to become a resident student, the city was rife with military activity. Cordons of barbed wire divided one zone from another, while, day and night, military lorries and tanks rumbled through the streets, leaving fear and terror in their wake. Searchlights intimidated those who might attempt to move under cover of darkness. There were thousands of soldiers everywhere — regulars in khaki with steel helmets and fixed bayonets, Auxiliaries in black, and the oddly uniformed Black and Tans. And of course there were the outsized DMP men. But greatest of all these menacing forces was the Dublin Castle G Division: plainclothes detectives employed in political espionage, to be seen lurking at every vantage point. That a Republican dare move out of shelter was extraordinary. That one with a price of £10,000 on his head should go about his daily work — work of the highest national importance — on a rusty bicycle brought nothing short of amazement. It is hardly surprising that Collins' name captured the world's press. Even in England, his escapades earned him a measure of admiration.

All this was a contrast to life as a resident student at Mercers' Hospital, where Brigid now came face to face with the casualties of the Anglo-Irish War. She expected the consultant staff to be West-British ascendancy types. But she found that it was not that way at all. Even the medical and surgical knights had a kind of reserved regard for the aspirations of the Republicans. Their condemnation of the Black and Tan terror, they never hesitated to express with vigour.

Hospital experience stimulated still more Brigid's desire to be a doctor.

I remember one of the first pinnings done by Sir William Wheeler on a man's knee. Sir William was very proud of it. One evening when he was a little fitter, the man — a Republican casualty — was suddenly abducted from his bed by his Volunteer colleagues. Obviously he was important in the Movement, and they feared his arrest if they left him in the hospital any longer. I was quite unaware of the man's identity. Sir William, however, had a sense of humour. Every morning, he'd ask me had I yet taken out the man's pin, and gave me instructions on how I was to do it, and how I was to care for the knee afterwards. He practically convinced me that I was in league with the man's rescuers, and that I was still in charge of the patient. I couldn't be certain whether Sir William knew anything about my own activities, and if so, how he had found out. This was one affair, however, in which I wasn't involved.

This incident is recorded by Dorothy Macardle. Erroneously she refers to an amputation:

A Volunteer wounded in Pearse Street when a corps of seven, under Seán MacBride, ambushed a party of Auxiliaries, was taken to Mercers' Hospital. His leg had to be amputated and he lay helpless, expecting capture and execution. Presently his young officer with three or four other comrades appeared in the ward, armed, held up the staff, carried him out to a car and drove him to a house where Mrs. Darrel Figgis kept him in safety and nursed him back to health.

Sir William Wheeler was an able surgeon but he had all the qualities of the crotchety consultant, particularly during operating sessions. Though his religious affiliation was to the Church of Ireland, he always carried a Miraculous Medal in his car. His reason, he used to say, was in case he was shot by the Tans — it would make them quite certain not to bring him to the Adelaide Hospital.

Brigid recalled accompanying him one early morning to assist at an operation:

Driving over Baggot Street Bridge we were held up by the Auxiliaries. Furious, Sir William was ordered to get out of the car. Pulling himself up to his full height — which wasn't very great — he told them who he was, and what he was about. We got by without further interference. Although he had reached high rank in the British Army, he despised the British policy in Ireland in 1920.

Unlike many consultants of the time, Sir William Wheeler was not against women doctors. Indeed, he was most considerate. He allowed Brigid to do a lot of surgery which she liked.

He kept me on as his team assistant, which meant I got in very little medical residence really. Although the food and the living quarters were poor at Mercers', there was a happy family atmosphere, and there was always a gallant male who would offer to take over at night.

Her time off she spent with Aunt Joe. Crossing a city gripped by a ruthless military machine was not pleasant.

For no reason whatever, a bunch of Auxies would suddenly start shrieking and whistling and rushing at passers-by, prodding them with guns and bellowing like bulls, 'Get back, get back out of the street'. The result was fearful confusion, people darting for cover anywhere they could find it. With two big revolvers, one strapped to each thigh, and their black Tam-o'-Shanters, the Auxies struck terror into women and children.

Under the command of General Tudor, they became known as 'Tudor's Toughs'. Indeed, General Macready, General Officer Commanding in Ireland, had requested the black tam-o'-shanters to distinguish the Auxiliaries from ordinary soldiers, so bad was the reputation of the Auxies. A Boer War general, Sir Hugh Tudor carried out his Government's mission of murder and destruction so well in Ireland that he spent the rest of his life cowering in corners in fear of assassination. His campaign was so inhuman that his deputy, General Crozier, resigned his Commission in disgust.

With Aunt Joe, Brigid visited old friends: Martin and Peg Conlon in Cabra Park and Mrs Tom Clarke who still lived with her three boys in an old-world house with a tree-shaded garden in Richmond Road. Mrs Clarke had opened a tobacconist's shop at the Fleet Street/D'Olier Street corner. Despite the formidable Tans and Auxies, Brigid made other visits. She was still acting as a custodian of papers and documents, including cheques, which had to be farmed out to 'safe' persons in case of raids. There was a new shop in Henry Street, built after 1916.

Upstairs was the Finance Ministry, from which Michael Collins, shortly before, had made one of his dramatic escapes. Regularly Brigid had to visit Paddy Sheehan there.

He had the heartiest laugh I ever heard. Whenever I went in, he'd rub his hands and say , 'Well, and what can Murray and Quirke do for you today?' This was the fictitious name on the door. The place was used for the exchange of documentation and the transmission of information. Ever after, I always called Paddy Sheehan Mr Murray and Quirke. He was one of Mick Collins' confidants.

Another place I had to visit was on Wellington Quay where Madge Clifford held the fort for Austin Stack. It was the Department of Home Affairs. Still another was in North Earl Street over Tyler's shoe shop. That was the Ministry of Lands with Conor Maguire, Art O'Connor and Kevin O'Sheil in charge.

On 12 July 1920, in Belfast, Sir Edward Carson indulged himself in an outburst of Orange oratory against the hated Sinn Féin. As a result, Belfast became a hell. Protestant mobs killed, burned and looted, and Catholics hit back. In four days, eighteen people died, and hundreds were made homeless. The campaign fought between 'Fenian Papists' and 'Rotten Prods' was called a pogrom. Indirectly it caused Brigid a fright.

Once I was given a cheque for an enormous sum of money to look after. It came from the Dáil Loan and was for the relief of the Belfast refugees. I hid it in a magazine which I carried with me, even to the Richmond Hospital where I went to visit my brother who was then a patient. When I was coming away, I thought, 'Why not leave him that magazine to read?' And I did, quite forgetting its contents. Like the loaves in Church Street in 1916, something inspired me to take it back. Still not remembering why, I went back to the ward and collected the magazine. When I got home, I found the cheque inside. Looking back, I realise that minding important papers, however temporarily, was a very serious responsibility.

As 1920 wore on, tragedy was piled on tragedy. In August, the Restoration of Order in Ireland Bill was introduced in the Commons by Sir Hamer Greenwood; it became law in September. It provided for trial of civilians by court martial, imprisonment of Sinn Féiners on suspicion, imposition of curfew, and military courts of enquiry instead of inquests. This last was to stop Irish juries bringing in verdicts of murder. For possession of a 'seditious document' one of the first to be tried by court martial under this bill was Terence MacSwiney, Lord Mayor of Cork. Throughout that autumn, his marathon hunger strike, of 74 days, in Brixton Prison hung like an impending doom, affecting every Irish person still capable of human feeling.

In early August, Patrick Lyons died at Northyard, Scramogue, Co Roscommon. All his life, he had never known Ireland truly at peace. And he had died when she was engaged in her most bitter war. Despite transport difficulties, Brigid got to her father's funeral. She watched the Volunteers of another generation lay the old Fenian beside the woman who had given him the four happiest years of his life. It was a break — how much of a break she was to realise only when it came time to return to Dublin.

My only brother was then left in the old home with Aunt Annie, now a very old woman — she who had looked after us so well and spoiled us as children when my mother died.

September brought more excesses, 20 September being its blackest day. A head constable was shot dead in a pub quarrel in Balbriggan, after which the Black and Tans from nearby Gormanstown Camp sacked the town. A factory, four pubs and nineteen houses were burnt out and thirty others wrecked. Two young men were bayoneted to death in the street, and the population fled into the surrounding countryside. On the same day, Tuam was wrecked for the second time. And also on that day, a British rations party was ambushed outside Monks' Bakery in Church Street, Dublin. Three British soldiers were shot dead, and Kevin Barry, an eighteen-year-old medical student, was captured.

On 20 October, Kevin Barry was sentenced to death. About the same time, another medical student, nineteen-year old Frank Flood, was arrested. He too was to die by hanging. Six Flood brothers had been in the Movement, including Seán, whom Brigid knew as 'the great provider' for the Four Courts garrison in 1916. In supporting the Cause, these boys had rebelled against all their family traditions. Their youngest brother, Deputy Commissioner Alfred Flood, retired in April 1972, from the Garda Síochána after forty-seven years' service, a record for the force.

Despite the prayers and novenas, MacSwiney died on 25 October. Brigid was on her way to the clinic at the Mater Hospital when she heard a Stop Press. She searched her pockets for a penny to buy a paper. She didn't have one. She recalled: 'We both knew — the boy was so distressed … the memory of it stays with me.' The death of Terence MacSwiney, together with Kevin Barry's court martial and execution by hanging, aroused the nation's deepest indignation.

Brigid had grim memories:

We prayed outside Mountjoy Prison when many of these young men were dying. We used to get up early and be there by 6 a.m. It was usually cold and dreary. Eventually a bell tolled and an officer would come out and post up the latest death notice on the door. Whichever of your friends was due to go, you knew he was gone when you heard that bell. Then we'd go away until the next execution.

The wholesale sacking of towns continued. In reprisal for the shooting of Black and Tans, Tralee and Templemore suffered. On 4 November, the town of Granard was burned and looted. The Greville Arms Hotel — the home of the Kiernan family, once a refuge for all associated with the Movement — was burnt out that night. Seán Mac Eoin of the Longford Flying Column paid the debt by ambushing a convoy of eleven lorries of Tans returning from the sacking of Granard. In December, came the burning of Cork with damage up to £5 million. All this takes no account of the continual shootings, many of the victims being innocent people, including women and children.

In the United States, there was outrage at the conduct of the British forces in Ireland. An American Commission of Enquiry was set up. Amongst Irish citizens invited to give evidence was Fr Michael

Griffin of Barna, Co Galway, brother of Annie Griffin, Brigid's medical student friend at University College Galway. Fr Griffin subsequently disappeared. At the time, Annie was doing her hospital course with Brigid at Mercers' Hospital. Like her family, she felt grave anxiety about her brother. Terrible things were happening, and Galway was suffering a particularly grim period.

On the morning of Sunday 21 November, Brigid received an urgent message to go to Annie Griffin immediately. On arrival at her digs in Sandymount, she found her friend distraught. Annie had had a message from home: riddled with bullets, Fr Michael's body had been found in a bog in Barna. People out searching had seen a piece of his cassock sticking through the turf. Annie must get to her family in Galway — but how?

On the hoardings that weekend there was an advertisement:
GAA Challenge Match. Football.
Tipperary (Challengers) v Dublin (Leinster Champions)
An All-Ireland Test at Croke Park on
the 21st inst. at 2.45 p.m.
A Thrilling Game is Expected.

How thrilling that game proved to be is recorded in Irish history. The fixture gave Brigid Lyons an idea.

I brought Annie to the Belvedere Hotel. My uncle used to stay there and we had contacts. But it was no good. Nobody could help us. Then we went to Vaughan's Hotel. At the corner of Rutland [Parnell] Square, a cavalcade of lorries filled with Tans careered past towards Dorset Street, never with such speed and fury. We wondered where they could be going. In Vaughan's Hotel somebody told us about the fourteen British intelligence officers ['The Cairo Gang'] shot dead that morning. Before the evening was out, we heard of the reprisals at Croke Park. The Black and Tans opened fire into a crowd of eight thousand people watching the football match. Fourteen people died, and many were injured or trampled on in the stampede, including a woman. Amongst those shot dead were two small boys as well as Mick Hogan from Grangemockler, the captain of the Tipperary team. That day was to be remembered as Bloody Sunday.

We continued to try to contact anybody who might be up from Galway for the Croke Park match. Finally we had to give up. I stayed that night with Annie in Vaughan's Hotel. Next morning, we went to the Lord Mayor, Alderman Larry O'Neill, to see if he could find any means of transport for Annie to Galway. He failed too. By midday on Monday, when we got back to Annie's digs, somebody had arrived from Galway to collect her. It was a chap from college whom we both knew as 'Baby' Duggan, a Volunteer.

And so at last, Annie Griffin reached her bereaved family in Galway. Fr Griffin was at first buried in Barna, but was later transferred to Loughrea. Meanwhile, Brigid was still in Dublin where tensions were high:

On that Sunday night, I called to Margaret McEntee's flat in Rutland Square. Dublin was buzzing with wild rumours. Visiting her was Beatrice Brady from Belfast. (It was at her house I stayed when I went to Belfast as a courier in May 1921. She later became a Carmelite nun.) Frank Gallagher came in and we comforted ourselves by drinking cocoa. There was terrible anxiety about Peadar Clancy and Dick McKee who'd been arrested in the early hours of that morning. On Saturday night in Vaughan's Hotel, Conor Clune, a young innocent up from Clare for the Croke Park match, had also been arrested. We all felt the worst would happen to all three men.

Worse than the worst happened. On Bloody Sunday night, all three were done to death in Dublin Castle 'while trying to escape'. Afterwards, post mortem examinations arranged by Collins showed that the three men had been shot in the head at close range, and that Clancy and McKee had first been brutally beaten. Against all advice, Collins attended their Requiem Mass and funerals, although since Bloody Sunday he had become the most wanted man in the British Empire.

To Brigid Lyons, the death of Peadar Clancy was most distressing. She had served with him in the Four Courts. She had shared with him the last hours of that fight in 1916 in the little Church Street outpost to which Ned Daly had promoted him. Later, she had worked with him in electioneering campaigns. Like all who knew him, she admired his courage and forthrightness. That his death should have been so horrible was particularly distressing. 'Peadar Clancy was an outstanding character,' she stated, 'who might have done even greater things for his country.'

Brigid went to Longford for Christmas. Her cousins, the McGuinness girls, travelled often to Dublin to collect supplies of ammunition for the Longford Flying Column.

As I was free just then, they decided it was my turn. With £50 and a large suitcase, I was sent back to Dublin by Brigadier Reddington to buy all the equipment and ammunition I could get. I was instructed to go to the home of Leo and Billy Fitzgerald in Pearse Street where the Quartermaster General, Seán McMahon, operated. I had known him from the 1917 South Longford election when he had worked like a Trojan.

I made my appeal. Seán Mac Eoin and the Longford Flying Column were very active and were short of ammunition. He said munitions were very short, but he'd do his best for Longford. Whatever could be spared would be taken to the train for me. Three days later, at Aunt Joe's, I got a message to be at the Broadstone Railway Station for the 1 p.m. Sligo train on the next Monday. I sent a wire in cypher to Edgeworthstown giving the time I would arrive there, where the stuff was to be collected from me, as Longford was too dangerous.

At Broadstone, I got on the train and waited at a carriage window. Presently one of the Fitzgerald boys appeared. He said, 'Just wait around and a fellow will be along shortly with all the supplies we can give you.' Then a little hunchback arrived carrying the case on his back. He was a well-known messenger in the Movement. It was a great big leather hold-all, but he managed to get it under the seat of the third-class compartment. While he was still talking, four young fellows got in and sat down. Just then a siren sounded. I heard lorries and, in a few seconds, a crowd of Auxies dashed into the station brandishing revolvers. The hunchback said, 'You're caught.' My heart stood still. I said, 'You'd better get away anyway.' And he went.

The Auxies swarmed along the platform, opening carriage doors and calling, 'All males out.' The four men in Brigid's compartment were taken off to the waiting room. At first, she was concerned for them.

Then I thought of my own position. I became terrified, because at that time if you were found with as much as an empty cartridge case, you were shot. No hope, no escape for you. I tried to think: will I own up? Or will I say the case happened to be in the carriage when I got in? It wasn't an easy decision. I prayed in a sort of way and somehow, instinctively, feminine guile took over.

Without consciously deciding anything, I put my head out the carriage window and called to an officer, 'What's going on? What's wrong?'

He said, 'We're searching for munitions.'

I said, 'Surely nobody would be carrying munitions these days?'

'Oh,' he said. 'You never can tell. These Sinn Féiners can get up to anything.'

'That's a terrifying thought,' I said. 'And I have to get to Longford.'

'Oh well, you won't be delayed too long,' he said. He was courteous and I played it that way too. I asked him again, two or three times, how long more we'd be delayed. He replied, 'You don't have to worry. You'll be off as soon as we've finished searching these fellows.'

The men were allowed back to the carriage, and Brigid thought that all was well. Then the Auxies boarded the train and began searching the carriages and pulling out luggage.

By then I don't know what my feelings were. I was paralysed — numb — but I prayed hard, never as hard before or since. They arrived at my compartment, opened the door and pulled a few things down from the racks. An Auxie was stretching for the case under the seat when that officer appeared again. 'The little lady's luggage,' he said. 'Leave it alone.'

For all I've said about the Black and Tans and the Auxies, that man was an officer and a gentleman! I'll never know why I didn't collapse that day at Broadstone Station.

The train set off, but Brigid's ordeal was not over. At Mullingar, she found that she was in the Galway section of the train instead of the Sligo section.

> That was a bad setback, because I daren't trust the bag to a porter. I was trying to manhandle it out of the carriage when somebody offered to help. It was a Galway student whom I knew only vaguely. As he pulled it out, I said, 'Books weigh heavily' — and then the handle broke. He had to get back on the Galway train as it was leaving so I had to carry the dead weight in my arms all the way through the underground passage and up to the platform for Sligo.

Brigid was to be met at Edgeworthstown. The family was too well-known in Longford.

> My McGuinness cousins and myself were always held up and searched on arrival by a vicious RIC man who always watched our movements. That was why I hoped my wire had arrived and that somebody would be at Edgeworthstown. But my luck was out. There was no one to be seen. Leaning out the window, my eyes were out of my head watching for someone to come, and, unbelievably, the train was moving again before I realised. From Edgeworthstown to Longford were the worst moments I've ever endured. Having got through at Broadstone, to think the stuff might be taken from me at Longford was the last straw. Maybe I should have got off the train at Edgeworthstown, but I didn't think quickly enough. It would have made more sense to do that, but then there were RIC men there too and I'd soon be noticed with the heavy baggage.
>
> For no reason I can understand, excepting prayer, there was Johnnie Galvin, our workman, standing on the platform at Longford. He was a frail man, but with a superhuman effort he got that case on his back and we set off boldly. The hated RIC sergeant watched us, but miraculously, for once, he didn't interfere, and Johnnie carried it non-stop all the way to No. 2 Main Street. There I was greeted with consternation. Nobody expected me. The arrangement was for Edgeworthstown. Commotion and furore broke out. Apparently my telegram in

cypher had been delayed by the police and was delivered in Edgeworthstown only after the train had passed. Realising I'd gone through to Longford, there was even greater concern in Edgeworthstown.

Brigid and her cousins decided to get rid of the contents of the bag as soon as possible, because anything could happen at any moment. They opened the case.

It was then I discovered fifty hand grenades was all I had. They [my cousins] set out in the dark by devious routes to distribute them to the Longford Flying Column in the country. They succeeded, but they'd hardly left our house in Main Street when one of the numerous raids took place. Nothing was found.

In spite of the risks, I was more disappointed than proud about that escapade. I had set out with £50 and that was all the munitions we were given for the Longford Flying Column, a force which — thanks to Seán Mac Eoin — was putting up one of the best fights of the whole Anglo-Irish War. It was probably some of my grenades Mac Eoin used in some of his famous skirmishes. That idea made me feel proud.

Asked about the system of paying for munitions, Brigid said that the Flying Column had to pay for every bullet they got:

That's why I've never forgotten the people who wanted to go another round with the British when the Truce came, and again after the Treaty. People who weren't in the country and who didn't know what was going on were most anxious to fight on rather than accept the Treaty, although at the time we hadn't another round of ammunition to fight with. Of course, during the Truce period we were buying munitions and making it in backyards and kitchens. We were raiding barracks and buying ammunition from British soldiers — getting it anywhere we could get it. Cash was always easier to get than munitions.

Knowing the consequences if she were caught, Brigid Lyons personified the young people of the period in her contempt for the word fear:

You're only concern was how much stuff you could get to bring back. Your fear would be the disappointment if you only got very little, as I did on that trip to Dublin. You couldn't go on if you were to think about the risks. Besides, it wasn't my first time. I'd often carried ammunition in Galway. In spite of the raids, we kept ammunition hidden in all sorts of places in the house in Longford.

Her familiarity with munitions notwithstanding, Brigid, unlike Constance Markievicz, for example, was never interested in the personal use of firearms:

I was too awkward. My cousins learned how to unload a revolver to clean it. But for one who can't drive a screw, I was never competent to handle firearms. In Galway, somebody once gave me a very small automatic. It was so tiny it was like a toy. I was standing at the door of George Nicholls' house when one of 'the boys', Fred O'Doherty, came over to talk to me. He said, 'I know you have a revolver. You should give it to me'. I refused and he asked me then to let him just see it. I went and got the revolver and whatever I did, a shot went off. It hit nobody, but I never forgot that incident. I'd rather try to talk my way out of a situation — as I did at Broadstone Station — than try to shoot my way. Besides, my generation looked on shooting as a man's job!

Apart from the grenades affair, Christmas 1920 was remarkably un-festive in Longford. Uncle Frank was in jail again. There were rumours about peace feelers. Dr Clune, Archbishop of Perth (an uncle of Conor Clune, who had died in custody in Dublin Castle a month earlier) had come to Dublin and talked to Arthur Griffith (then in jail) and to Michael Collins. He was said to be an emissary from Lloyd George. Emissaries had also gone out from the McGuinness household to members of the Longford Flying Column to say that there would be Christmas dinner for any who came. There was, however, no let up in the fighting. Two turned up for a quick bite: Brigadier Reddington (shot accidentally afterwards) and Michael Robinson. It was a short, pleasant reunion.

I didn't know the Longford Flying Column in the way my cousins did. In fact, I never met Seán Mac Eoin until he came to Dublin in 1921, and was brought by Martin Conlon to see Uncle Joe.

Christmas 1920 also marked the return of de Valera, on Christmas Eve, after eighteen months in the United States. He wanted to change the pattern of the fight being waged by Collins. Asked about reaction amongst the Volunteers, Brigid said, 'The fight was at its height. Collins was the man of the moment, and everything was geared for fighting rather than political argument.'

# 18

# A FRIEND IN NEED

IT WAS A DISMALLY abnormal Christmas in Longford. The McGuinness family members were still sleeping wherever they found a bed. The only redeeming feature of Brigid's journey home had been the glowing accounts of the feats of the Longford Flying Column under the command of Brigadier Reddington, and the legendary Seán Mac Eoin.

Dublin was no better on her return. Curfew continued and the Black and Tans seemed to excel themselves in their campaign of terrorising the population. It did not even require a misunderstanding to get yourself shot.

One night in Gardiner Street I was trying to let up a Venetian blind. It was stuck and I was rattling it to free it. Just as I succeeded, I saw about six soldiers outside, their rifles levelled at me. Apparently they'd been shouting at me, but I hadn't heard. There was no possible reason for their attitude — just devilry.

A few nights later, there was a round-up of all men in the vicinity of Gardiner Street:

In the morning there were lines and lines of men in the street being searched at gunpoint. I recognised Kevin O'Higgins amongst them. I was upset to see him there. He had been staying in various hotels in Gardiner Street and he'd be a terrible loss if the Tans identified him. The locals could be trusted to give nobody away. It was the RIC we feared — those we called the 'bad' members of that force. But for these, the British could not have picked up as many of our men as they did. The terrible tragedy was that there were good and bad amongst the RIC men, but you didn't know which was which.

I didn't get to my lecture that day. My Uncle Frank was staying at the Belvedere Hotel. It was no longer considered wise for him to stay in Longford. I spent the day with him until near curfew time. It was only then, after many hours, the Tans allowed the men back to their homes. Reluctantly, they had allowed the men to take the tea brought to them through the long day by their womenfolk.

Early in January, exciting news came from Longford. District Inspector McGrath had led eleven Black and Tans to Miss Martin's cottage, Seán Mac Eoin's headquarters near Ballinalee. Single-handed, and to draw fire away from the cottage where there were women and children, Mac Eoin shot his way out through the attackers and escaped, but D.I. McGrath was shot dead. The newspapers were never short of headlines in those years. Three weeks later, Mac Eoin was top news again. At Cloonfin near Ballinalee, with eighteen men, he attacked a motor patrol of twenty Auxiliaries who, after an hour's battle, surrendered with three of their men killed and fourteen wounded. Mac Eoin then took on the newly arrived reinforcements. Later he gave the enemy a captured lorry to remove their wounded to hospital. 'We were continually hearing of Mac Eoin's exploits,' Brigid said. 'And we were tremendously proud of his Longford Flying Column.' Others too heard of the intrepid Mac Eoin.

Cathal Brugha, Minister of Defence in the outlawed Dáil, had conceived a plan to assassinate British cabinet ministers in London. Mac Eoin was his choice for the job. He summoned him to Dublin. Very much a countryman, Mac Eoin, already feeling obvious, even in Dublin, was certain that he would stand out more in London. It was Michael Collins who quickly stepped in and countermanded Brugha's order to Mac Eoin. Collins required his military initiative where it could inflict the greatest punishment on the enemy — namely, Co Longford. This was one of the incidents which contributed to the

Collins/Brugha estrangement. Brigid added to the story:

One evening in March, Martin Conlon arrived at Aunt Joe's with a strange man. They were looking for Uncle Joe, but he was out. Then Martin said to me, 'You know this man?' I looked at the bronzed, handsome man. I guessed he was someone important. 'Oh, yes,' I said, though I didn't recognise him. The times made one devious. I made tea. Shortly I discovered who he was. I had never seen Seán Mac Eoin before.

After Martin Conlon left, Nancy Killeen and Mary Brady, mutual friends, dropped in, and the four of us chatted happily. When he was about to leave, Seán turned to me: 'If I'm arrested tomorrow, I want you to deliver some messages for me.' He gave them to me. He was in great humour until it came to saying goodbye. Then, suddenly serious, he said, 'We may never meet again.' And then he left.

When Uncle Joe came in and heard my story, he was furious. He said it was an unnecessary and terrible risk for Seán Mac Eoin to come to Dublin. At the time we didn't know who had brought him — and why. All evening, Uncle Joe repeated his hope that nothing would happen to Seán. In the afternoon of the next day, Uncle Joe came in looking like a ghost. 'Mac Eoin has been shot in Mullingar,' he said. We were utterly shocked.

A Stop Press announced that if Mac Eoin did not die from his wounds, there would be no escape from the rope for him. He had been removed to Dublin, but we didn't know where. Remembering his visit, and particularly his remark on leaving, I decided to try George V Military Hospital [now St Bricin's Hospital] to see if I could be of any help to him. Without telling me whether Seán was there or not, they interrogated me. I said I'd like to see him. I was anxious to send some news to his family. Utterly impossible, they said, so I asked if they'd take him in a message. I was allowed to write a note. I told him I was there and asked was there anything I could do.

To Brigid's surprise, a reply from Seán, written in pencil, was brought to her:

11.3.'21
My dear Friend,

I am so delighted to hear from you. I was just wondering if you couldn't get in to see me and how I did want to see you. There is so much we have to say to one another, but sure, as you say, it will keep.

I am feeling fairly well, but must keep quiet as there is a danger of wound getting bad again. Many thanks for your kind presents and I know that you give them in the right spirit.

Remember me to all and do not forget to call now and again and send up a note even if you cannot get in to see me.

Dóchas go deo,

Seán Mac Eoin

After that, Brigid called regularly to George V Hospital. Then one day she was told that Mac Eoin was gone. They could not say where. Time revealed that his sudden transfer had foiled Collins' first attempt at his rescue. Brigid assumed that he was in Mountjoy Prison. This was soon confirmed by a letter from Remand Prisoner J. McKeon.

Mountjoy Prison.
Wednesday.
Dear Friend,

I want you to come in and see me. You will have to write to the Prisons Board for a permit…

What happened you Sat. and Monday that you did not come in? I was moved Tuesday over here to prison. The wounds are healed and I am in perfect form.

[He goes on to ask her to write to his relatives, particularly advising his brother Michael not to attempt to visit him just yet.]

… write to me and let me know how you are as I miss you very much. Remember me to all. I must conclude now, hoping to see you soon.

Do chara go deo,

Seán Mac Eoin

Brigid approached the Prisons Board in Dublin Castle and got a permit to visit Mountjoy. She saw Mac Eoin in the prison hospital. Her visits continued as often as it was possible to obtain a permit. Between visits, a correspondence was carried on. If there is a touch of boy–girl romance about Remand Prisoner J. McKeon's letters, who should deny it? Least of all the British authorities who apparently accepted that even Irish rebels might be capable of deeper feelings. As far as this relationship was concerned, they were encouraged to continue in that belief, its blade made keener in times of war.

On 19 April, Seán wrote:

I am sorry to hear you didn't get to see the Sec. of the Prisons Board, for if he met you he couldn't refuse you, but no matter, you will get in to see me yet please God. I don't want anything but matches and don't be afraid of me burning myself. Send me a half dozen boxes. The family is big and you know the old adage: 'The beggar can ask the King for a match' and vice versa. We do have to put that in force regularly…

One day in early April, Joe O'Reilly, Collins' amanuensis, dashed into Aunt Joe's place, full of zest as usual. O'Reilly was the man of whom Collins said, 'I'm in no danger while I have that lad praying for me.' Collins had many loyal friends, but none with the same single-minded and dog-like devotion as Joe O'Reilly.

'Mick wants to see you, Bridgie,' he blurted breathlessly. 'Tomorrow, eleven thirty, 46 Parnell Square.' Then he was gone like the wind, on his bicycle.

Next morning, Brigid attended Sir John Lumsden's lecture at Mercers' Hospital. Like many another morning, her mind was not entirely on the subject of medicine.

I wondered if anyone in that ward could know where I was going, and for what reason, how shocked they might be. Michael Collins, still with a price of £10,000 on his head, was the most loved and most hated man in Ireland.

Number 46 Parnell Square housed the Keating Branch of the Gaelic League. Though a dreary, unexciting place, it was a rendezvous used by Collins and his intelligence people. It was also the centre where members of Cumann na mBan circulated information. That morning, there was a little girl taking a dancing lesson in one of the rooms. On the dot of 11.30, the Big Fella charged in, greeting Brigid with an iron-like handshake. He was eager for business.

'Have you seen Seán?' he asked.

Brigid told him that she had. She recalled, 'I suspected he knew and this was the purpose of this meeting.'

'Where did you see him?' he went on.

She explained the whole position. He followed her carefully. Then he came to the point.

'I want you to get detailed information on where he's confined in Mountjoy,' he told her. He emphasised the word 'detailed'. 'Pay particular attention to exactly where you see him — the room, where its situated, how you get in, where you go inside, the number of locked doors, the number of sentries, who is present at the interviews, and all the details concerned with your visits.' She was to report back as much information as she could.

I knew immediately Mick Collins was planning another attempt at Seán's rescue. At any cost he wasn't going to lose his warrior friend, Seán Mac Eoin.

At the time, I was seeing Seán in the prison hospital in a ground-floor cell. It was a long way round through the buildings. I was always searched going in — wardresses did it. They were courteous enough, but they made certain you couldn't have carried anything in. Gifts, like cigarettes or matches or sugar [Seán asked for sugar — to prevent him going sour, he said] had to be left at the gate.

A warder — sometimes an armed Auxiliary — was present all during the visit. We had to talk double-talk or pass the odd vital word very quietly. I usually held a written note between my fingers and I managed to slip that to him, and collect his note, when I first went in or as I was about to leave. Once while he was in the prison hospital, I failed to get the note to him. As usual, it was ready, hidden between my fingers. When it was time to go, Seán, in desperation, said, 'Brigid, have you nothing to say to me?'

'I have,' said I, putting a break in the voice. 'But I can't say it with that fella looking on.' Turning his back, the Auxie said, 'Get on with it, Missie, and be quick.' In a flash, I slipped the note under Seán's pillow.

At Mountjoy, the officials suspected nothing. They took this frequent visiting as a boy–girl relationship. 'I played it that way too,' Brigid said. 'And Seán's letters also gave that impression. That was what we allowed them to think. But it was different at Dublin Castle where I had to go for permits to visit. I was always closely cross-questioned: what was my interest? Why was I so anxious to visit this man, Mac Eoin?'

In the middle of April, Dublin Castle suddenly clamped down on visiting. All Brigid's appeals proved useless. She reported the development to Mick Collins. He wrote to her on 23 April:

> I don't think that there is anything insidious about that request. It is probably due to the forthcoming execution in Mountjoy. What you should do is to write at once and call on Monday protesting against the thing. You could also say you had received a couple of urgent messages from his home. You could adopt the attitude that it was a breach of faith on their part, having promised you a permit.
>
> Do chara,
>
> Micheál

Collins' surmise was correct. Thomas Traynor, the father of a family and a friend of Seán Mac Eoin's, was under sentence of death. He was hanged on 26 April. Four days earlier, District Inspector Potter, RIC, had been taken prisoner in an ambush on the Clogheen/Cahir road and was held hostage for Traynor. On 27 April, Potter was shot in reprisal. As an 'official reprisal', the Black and Tans then blew up ten farmhouses in South Tipperary.

Mac Eoin had shared the exercise yard with his friends Thomas Whelan and Thomas Traynor while Traynor was under sentence of death. One afternoon, Traynor was called from the yard and led away. They all knew that he was going to the condemned cell for the all-night vigil in preparation for the hangman in the morning. Seán Mac Eoin recalled his feelings when he said goodbye to Traynor: 'it made my heart heavy. I wondered what I would feel like when my time came. For I knew that a court martial would be only an outward show of justice.'

The details of it unknown to Brigid Lyons, the Collins plan for the rescue of Mac Eoin was underway. Her job was to resume her visits as soon as possible. She kept Mick Collins fully informed. On 28 April, he wrote to her on notepaper headed 'Dáil Éireann, Dept. of Finance, Mansion House, Dublin.' Dictated by himself and typed by 'E.L.', the letter reads:

I am awfully sorry that I did not get your letter of the 25th until the same time as yours written yesterday. Evidently the Labour Department does not put itself out very much in the transmission of messages. Please do not use that way again, but the other.

I was going to suggest, but of course, as Miss McKeown has gone back it is late now, that you should both go to the Castle, and that she should give you a kind of authority to act for the family here and she would also introduce you over there, but go again on Thursday and you might write a line to them at home to write for a permit, and if you can get any cousin to write also let her do the same.

Do chara go buan,

Micheál

Anxiety outside was matched by an even greater anxiety within the 30-foot-high walls of Mountjoy. On 29 April, Seán Mac Eoin wrote:

A Bhrighid, a chara, dhíl mo chroídhe,

I have given up hope of seeing you this week so now I just write you these few lines to let you know that I am washed and painted every day all week waiting for you. Can you not get to see me?

[Having requested a tin of polish and a pair of laces (tan) and enquired for mutual friends, he goes on] You seem to be surprised at me being good looking when you saw me last. I thought you knew that I was always that. You know it runs in the family!

When she was allowed to resume visits, Brigid found that the prisoner had been removed from the hospital section. For the sake of his health, the prison doctor had moved him to a cell on the upper floor. The planning had to start again. Later, she saw him only in the Deputy Governor's office and always in the presence of an armed Auxiliary. She made detailed notes and passed them to Collins, including any incidental changes in the routine that she might have noticed. The Collins plan had now taken its final shape. The rescue was to be made from the Deputy Governor's office, conveniently situated near the main gate.

Many years later, Seán Mac Eoin recalled Brigid Lyons' first visit in the Deputy Governor's office. It came at a time when his hopes were low. The plans had been altered so many times to meet the new contingencies.

In the Governor's office I recognised the girl visitor, a medical student she was, a member of Cumann na mBan, the women's section of the Irish Republican movement. We talked guardedly. The Deputy Governor and the Auxiliary who was with him were a chivalrous pair. They discreetly turned their backs while we said goodbye.

In those seconds Brigid Lyons informed him of the latest plans — now ready to be put into action. According to Mac Eoin,

My admiration for Collins soared as I went back to my cell that day. In my hand — it had been palmed to me by the girl — was a plan showing that they knew what cell I occupied. And within 24 hours I was involved in a plot that seemed to belong to the world of escape fiction. Details of a get-away were passed to me.

In the best tradition of fiction, the plan was simple. Its success would lie in the effectiveness with which it was carried out. Every morning, a Rolls-Royce whippet armoured car called at the abattoir on the North Circular Road to escort meat deliveries to various barracks, including Mountjoy Prison. The whippet and its crew would be seized. The IRA would don the British uniforms. The whippet would be driven into Mountjoy and would emerge with Mac Eoin, a free man. Observations on timing and movements began. Through Brigid's continuing visits, Mac Eoin was kept advised. If a visit could not be contrived to coincide with the whippet's expected arrival time, Mac Eoin must invent a complaint necessitating his going to see the Deputy Governor. If necessary, he must invent a few more complaints and play for time, but he must be in that office when the 'British' crew and the whippet arrived.

During this time, Brigid was preparing for her final exam. As if that stress, with a little espionage on the side, weren't enough, she was suddenly immersed in urgent political problems. A general election, the Partition Election, was scheduled for 19 May 1921. She was sent to Belfast with dispatches concerning the election, having first been warned of the danger of her mission. Under instruction, she went to a certain hotel where she was met by a priest. He warned her that she was in a dangerous area and advised against her staying in that hotel. He took her to the home of a Mr and Mrs Brady, who were sympathetic to the Cause.

'It was a most luxurious house,' Brigid recalled.

Their daughter, Beatrice, was with me at University College Dublin. She was a great camogie player. Her parents were most hospitable. On the Sunday morning, they showed me the Falls Road and Sandy Row and Queen's University. Later that day, I was brought to a meeting with several local girls and Eamonn Donnelly who was Director of Elections for Belfast. I delivered my dispatches and collected more for Dublin. I was to return on a late train on Monday, but Eamonn Donnelly sent me a message that I was to go on the earlier train as there was a feeling I'd been followed in Belfast. I came on the earlier train and delivered a message to Mrs Sheehy-Skeffington in Belgrave Square, and another to Kate Brady, another member of the Brady family, who lived in Leeson Street. Still another living in Dublin was Frances, wife of Harry MacAuley, the surgeon.

On her arrival at Aunt Joe's, there was another mission awaiting her, this time to Sligo. She was empowered to represent headquarters in the selection of candidates for the General Election at the local convention in Sligo. Her letter of credential reads

Sinn Féin,
6, Sráid Fhearchair,
Áth. Cliath.
11.5.21.

A Cháirde,

The bearer, Miss B. Lyons, is given full power by the Standing Committee of Sinn Féin, to make necessary arrangements with regard to the selection of candidates for the constituency of Sligo–East Mayo.
Mise le meas,

Máirtín Ó Conellain
Director General of Elections.
Cumann Ceanntar,
E. Mayo and Sligo.

The prospect of visiting Sligo appealed to Brigid.
I was excited. I'd been at school there. I wondered how the Ursuline nuns would receive me and what they'd think about my activities. I thought I'd better look my best, so I borrowed my aunt's costume which was about four sizes too big. Whatever I looked like, it made me feel respectable.

The journey was roundabout because of blown-up bridges on the direct line to Sligo. A slow train brought her to Claremorris, arriving late at night. Next morning, she got a lift to Swinford, and another to Tubbercurry, from whence she got a train to Sligo. As instructed, she went to the Harp and Shamrock Hotel.

> There were two young men sitting at the fire in the Commercial Room. They lowered their voices when I came in. I sat in a corner wondering what would happen next. Presently three more joined the two. There was a confab which obviously I wasn't meant to hear.
> 'But we met the train and he wasn't on it.'
> 'You mean they didn't send him down?'
> 'And what other way would he come but the train?'
> I was listening keenly. Then I approached them, saying, 'I think you're looking for me.'
> There was alarm on their faces so I produced my letter of credence. A woman — a girl in an ill-fitting costume — was the last they expected to arrive with 'full power' for the selection of candidates. After a meal, they took me through back streets to a room where we held the meeting. One of the party was Eamonn Coogan, afterwards Deputy Commissioner of the Garda Síochána, and whose wife, Beatrice, was a novelist.

The meeting was a bit stormy. There was disunity. One of the sitting TDs was unacceptable to the Volunteers. He had expressed disapproval of their activities and they were determined that he would not be selected again as a candidate. Brigid took the line that the choice was theirs:

> I felt that the Volunteers were the people in the fight and I fully understood if they didn't want a man who was in any way opposed to their activities. Whatever the Volunteers wanted must be done.

Sadly, the wise contribution that might have come from Alec McCabe was missing — he was in prison. A distinguished Volunteer, McCabe had been acquitted by a jury of a charge of possession of explosives, but for his politics he had also lost his job as a teacher in Kesh in South

Sligo. Brigid regretted his absence from the meeting that night for, in addition to his advice, she remembered that Kesh in South Sligo was near enough to Scramogue in North Roscommon to make Alec McCabe a neighbour's child.

Eventually I ratified the nominations for the Sligo–East Mayo constituency as follows: Alec McCabe [in prison], Dr Ferran, Frank Carty, Thomas O'Donnell and James Devins [also in prison]. All were elected without opposition.

The following morning, past-pupil Brigid Lyons was welcomed at the Ursuline Convent. When the nuns heard the nature of her mission to Sligo, there was a flutter of excitement.

I was very glad I'd worn my aunt's costume. It made me feel good. I was bombarded with questions, particularly about Michael Collins. The nuns adored his exploits. What was he like? Was he of this earth at all? They were wildly enthusiastic about the Movement and what the Volunteers were doing. The only blot on that visit to the Ursuline was when a Fr Crehan from Boyle came in. A great Gaelic League man, he didn't approve of my decision of the previous night. He thought the sitting TD should have been ratified. That worried me until I got back to Dublin. The only fault found there was that I should have spent more money. Setting out, I'd been given £2 and my travel ticket. I explained I didn't have any reason to spend more money.

Awaiting her was a letter from Seán Mac Eoin, dated 11 May:

Brigid, a chara dhíl mo chroídhe,

How are you or what has put you from coming to see me? I was expecting you and Maggie [later the wife of Major-General Richard Callanan, this was Brigid's cousin Peg McGuinness] to pay me a visit. I hope she is in real good form after her holiday [she had done three months' imprisonment in Mountjoy]…

I have no news except that a summary of the evidence was taken yesterday on the charge, D.I. McGrath. I suppose you may have heard of the case. The evidence is very strong, but sure worse could happen...

Brigid visited Seán again. Her visits were becoming increasingly important. She knew that what she was doing could greatly assist Collins in the successful rescue bid. Then something happened which was to have repercussions:

> I discovered to my horror that a new sentry had been posted over the door leading to the main building. He was surrounded by sandbags. I felt this was against anything that could be done to rescue Seán by that route. Security seemed to be tightening up. I was still seeing Seán in the Deputy Governor's office. One of the plans had been to rescue him from that office during such a visit. That had been abandoned in favour of the armoured car plan. I immediately reported to Collins on the position of the new sentry.

Early on the afternoon of Saturday 14 May there was a Stop Press in the streets. Michael Collins' audacious attempt to rescue Seán Mac Eoin from Mountjoy Prison had failed. Something entirely unforeseen had occurred. Mac Eoin had demanded yet another interview with the Governor and this had been arranged. A new group of Auxiliaries and Black and Tans had, however, taken over prison duties that day, and their commander insisted on interviewing every prisoner personally. Mac Eoin's insistence on his right to see the Governor, as arranged, was refused, the new commander insisting equally strongly that his inspection took precedence. Thus Mac Eoin was not in the Governor's office when the 'British' senior officers (Emmet Dalton and Joe Leonard) arrived to 'transfer the prisoner to Dublin Castle'. The fact that he wasn't there gave the Governor time to inspect more closely their bogus document stamped with the seal of Dublin Castle. He lifted the phone to verify with the Castle, whereupon Dalton and Leonard pounced, binding and gagging him. There was still the hope that Mac Eoin would appear in that office.

Meanwhile, a shot was heard from outside. The sentry on the main gate insisted that it be shut until the armoured car was ready to leave. With the car's engine running, the 'British' crew played for time, insisting that it be kept open as they were leaving directly. The sentry remained adamant and a Volunteer covered him with a revolver. The new sentry behind his sandbags on the roof was watching. He raised his rifle and another Volunteer fired and hit him. Dalton and Leonard then appeared and the armoured car tore through the main gate of Mountjoy, its crew safe, but sadly without the man they had risked so much to bring out.

Brigid felt desolate at the news.

I wondered if I had failed in any way in my reports on my visits to Mountjoy. Because the whole purpose of my visits was to report exactly when and where Seán was to be seen, to help Collins formulate his plan. One plan had been to take him from the Deputy Governor's office during a visit. That's why Mick was asking others to get visiting permits as well as me. Holding a few permits, two or three people — in disguise of course — could go in and carry out the rescue. Before that sentry was posted over the door, it all seemed feasible enough. When the bad news broke, there was terrible excitement. People began calling at Uncle Joe's. They expected to hear at any moment that Mac Eoin had been killed. It would be the usual British excuse: 'shot while trying to escape'.

At the height of the excitement, at about 4 p.m. on that Saturday, Joe O'Reilly rushed in and handed Brigid a letter. It was from Michael Collins.

To Brigid Lyons,
27, Lower Dorset Street,
Dublin.

A chara dhil,

I have a heavy heart now. We just failed to get him. A slight alteration somewhere or other. Try the visit anyway. No doubt he'll give you the devil's own searching now. Perhaps it would be as well to get the other girl to have the visit and keep your permit in reserve.

We have had very hard luck with Seán, yet there must be something good somewhere. It's only to start again now.

Do chara go buan,

Micheál

That letter, one of her most cherished, gave her consolation as well as a new confidence in the future. Despair had no place in the philosophy of Michael Collins, and he had little patience when he detected it in others. Setbacks were part of life — to be put behind you and forgotten. The future was all that mattered, and he had the gift of making his friends see it that way too. The pity was, in that hour of disappointment, that it wasn't possible for Collins to communicate a ray of hope to the man left behind in Mountjoy.

Seán Mac Eoin has recorded his own feelings at the time.

Dejected, I sat on my bed and considered how near I was to my end. I decided I would prepare for death. Escape from Mountjoy was now impossible. I wrote my last letter to my comrades and I roughed out my speech from the dock, the one I would make before the death sentence was pronounced on me.

Joe O'Reilly had hardly left when a telegram arrived for Brigid. Aunt Annie was critically ill in Scramogue, Co Roscommon. More depression, more sad memories, for this was the kindly, loving person who had stepped in and reared the children of her dead sister-in-law. It seemed imperative to go immediately, but trains were uncertain. Aunt Joe advised against it and, on the Sunday evening, they went to see Mrs Tom Clarke. The garden was full of May blossom, but the talk was only of the terrible shootings and reprisals all over the country and, of course, the fate of Seán Mac Eoin. All evening, Brigid's thoughts were with her Aunt Annie. Was she still living? Flinging caution aside, she set out early next morning for Roscommon. A slow train meant that her aunt had just died when she arrived. But she was glad she had gone. Aunt Annie had been a very special aunt — the only mother she had ever known.

# 19

# LLOYD GEORGE WIZARDRY

THE RESULT OF the general election was another overwhelming victory for Sinn Féin. De Valera, Collins and Griffith were elected in northern as well as southern Ireland. Awaiting his trial for 'murder', Seán Mac Eoin in Mountjoy Prison was elected, unopposed, for Longford–Westmeath. On 28 May, he wrote thanking Brigid for parcels safely received.

> … The boys are all delighted and send you their fervent gratitude and love. I am almost jealous, but I know that unkind locks and keys and gates and doors are between you and them and that they cannot, for the present at any rate, say or do anything that would annoy me much…
>
> I am expecting you in every day. Yes, you will receive that photograph. All the difficulties that were in the way have been overcome I believe. Let me know if you get it.
>
> My trial will take place in the City Hall on Wednesday 8th June at 10 a.m. So now, pray for me your best…

The photograph to which Mac Eoin refers had been smuggled out to Collins. It is a snapshot taken by a friendly warder and shows Thomas Traynor (executed on 26 April 1921), Seán Mac Eoin and Thomas Whelan (executed on 14 March 1921) standing in an exercise yard with a prison block for backdrop.

Aged twenty-two, and from Clifden, Co Galway, Thomas Whelan

was accused of shooting a British officer on Bloody Sunday. He died protesting his innocence. The father of ten young children, Thomas Traynor, a boot-maker from Tullow, Co Carlow, had been a member of the Boland's Mill garrison during Easter Week 1916. The memory of both men was honoured in 2001 when their bodies were included amongst those exhumed in Mountjoy Prison and transferred to Glasnevin Cemetery.

Michael Collins sent this treasured photograph to Brigid with a note:

3.6.1921
A chara dom,

The attached is for you from Seán. Keep it carefully. See note on back. Photo very like him. You can almost see the fiery energy rushing from him.

Best wishes,

M.

Brigid was by now a student at Holles Street Hospital. As babies frequently make their appearance in the small hours, midwifery on the district brought a new risk factor. The Auxies and the Tans were no respecters of doctors, let alone medical students, when they broke curfew, even to attend the sick. Passing along a deserted St Stephen's Green at two o'clock one morning, going to a case in Camden Street, Brigid and a student called Theo McWeeney were challenged by a lorry full of Auxiliaries spoiling to shoot.

'Theo had been in the British Army and had the best possible accent to deal with them,' Brigid said.

He negotiated skilfully and having displayed the maternity equipment in our bag, we were allowed to proceed. But frequently they wouldn't even listen — they just hooshed you into the lorry and brought you off to the nearest barracks.

Appalled at the squalor and overcrowding of the 'homes' in the district, Brigid was also deeply impressed by the charity of the poor towards one another, by their love of children, and by their sense of political indignation at the state of the country. And — short of her latest baby — every mother idolised Michael Collins. In the hospital, too, he was continually discussed, not always with the same adulation. According to Brigid, 'Some of their opinions of the man were so wide of the mark, so crazy, I longed to tell them how wrong they were, but I never did. I feared I'd ever let a word slip — but I never did.'

She continued her visits to Mountjoy. Collins had another rescue plan in train — in fact two. He was determined to save the indomitable Mac Eoin. Far from being depressed, Mac Eoin was spreading cheer from the gloom of his prison cell. On 7 June, he wrote to Brigid:

> … Do for goodness sake get cheerful and don't grumble so much over the disappointment that His Majesty's Prison Board has thought well of giving you. You know very well that a small person like you cannot know what is right and wrong…
>
> I think you should see Mr. Noyk, Solicitor. He may be able to get a summons for you to attend the trial on my behalf. You ought to have valuable evidence as to my character which might weigh with the Judges who are to decide whether I am a fit person to be at large…

Four days later he wrote:

> … I have not gone out for trial yet — not until Monday now, I believe. I'm glad to know you got the photograph. I can assure you the same poor piece of paper is very dear to me, with my companion [Thomas Traynor] on it. I had a tough struggle to keep it from falling into other people's hands. Mind it, now that I succeeded in minding it so far. It is for you to go the rest of the way.

On the morning of 14 June, Seán Mac Eoin, the legendary rebel, stood handcuffed before a court martial in the City Hall. He had noted the position of the window. Another rescue attempt was imminent. Across the road in the Exchange Hotel, Collins' men were watching and waiting. In due course, the defence lawyer would request removal of the prisoner's handcuffs to enable him to consult his notes. It was then he might club the guard, grab his revolver and, having thrown the court into confusion, leap through the window to the waiting rescuers. But in his pocket Mac Eoin had put two pieces of paper. On one he had written, 'Trust in God, go ahead and do your best.' On the other: 'Trust in God, have patience and wait.' At the critical moment he would conduct his own lottery by drawing one piece from his pocket. Whichever it was, he would abide by the decision.

When the handcuffs were removed, Mac Eoin withdrew one of the two pieces of paper. It read, 'Trust in God, have patience and wait.' The decision made, he calmly turned and addressed the court.

Officers and gentlemen of the court martial, I am being tried not as an officer, but as a murderer… From you I crave no mercy. But as an officer of the Irish Army I claim the same right as I would be prepared to give if you fell into my hands.

Although pleas were made on his behalf by relatives of the dead District Inspector and by his former British prisoners, Seán Mac Eoin was found guilty of murder and was sentenced to death by hanging. The sentence was subject to confirmation, but like the trial, it was felt that too would be a mere matter of form.

Two days later, on 16 June, he wrote to Brigid to let her know

… that I am back in the home of locks and keys and that I am in the very best of form. Is there no reasonable chance of your coming in to see me?

… There is no use in me saying anything about my trial. You have seen the papers. The only other news is that I am not to live long, in the opinion of the court that pretended to try me and give me justice…

There is a P.S. to this letter: 'Matches, matches or we perish for a smoke.'

On 19 June, in an otherwise bantering and cheery letter, he wrote, Yes, the trial is over, in a sense, and to tell you true I am not sorry, even though I was found guilty and sentenced to death by that part of it which is over. You see it has to be confirmed yet, but that means…

The sentence was confirmed. Seán Mac Eoin wrote what he believed to be his last letter.

My dearest friend,

I take this opportunity to write to you to thank you for your kindness to me. I know you will say that isn't necessary. I agree that if I never wrote, you would know that I cannot express my feelings for your attention to me. So I leave it at that and won't attempt it.

My dear friend, as this may be the last opportunity I may get of writing to you on the q.t., I want you to say goodbye for me to all my boys and girls [a list of names follows]. I may quit for I cannot name them all. There are scores of fellows I should name, but I cannot. All I can say is: to the boys of the Brigade, Beannacht Dé Libh.

I was going to send you a list of names to give a few copies of the photo to, but in this also I would only be rising rows so all I want you to do is send a copy to Tom Reddington or Michael Geslin and let them get copies for whoever of my friends may want them. I sent out the photo to Mick a week or more ago. You should have it by now.

I cannot write so I will ring off. Hoping to see you sometime. May God bless and guard you and all my friends.

Do chara go deo,

Seán Mac Eoin

Brigid Lyons conveyed the contents of that letter to those for whom they were intended: the members of Commandant Mac Eoin's Longford Flying Column. It was a depressing period. Her friends were dying in the flush of youth. Two weeks earlier, on a sunny afternoon as she had walked down Gardiner Street with Aunt Joe, the Custom House had erupted into an inferno of smoke and flame. In a city garrisoned by tens of thousands of British military, a comparative handful of IRA guerrillas in broad daylight totally destroyed the headquarters of the British Civil Service in Ireland. Not without cost. Five Volunteers were killed and eighty taken prisoner. 'We came on it unexpectedly,' Brigid remembered.

It was a horrible sight. Then we heard of those burnt inside. The O'Reilly boys — brothers — were trapped and lost their lives. The burning of the Custom House seemed significant at the time. We felt the end must be near when the Volunteers could achieve this under the very noses of the British military might that existed in Dublin.

Later Brigid's Uncle Joe revealed that he had participated in the destruction of the Custom House. Nor was he very proud of the handiwork of the Volunteers on that May afternoon — despite the plaudits of the public for their display of bravery. The price in prisoners and deaths had been too great. Covering the approaches, he had managed to get his men away as the screaming of the Tans Crossley tenders swarmed into the area.

On 22 June 1921, King George V opened the first Northern Ireland Parliament at Stormont and appealed 'to all Irishmen to pause, to stretch out the hand of forbearance and conciliation, to forgive and forget.' That night, the IRA mined and derailed a train bringing back to Dublin part of the King's escort from Belfast. Nonetheless, the King's speech had made an impact.

There was, however, no news in Mountjoy. Writing on 25 June, Seán Mac Eoin said, 'Everything is just the same here. All I can tell you is that my supply of sugar has come to an end. So if you would like to keep me from turning sour, send me in a small grain.' Brigid continued to visit. There was still the hope of rescue — even if it meant dynamiting the 30-foot surrounding wall.

Nevertheless, things were changing in a barely perceptible way. There were rumours of peace-feelers from Britain. Nobody took them seriously. Then de Valera was arrested and hastily released the following morning. People tried to draw conclusions. Even in Mountjoy, things were going topsy-turvy. Writing on 4 July, Seán Mac Eoin is

> Very vexed with everybody outside the prison walls and at the Castle. I had no less than three visitors who shouldn't have got permits and that I considered cheeky coming to see me. Another has got a permit to see me today, a person I don't know and never heard of. The next time you are up at the Castle I think you should create a small riot...
>
> I expect to see you soon so don't be put off — get a permit.

News of a peace conference had now broken. There was speculation everywhere. On 8 July, General Sir Nevil Macready, British Commander-in-Chief, drove in an open car to a peace conference at the Mansion House. He exchanged salutes with Irish Republican sentries. Brigid Lyons watched the arrivals.

> Rumour was rife. England feared world opinion. Something must happen. But was it going to be peace? Or would the conference break down again? The people wanted peace. They'd been through a terrible time. We were all hopeful and dependent on prayer.

On the Sunday before the Truce, she had been at Mass at Berkeley Road Church. Passing Mountjoy Jail, she had been struck by a silly impulse. She had no permit but she thought she'd ask to see Commandant Mac Eoin.

> I went up to the Jail gate and rang. A warder looked out through the wicket. I told him what I wanted. He turned to another and said, 'There's a one outside wanting to see Mac Eoin.'
>
> The other looked through the wicket and snapped abruptly, 'What d'you want to see him for — have you a permit?'
>
> I said I hadn't and he banged the wicket closed. Then I heard bolts being withdrawn and a well-dressed gentleman came out. He paused, looking at me.
>
> 'I'm trying to get in to see Commandant Mac Eoin,' I said, 'and they won't let me.'
>
> 'That's too bad,' he replied. 'Are you a friend?' I said I was and

he turned to the warder.

'Take the visitor in to see Commandant Mac Eoin,' he said. And to my surprise — and to Seán Mac Eoin's — I got in. It was a surprise to everybody. Even the use of the title 'Commandant' was unusual.

Brigid discovered that the man was Sir Alfred Cope, Under-Secretary for Ireland. She had seen him before on her calls to Dublin Castle for permits. His charm that morning reflected the new approach in view of the current peace talks — what might nowadays be called the softly-softly approach.

At midday on Monday 11 July 1921, the truce between the IRA and the British forces in Ireland came into operation. The War of Independence was over. The IRA was recognised as the army of Ireland, and therefore retained its arms. It was a glorious summer day and Dublin — all Ireland — went mad. The hoardings in Sackville Street, which screened wrecked buildings, were pulled down and, using bits of the wood, youngsters marched with 'guns' on their shoulders, imitating the Black and Tans. The evening was bright and warm, and Dublin became like a Mediterranean city at carnival time. A sense of relief was everywhere. Crowds came out to walk and to sing and to savour the new freedom.

That night, Brigid received a message from Michael Collins: he would like to accompany her to see Seán Mac Eoin on the following Wednesday at 2.15 p.m. She made arrangements for a visit by James Gill and herself to the prisoner, still under sentence of death. As nobody knew how long the Truce might last, Collins did not wish to reveal himself.

I met Mick on Wednesday 13 July. With the usual twinkle in his eye, the first thing he said was, 'I was in Granard yesterday.' It was the first time he dared leave Dublin for a long time.

'Did you miss the Greville Arms?' I asked him. [The hotel had been burnt out by the Tans.]

'Yes, I missed it,' Mick said. 'But the people are still there.' He meant the Kiernan family, Kitty Kiernan in particular. His friend Harry Boland and himself were both interested in Kitty.

It was a joy to see Seán Mac Eoin's surprise when he saw Mick Collins walk into Mountjoy that day. As usual, there was a warder present. But Mick's incognito was honoured. We all felt tense, each of us knowing what we knew, and yet unable to speak freely. Seán just greeted him as a visitor, but there was no hiding his inner delight. Collins too had an immense admiration for Mac Eoin. He had put up such a magnificent fight in Longford with the minimum of men and munitions. They talked happily, the warder hardly taking any notice. In fact, it was all much less formal than I had been used to in the Deputy Governor's office when I had to pass and receive messages in the presence of the Deputy, an Auxiliary, a warder and sometimes even a policeman.

The following day, Seán Mac Eoin summed up his feelings in his letter to Brigid:

I don't know how to explain to you how grateful I am to you for your visit of yesterday. My old heart beat high with joy and all I could do was stare and murmur to myself 'Thank God'. I am sure you understand how I felt…

I will be ever grateful to you for that visit, not but that you came often to see me before, but never were you so welcome and that welcome will always remain so long as I remain.

Discreetly, no reference is made to Michael Collins, alias Mr Gill, Brigid's companion on that visit. A truce there might have been, but it was still a truce without trust.

In the ensuing weeks, however, Ireland became a different country. Friends were reuniting, people were meeting who had not met openly for years. The British Army was keeping discreetly out of sight. For the first time, the British learned how comparatively few soldiers there had been on the Irish side. They learned that it was the will of a people that was more powerful than legions of men and armouries of weapons. There was even a sneaking admiration for Irish grit and spunk. In country towns, the Flying Columns came in and fraternised with British soldiers and swapped stories, the rancour and bitterness suddenly forgotten. But the Flying Columns — like the people — limited their new social intercourse to British Army regular soldiers. The Tans and the Auxiliaries were still hated. In memory, they would always be hated.

The Truce threw up a new kind of Irish patriot, a Johnnie-come-lately of the armchair warrior type. 'The number of them was amazing,' Brigid recalled.

People who came out and wanted to be regarded as prominent activists and fighters. They were called 'the eleven-thirty volunteers.' [The truce had begun at noon.] Another nickname was 'The Trucileers'. Collins called them 'The Sunshine Soldiers'. They didn't really get into full spate until the Treaty was signed. Then they were wildly enthusiastic for a Republic. Nothing less would do them.

After the first jubilation of the Truce, public tension began to rise again. Brigid remembered 'on the North Circular Road seeing teenage girls barging young British soldiers. We thought how very bad it was. They were kids but they were very hostile to those boys. It was hardly in the spirit of a truce.'

There were occasional explosive breaches of the Truce too, perhaps accidental or misguided or the result of alcoholic braggadocio, but they did not help relationships with London. De Valera had met Lloyd George, who was afterwards to say, 'When I tried to bring him down to the present day, back he went to Cromwell again. It reminded me of a circus roundabout.'

Lloyd George was giving Ireland Dominion Status, but de Valera wanted External Association. In this demand, he was ahead of his time. It was to be many years yet, and would require the disintegration of her Empire before Britain's prime ministers would learn the niceties of External Association. De Valera returned to Dublin, the unacceptable Dominion Status being the best he could get. A tortuous and semantic correspondence followed in which Lloyd George accused de Valera of 'playing with phrases'. It was as if de Valera were meticulously adhering to the advice of Cathal Brugha: 'Keep them talking.'

Dáil Éireann was to meet in August to accept or reject the British terms. On 6 August, Dublin Castle announced the release of all interned and imprisoned members of the Dáil — with one exception: 'J. J. McKeon who has been convicted of murder, cannot be released.' There was an outcry. Collins had first made representations for his release immediately after his visit to Mac Eoin. Now he made a furious protest. There would be no discussions without Mac Eoin. On 8 August, de Valera issued a statement:

> If the detention of Commandant Mac Eoin is persisted in, I cannot accept responsibility for proceeding further with the negotiations...
>
> In British legal phraseology he is termed a murderer: but for us, I believe, for the world, he is a heroic Irishman.

Late that night, Mac Eoin was released.

Four decades later, General Seán Mac Eoin, in a television interview, told a story alleged to have occurred that day. Lloyd George had been playing ball with his little granddaughter in the garden of 10 Downing Street. Then he took to walking up and down the path, thoughtfully. She begged him to go on playing, but he said that he was worried. The child asked him why and he replied that a man was going to die and he didn't know what to do about it.

'Let the man live,' she said. 'And come and play ball.' That turned the tide. Lloyd George dispatched a message ordering that Mac Eoin be released.

General Mac Eoin told Dr Brigid Lyons Thornton that many years later, the child, now a woman, came to Dublin and visited him. After dinner, they went to the RTÉ television studio in Montrose, to see the videotape of the interview in which he had related that story. But alas! The tape was not to be found.

Brigid Lyons was busy on the morning after Seán Mac Eoin's release.

> I was doing dressings in a ward at Mercers' Hospital. The porter threw the door open and called out, 'Commandant Mac Eoin wants to see Miss Lyons.' If you'd thrown a bomb into that ward, it couldn't have been more devastating. The patients and nurses went mad when they heard he'd been released. When I got to Aunt Joe's in Gardiner Street, there he was, looking well and delighted

with himself. I could hardly believe it. The soldier we had all stormed heaven and earth to save from the hangman's noose.

As soon as news reached Longford, people began to come to Dublin to see Mac Eoin. An old friend, a cattle dealer called Dick Tuite, wanted to know, on behalf of the people of Longford, the date Mac Eoin was going to Longford, so that a civic celebration could be arranged. Having got the date, Tuite sent a telegram in code to Longford: 'The cow has calved. She's going home on Thursday.' The celebrations in Longford went on for days. There was also a municipal reception for him in Mullingar, where he had been shot and arrested.

In Dublin, too, the fabulous Mac Eoin was fêted.

He got a new Volunteer uniform made. He could wear it publicly now and he'd never had one while he was on the run. He wore it for the first time when we all went to a reception given by Mrs Tom Clarke.

For the young heroes, life was good and it was grand to be around again. But behind the new leisure, the new communal gaiety, the Volunteers (now the Irish Republican Army) were actively engaged in recruiting and training, for who could trust an Englishman's smile? Who could believe the British were sincere in their desire for peace with Ireland? The British garrisons were not idling either. They were concentrating their forces for the resumption of the bloodiest war ever, if the peace negotiations failed. Hadn't Lord Birkenhead warned in London that Great Britain would be committed to 'hostilities on a scale never hitherto undertaken by this country against Ireland'?

In these lengthening shadows, the Dáil met in public session on 16 August 1921, to consider the British offer of Dominion Status. Brigid Lyons listened to the debate. Her memory of it reflected something of the confused emotionalism of the time.

I was shattered to hear de Valera say his oath to the Republic was the best measure of freedom he could get. For me, I didn't think that was enough, or for him either. When I look back on it, of course, it was a sensible statement, and the only one anyone could make, but at the time I thought it was the Republic or nothing for me — still, like a lot of others not knowing exactly what a Republic was. The Dáil rejected the British offer and stalemate followed.

Through those weeks, Collins toured the country. The IRA must be kept up to fighting pitch. Too many had taken to strutting round like victors in uniform, too willingly accepting the adulation due to heroes. With Harry Boland now back from America, Mick enjoyed the old horse-play companionship. Together they went to Granard whenever possible. Brigid thought that if Fate had not intervened, Michael Collins rather than Harry Boland would have won Kitty Kiernan. 'Neither had great prospects in a worldly-wise way, but I think if your heart ruled you, you'd have taken Michael.'

Collins visited his constituents in Armagh and made a speech. His prophecy is remarkable, given the plight of Orange Unionism in an EU-dominated Europe:

The Orangemen have been used as a tool in preventing up to the present what is now inevitable. The moment is near when they will no longer be of use as a tool, when they will, in fact, stand in the way of an agreement with Ireland which now has become essential to British interests. Then they will be thrown aside and they will find their eyes turned to an England which no longer wants them.

He invited the Orangemen 'to come in and take their share in the Government of their own country.' His reward was a pelting with stones.

A soldier, with no ambitions as a politician, Collins objected strongly to his nomination by de Valera as a member of the Treaty negotiating team. If a man with de Valera's charisma had failed to wrest an Irish Republic from Lloyd George, why send self-confessed second-rate negotiators and expect them to bring back that cherished prize? 'In going,' he said, 'I'm signing my own death warrant.'

The Treaty delegation left for London on Saturday 8 October 1921. Michael Collins was not with the other negotiators. Brigid was at Kingstown (Dún Laoghaire) to see them off.

I had seen less of my nationalist friends since I was studying hard for the first half of my final in October. But, of course, I was still absorbed in what was going to come as a settlement with England.

On that Saturday, Michael Collins became engaged to Kitty Kiernan. He joined the delegation in London on Monday 10 October.

Brigid passed her examination. For the time being, at least, she could again meet people and listen to and express opinions.

Throughout October and November rumours flowed from London: what we were going to get and what we weren't going to get. I met Dr Kathleen Lynn at Mrs Tom Clarke's and she said, 'We're getting everything but the name of a Republic.' I still felt I wanted to hold out for the name too. I loved the word Republic. I don't know why. It was idealistic and attractive and in wanting it I think I represented the average outlook of people of my age group. It was the name Free State which turned so many people sour. It was unattractive and to this day I dislike it. But maybe a name isn't that important. It certainly wasn't worth a civil war with its terrible loss of life.

As the London negotiations dragged on, maintenance of the Truce in Ireland became more precarious. With munitions still in the hands of the IRA, it became increasingly difficult to control trigger-happy youths. Writing on 2 November, on notepaper headed 'Irish Republican Army, The First Midland Division, Headquarters, Longford', Seán Mac Eoin expressed his concern.

> I do hope Uncle Joe gets back before the Truce goes wallop. It was expected to go so soon last week that I was raced and chased all over Dublin last time I was up.

The Treaty accepting Dominion Status was finally signed in London at 2.10 a.m. on 6 December 1921. The news broke in Dublin later that morning, bringing even greater confusion to an already confused population. The people continually looked for guidance, for straightforward explanation. What they got was circuitously expressed hypotheses wrapped in semantics beyond general understanding. It may be that that was the intention. Today it is known as 'keeping your options open'.

Nevertheless, the drift of public opinion was immediately discernable. That morning, at a clinic in the Mater Hospital, Brigid heard the medical students express it. 'It's a split,' they chorused. 'It's a split. Ireland is split again.'

Indeed, the weeks ahead showed all too clearly how seriously Ireland was to be split. An acrimonious Cabinet meeting took place on 8 December. High on the agenda was the failure of the plenipotentiaries to consult Dublin before signing the Treaty. Dublin, it seemed, misunderstood the meaning of the word plenipotentiary, for it was in that capacity that the delegation had been sent to London. *Figaro*, the French newspaper, derisively defined plenipotentiary, as understood in Ireland, as 'a man with full powers but powerless'. By a majority, the cabinet accepted the Treaty.

Cabinet dissension was, however, revealed by the issue of a statement to the press: 'The terms of the agreement are in violent conflict with the wishes of the majority of the Nation.'

The news of the Treaty had, in fact, brought immeasurable relief to the majority of the people of Ireland and when, eventually, through the democratic process, they voted on the matter, there was no doubting their answer. But that was still in the future.

In the gloomy Convocation Hall of University College Dublin, the Dáil met on 14 December, ostensibly to ratify the Treaty. The records of that ill-fated marathon meeting reveal that for three days, spite, abuse, vilification, vituperation, vindictiveness and parish platitudes poured from ill-tempered men and emotional women. Most of it concerned not the terms of the Treaty, but the personal reputations of two of the 'plenipotentiaries', namely, Griffith and Collins.

In an atmosphere devoid of the logic and detachment necessary for clear thought, de Valera introduced his Document No. 2, his alternative to the Treaty. Those who examined it seriously could find little or no difference. Griffith said the difference 'was a quibble and so far as my power or voice extends not one young Irishman's life will be lost on that quibble.' De Valera refuted this in what was called 'a long passage of bleak sincerity'. Collins pointed out that the Treaty 'gives us freedom, not the ultimate freedom that all nations desire and develop to, but the freedom to achieve it' — his stepping stones to the Republic thesis. He reminded them that the Dáil was 'perfectly free to accept or reject' the agreement. Having introduced Document No. 2, de Valera then withdrew it without making its contents known publicly.

At the end of three days, the Dáil adjourned for Christmas.

# 20

# ENTER THE DOCTOR

IN THE CHRISTMAS recess, the political confusion initiated by the Dáil spread throughout the country. Depending upon the force of personality of the last person he talked to, a man switched his allegiance for or against the Treaty from day to day, from hour to hour. Yet the people were deeply concerned as to what was to happen. The leadership they sought came only from the press and the pulpit, both having indicated their acceptance of the Treaty. Discussion centred on the mystery of the Treaty vis-à-vis Document No. 2. Nobody could sort out any difference. People were confused. According to Brigid:

People who'd never fought, people who'd never even been in the Movement were the most adamant that we couldn't accept anything less than a Republic. There were many such among my own friends — those who said, 'Oh, but wouldn't it be dreadful now to take less than a Republic? Isn't that what you fought for all the time?' If they had analysed the Treaty, we'd got everything on which we could work for a better future. The reality was, like it or not, we couldn't have gone on in arms any longer. We had no more arms. Our economy was on its knees. Crops weren't being sown — nothing was being done. And many young people weren't prepared to go out and fight again for the difference between Document No. 1 and Document No. 2. Most people remembered only too well the horrors they'd just gone through.

I too was against the Treaty at the beginning. It hurt, for

instance, that we should pay gratuities and pensions to our late and hated enemies, the RIC. I didn't want to see the Royal Navy still in possession of our ports, and taking an oath to the King of England was something I just couldn't approve of. It was comparatively minor things like that which stuck in our minds, rather than the bigger issues, like the immense possibilities ahead in moving peacefully towards more and greater measures of freedom — Collins' stepping-stones idea.

Of course I had wanted a Republic. Like the others, hadn't I done my bit for it, given it all my hope and interest — even my prayers? I used to say my prayers in Irish. I decided never to say them any other way until we got the Republic. I hoped God was more likely to hear them that way and act accordingly! Now it struck me for the first time that I was faced with having to make a serious decision. Most of us weren't clever enough at politics: we were young and inexperienced and we couldn't see where the politicians were leading us. It was fine while we were still fighting for the Republic and not knowing really what a Republic meant, beyond getting the British out of the country and getting control of our own national affairs. But wouldn't the Treaty do just that? When I had time to talk it over rationally with sensible people, I realised Britain couldn't possibly give us more than we got *at the time*. We'd got our own country, our own army, our own police and control of our own affairs, and there was no limit to what else we might get, given time. We'd just have to be patient and carry on the fight for a bit longer, in another way. If God hadn't heard my prayers for a Republic, I like to think He helped me to make a sensible decision on the alternative.

Thus opinions hardened and divisions widened. Opinions ranged from positive black to positive white with a grey area of confusion between. People still craved guidance. In its absence, they latched onto personalities: 'If the Treaty's been signed by Michael Collins, that's good enough for me.'

On 3 January 1922, the Dáil resumed the Treaty debate. Efforts were made to break the deadlock of personal abuse and parish rhetoric.

De Valera offered to produce his Document No. 2 on condition that it be put as an amendment to the Treaty. Griffith protested: it must be a straight vote on the Treaty. On the following day, de Valera gave notice that on 5 January he would move that his Document No. 2 be brought forward as an amendment to the Treaty. Griffith replied, 'I suggest that President de Valera should hand that Document to the Press, as we asked him a fortnight ago.' When Document No. 2 had been circulated to members in readiness for 5 January, Griffith noted that six clauses of the twenty-three in the original Document No. 2 had been dropped. De Valera accused him of quibbling.

On 5 January, Collins proposed that the opponents of the Treaty abstain from voting. The opposition would thereby make clear their stand on the Republic 'and we can have all the shame and the disgrace'. Differences prevented acceptance of his proposal. De Valera made a long speech on 6 January, on his difficulties since 1917 in keeping the balance between disparate elements. He would throw out the Treaty and offer the British his alternative even if 'there was not a gun (left) in Ireland'. His Document No. 2, he claimed, accorded with the wishes of the Irish people. He had always been able to examine his own heart 'and it told me straight off what the Irish people wanted.' He then resigned and promptly offered himself for re-election and, ignoring the Treaty motion before the house, he challenged Griffith to a vote on personalities.

Griffith's motion, 'That Dáil Éireann approves of the Treaty between Great Britain and Ireland signed in London on December 6th, 1921' was still before the House and, until it was dealt with, de Valera's proposal was out of order.

De Valera then endeavoured to have Standing Orders suspended. Griffith protested that he had listened for days while attacks were made on his honour and he was patiently waiting to wind up the discussion. He saw no reason why, in the middle of a discussion of the Treaty, a vote on the personality of de Valera should be sprung on the House. Standing Orders were not suspended and the debate resumed on 7 January. Cathal Brugha attacked Collins: the press and the people had 'put him [Collins] into a position which he never held. He was made a romantic figure, a mystical character such as this person certainly is not. The gentleman I refer to is Mr. Michael Collins.' He then appealed to Griffith and the other signatories not to vote on the Treaty. In that way, Griffith's name would live forever in Ireland.

Griffith replied, 'I cannot accept the invitation of the Minister of Defence to dishonour my signature and become immortalised in Irish history. Though I have not now, and never had, an ambition about either political affairs or history if my name is to go down in history I want it associated with the name of Michael Collins.' He then referred back to a cabinet meeting where he had said, 'If I go to London I can't get a Republic: I will try for a Republic, but I can't bring it back.' The plenipotentiaries had been sent 'to make some compromise, bargain or arrangement. We made an arrangement. The arrangement we made is not satisfactory to many people. Let them criticise on that point, but do not let them say that we were sent to get one thing and that we got something else.' He then quoted de Valera's letter to Lloyd George in which he had written, 'We have no conditions to impose, no claim to advance but one — that we are to be free from aggression.' Griffith said that the Treaty met that claim. He challenged de Valera to let the people know what his Document No. 2 involved: recognition of the King and association with the Commonwealth.

'There is no oath,' de Valera interjected.

Griffith said that de Valera had drafted an oath but had then omitted it from his Document No. 2 and he would not agree that 'the people of Ireland should be sacrificed for a formula. I do not care whether the King of England or the symbol of the Crown be in Ireland so long as the people of Ireland are free to shape their own destinies.'

De Valera replied, 'That document will rise in judgment against the men who say there's only a shadow of difference.'

At which point, Collins cried out, 'Let the Irish Nation judge us now and for future years.'

The vote on the Treaty was then taken, resulting in 64 for and 57 against, a majority of 7 for its approval. Thus another democratic step was taken in the acceptance of the Treaty. The third democratic step would be the voice of the people in a general election on its ratification. Thus, too, ended a historical example of political expediency in the public execution of convenient scapegoats. Mr de

Valera never explained why he should have expected others to extract from Lloyd George what he himself had failed to extract — namely, a Republic of Ireland. Listening to the Treaty debates, Brigid Lyons heard her Uncle Joe McGuinness make one of the briefest of all the speeches. He said, 'The Treaty has not been examined for the good things that are in it and I'm voting for it because of the good things that are in it.'

She also heard one of the longest speeches, that of Mary MacSwiney which lasted some three hours.

> She was bitterly unjust to Collins. She was an eloquent and convincing speaker, but very fanatical. Her arguments appealed to unthinking people. On the other hand, Mrs Pearse's [mother of Pádraig and Willie] short contribution was made quietly and with dignity. Likewise Mrs Tom Clarke when she said that 'it was a matter of sorrow that it should have come to this.' She and Uncle Joe were always great friends and he had advised her she should remain outside the turmoil of political rancour. Like her late husband, she wanted a complete break with England and we hadn't achieved that, any more than he had in Fenian times. While, therefore, she didn't approve of the Treaty, she remained reasonable about it.

In fact, she had reservations about the handling of the affair by de Valera.

On 9 January 1922, de Valera introduced a new issue. As President of Dáil Éireann, he represented the Irish Republic proclaimed in 1916 and reaffirmed by democratic sanction in 1919. To continue in that office, he would be a nominal president without a unified cabinet and, with a false appearance of democratic sanction, the subversion of the Irish Republic would be prepared by the Provisional Government. He was about to resign.

'Go and elect your President,' he said, 'I do not want office at all.' But he was willing, if re-elected, to take office as President of the Republic, his Executive to be drawn from the anti-Treaty group — government of the majority by the minority.

Some biographers make it appear that there was no scarcity of people prepared to propose de Valera's election as President. Reluctantly, and after great persuasion, Mrs Tom Clarke eventually did so — and then regretted it. She had never quite forgiven de Valera for an incident in Lincoln Jail. Eoin MacNeill's countermanding order in Easter Week 1916 had, according to some Volunteer views, sabotaged the Rising. Many would therefore resent his presence as a fellow-prisoner in Lincoln Jail. On the first day he made his appearance in the prison yard, de Valera ordered the prisoners to salute MacNeill to show that they no longer held against him his opposition to the Rising. They obeyed.

Of the Treaty debates, Brigid noted:

It was tragic and heartbreaking to see that people who had been so united had now become so mean and petty and inexcusably bitter. I remember someone with whom Uncle Joe had been in prison. He thought him the best friend he'd ever had — a jolly, pleasant fellow-prisoner. Because he was now pro-Treaty, this man spat at Uncle Joe going into Dáil Éireann.

In contrast, she remembered the tolerant demeanour of Griffith and Collins in spite of provocation.

Michael Collins looked harassed and worried. There was never any other expression on his face during those fateful days. He was a different man. He had to fight every inch of the way, listen to all that abuse, knowing as he did what they'd gone through in London. He knew the Irish people had had enough of war. He knew too that if the war was resumed, we hadn't a round of ammunition left. That's why the Volunteers and the IRB had advised him to sign the Treaty. Only once did he get very cross. Countess Markievicz said he was to be married to Princess Mary and appointed first Governor General of Saorstát Éireann. Michael thumped the table, 'That's an insult to the girl to whom I am betrothed,' he said.

At all hours of the night and morning, during the early months of 1922, Joe McGuinness TD, returned home more and more dejected. The changing of opinion, the switching of viewpoint, the continuous vacillation alarmed him. 'Yes, Uncle Joe went through a depressing phase of disillusionment,' Brigid said. 'And my aunt and myself suffered the same change with him.'

The Parliament of Southern Ireland (from which de Valera and his followers absented themselves) met on 14 January 1922, and elected Collins Chairman of the Provisional Government. Two days later, he led his ministers to Dublin Castle to take over the administration of the country from the Viceroy, Lord Fitzalan, on behalf of the British. It was a momentous occasion — the surrender of the citadel of British power and the symbol of Ireland's 700 years of subjugation. Thereafter, the Provisional Government set itself to building the new State. Meanwhile, the anti-Treaty faction skulked sullenly, or strutted menacingly, making the split an ever-widening chasm.

Instead of hope and sunshine, the spring of 1922 seemed only to bring foreboding. Brigid was studying again. She faced her final in March. Feeling physically and mentally tired, she did not expect to pass. Having been grilled by Sir John Lumsden from Mercers' and 'Joc' O'Carroll from the Richmond Hospital, she came out from the exam feeling 'well … a little more optimistic. But one never could tell.' Years of practice had given consultants distant manners and poker faces.

As with the politicians, the Army was divided on the Treaty issue. A convention was called in an effort to reunite the two factions, one of which intended to withdraw from the authority of the Dáil. They marched to a meeting at the Mansion House on 26 March (although the convention had been proscribed by the Cabinet). As they passed through Gardiner Street, Uncle Joe came in. Brigid noticed:

> He was tired and dispirited. I thought he was the most unhappy man I'd ever seen. He said, 'There they are — going out to divide and all the times we went out united.' That was a sad, sad day.

Preparations began for the General Election on the Treaty.

> Dan McCarthy asked me to work in the Committee rooms at 3 and 4 College Street, while I was waiting the result of my exam. I learned to type and sent out whips when they summoned the next Dáil sitting.
>
> Arriving at the office one morning, I saw some of my medical

student colleagues driving hilariously through Westmoreland Street on a side-car — some who'd done their final with me. They didn't wave to me or shout or cheer. I put in a miserable morning, went home for lunch and told Uncle and Aunt Joe I'd failed. Aunt Joe made an appropriate understatement: 'You didn't give it all the time you should have.'

That evening I went to University College to see who *did* get through. Trembling, I approached a list of 25 or 30 names.

I began at the bottom. I wasn't there so my eye climbed. Ninth from the top there it was! I kept rubbing the glass of the showcase with my finger, in case I wasn't seeing things too clearly. I decided I'd walk home across town and tell everyone I met I was a doctor. All the way from Earlsfort Terrace to Gardiner Street, I never met one person I knew. If it had been bad news, I'd have met everyone.

There was no celebration. Her success was spoiled by the prevailing depression. The split was opening wider. Next day, she was back in the College Street office with no wild urge to rush out to help suffering humanity. She didn't feel physically able. She had qualified and that was all that mattered for the moment. Her achievement, alongside her revolutionary activities, she summed up with characteristic self-effacement: 'A lot of it was prayer. And it was my good fortune to get the right cases.'

Although aware that, lacking resources, if for no other reason, the war could not be resumed, those who opposed the Treaty took to oratory. Malice, principally against Collins, ruled their outlook, rather than realities. As Joe McGuinness said, 'I could make a great speech against the Treaty. It's so easy to appeal to the mob instinct.'

De Valera repeated an ill-advised speech in several towns, forecasting such sinister ideas as that, for their freedom, Irishmen would yet have to wade through the blood of Irishmen. He denied the right of the Provisional Government to rule in Ireland. 'There are rights,' he said, 'which may be maintained by force by an armed minority even against a majority.'

An editorial in the *Irish Independent* described these speeches as incitement. In a letter to the newspaper, de Valera described the editorial as villainous. 'You cannot be unaware,' he wrote, 'that your representing me as inciting to civil war has on your readers precisely the same effect as if the inciting words were really mine.'

The Army Convention met again on 9 April. A resolution was proposed — and narrowly defeated — demanding an immediate military dictatorship, the elimination of the Provisional Government and the prevention of the general election on the Treaty issue. This was swiftly followed, on 14 April, by the occupation of the Four Courts by the Republican Army Council led by Rory O'Connor. Joe McGuinness became even more depressed. It was clear that the Republican faction meant to thwart the will of the people, to the point of civil war if necessary.

Efforts were made to find a basis for a peaceful compromise. With Arthur Griffith, Paddy O'Keeffe and Tom Hunter, Joe McGuinness served on a liaison committee in a last desperate effort to find some measure of agreement. He was very deeply concerned with the disastrous situation facing the country. At the time, Arthur Griffith was staying in Walter Cole's house around the corner, number 3 Mountjoy Square. Nightly, Joe worked late with him, coming home at all hours. One night, he was particularly late. Brigid remembered:

> My Aunt and I waited up for him. He came in shivering. It was May, but the nights were cold. He had been with Arthur Griffith again. Griffith and Collins were about to leave for London with a draft of the new Constitution. My uncle was all-in, mentally and physically. Next morning, he had a high temperature. He was unable to get up. In fact, he never got up again. There was no cure for pneumonia in those days. Uncle Joe died on 31 May 1922.

A TD for Longford, and an ardent supporter of the Treaty, Joe McGuinness died at a crucial moment, and his death was a grave loss for the Collins/Griffith group. He was honoured with a state funeral to Glasnevin. It proved to be a historic occasion, the differences of the two sides laid aside for one day to honour a dead colleague. It was to be the last time 'the lads' were to march together. All too soon, they were to march against each other, to be locked in the bitter enmity of civil war.

# 21

# KILMAINHAM ONCE AGAIN

A FEW WEEKS later, about 4 a.m. on 28 June, the newly widowed Aunt Joe McGuinness awoke to the sickening boom of artillery. 'I remember waking up too,' said Brigid. 'The first thing my Aunt said was "Thank God Joe's not alive to see this happening." She recognised it for what it was — the first shots of the Civil War. The bombardment of the Four Courts had begun.'

Events had been moving rapidly. There had been the new Constitution. There had been the 'Pact' election, which in effect was the third democratic step in the consideration of the Treaty. The result made plain the people's acceptance of the Treaty. Nonetheless, there were some who believed 'a nation has no right to do wrong'. As Brigid summarised it, 'Ratification of the Treaty by the people of Ireland wasn't enough for the death or glory boys. They were prepared to renounce democracy if necessary.' Frank McGuinness had been elected TD for Longford to fill his late brother's vacancy.

The Four Courts Republicans continued to defy the Provisional Government. Churchill was pressurising Collins. The assassination of Field Marshal Sir Henry Wilson — that strangely anti-Irish native of Co Longford — increased the pressure from Westminster. Unless the situation in the Four Courts were dealt with, the Treaty would be considered as violated. The defining moment came on 26 June when Leo Henderson, an officer of the Four Courts, was arrested in Ferguson's Garage in Baggot Street, while commandeering cars for the transport of arms to Belfast. That night in Leeson Street, Ernie O'Malley and Seán MacBride of the Four Courts group retaliated by kidnapping Brigadier J. J. ('Ginger') O'Connell, Deputy Chief of Staff of the pro-Treaty National Army. 'Ginger' was the romantic boy from Sligo of whose 'advanced views' Brigid heard through his sister Pigeon in the Ursuline Convent school.

Wednesday 28 June was a warm summer's day. Eager for information, Brigid went down O'Connell Street.

There was a hush — people were tense; they had fear in their faces. You sensed an atmosphere of doom. It was like back in 1916 — only there was glory in it then. Now there was only grief. I heard of the wounded taken to the Mater Hospital. I went to the Mater thinking to help. Yes, it was true. Serious casualties had come from the Four Courts.

She was bemused when she left the hospital. As if in mockery, the sun shone brilliantly, highlighting the mouldering fabric of the Georgian façades. Barefoot children played hopscotch and swung round the lamp-standards with bits of rope. Groups of blousy women stood expectantly on the steps of tenements, waiting ... waiting for any news that might bring reassurance. But Brigid Lyons felt sure that there would be no reassuring news. This was war, another war — as sure, as certain, as night follows day. It required no heart-searching to discover where lay her loyalty. She could not be but on the side of Michael Collins and the Treaty.

National Army Headquarters had been set up in the City Hall. She went there and volunteered her services to Dr 'Stetto' Ahearne, the first Director of Medical Services. Like many in the National Army, he had not yet acquired a uniform. New recruits were still to be seen in cloth caps and army tunics. There had not been time to organise all the details for the institution of the new State. Hadn't the anti-Treaty people said they would prevent the Provisional Government from governing? And weren't they already doing a good job? There was nothing requiring immediate attention at the City Hall. Dr Ahearne would call Dr Lyons as soon as there was need.

Activity soon spread from the Four Courts. On Friday 30 June, the building was reduced in a series of terrible explosions, and with its destruction went the accumulated treasure of the Public Record Office. That afternoon, in Berkeley Road, Brigid saw lorry loads of prisoners passing to Mountjoy Jail. Two men waved to her: Liam Mellows and Rory O'Connor, her friends and allies of a month ago and now … what? She was never to see either again.

After the Four Courts, Government troops concentrated on the east side of O'Connell Street: the Grenville, the Hamman, and the Gresham hotels where anti-Treaty forces had established themselves. As that war-torn week spent itself, the beautiful street was reduced to burning rubble. Towards the end, Cathal Brugha emerged from the flames, a gun blazing in each hand. Refusing their calls to surrender, he was fatally wounded by Government troops.

With Commandant Tom Flood, Dr Lyons one night went into a first-aid post in O'Connell Street during the height of the fires.

It was a tragic sight. What the British had done to the west side of the street in 1916, we, the Irish, had now done to the east side. As well, you kept hearing of men who'd been killed — people who had been your friends. It was the most heartbreaking experience I've ever gone through because bitterness was everywhere. Whatever the outcome, you knew it would bring no joy.

Meanwhile, the British were on the move — out of Ireland at last! On her way to the Abbey Theatre, Lady Gregory saw a crowd near O'Connell Bridge. A young man explained: 'It's the Tans, Ma'am. They're catching the Liverpool boats.'

'There was no booing or applause,' recalled Lady Gregory. 'Just a sort of delighted murmur, a triumphant purr.'

Brigid Lyons saw it differently. One afternoon, in Dame Street, she saw a contingent of British soldiers marching away to the docks, part of the great evacuation. Irish soldiers stood on guard outside the Bank of Ireland, and the Tricolour flew from the roof. For people like Brigid, this should have been their finest hour. It represented all they had fought for. But it didn't work out that way.

All the thrill had gone out of it. I had lived to see the British Army leaving Ireland, but the occasion was ruined through our own stupidity.

She continued to work in the College Street office. When it moved to Parnell Square, she went too. So far, she had not worked as a doctor. She had applied for a post, though, at Grangegorman Mental Hospital. In those days, you had to canvass votes.

> Then I withdrew my application when my uncle died. My aunt didn't want me to leave her. Later, I heard Dr [later professor] John Dunne beat me by one vote! Afterwards I got a message from Michael Collins: 'Why didn't you let me know you wanted a job in Grangegorman?' By then it was too late, but I had no regrets.

Looking troubled, Dr Oliver Gogarty walked into the office one day in early August. He had just come from St Vincent's Nursing Home. His patient, Arthur Griffith, was dead. Only a few days earlier, he had acted against Griffith's wishes by having him moved to the nursing home from Government Buildings where he had lain ill on a mattress on the floor. For their safety, ministers were living in Government Buildings at the time. If Gogarty was stunned, those working in the office were paralysed by the news. The death of Griffith was the most terrible blow. Recovering from the shock, they quickly had to turn to organising a state funeral. 'Seán Ó Muirthile was good at that,' Brigid remembered. 'In fact, we had all become expert at organising funerals.' Brigid stood near Nelson's Pillar as Griffith's funeral passed to Glasnevin. Amidst the mourning, she overheard the voice of anti-Treaty bias.

> When the university professors came past, wearing their gowns, I heard somebody say, 'That's the Privy Council now — they're the King's representatives.' That was the result of prevailing anti-Treaty propaganda: we had gone all British; we were more under the British than ever before; the Duke of Connaught, the King's uncle, would be coming to Ireland as Governor General; and Dublin Castle would become another Buckingham Palace. Unthinking people again, people who stupidly refused to see the rights the Treaty had given us.

A few days later, at his request, Brigid met Michael Collins in his office at Portobello Barracks. Resplendent in his general's uniform, he had just been appointed Commander-in-Chief of the National Army. He was a soldier again, a role he cherished more than that of the politician. He was intrigued that she was now a doctor. To Mick, doctors were for curing people, and he couldn't understand why she wasn't practising. That seemed greatly to concern the man of action. He had asked Dr Maurice Hayes to undertake the organisation of an Army Medical Service. It would shortly be launched, and would be recruiting doctors and nurses. He then asked her if she would fancy herself in an Army uniform. The idea was so absurd at the time that she took his suggestion as a joke.

Leaving for Government Buildings, he gave her a lift to the top of Grafton Street. She remembered:

It was a big open touring car with a military driver. We sat in the back, and I noticed that Mick unhitched his revolver placing it on the seat near his right hand. In the few minutes it took to reach town, he enquired for all our mutual friends, including those in Granard. He looked tired. A lot of the zest was gone. But then there'd been two recent deaths: his one-time bosom friend, Harry Boland, later his foe, and Griffith of course. With a cheery goodbye, he dropped me at Grafton Street. That was the last time I saw Mick Collins alive.

In the third week of August, feeling tired, Brigid went to Longford for a few days. On Wednesday 23 August, a beautiful morning, there was an urgent knock at the front door. It was Dick Callanan (later to marry Brigid's cousin, Peg McGuinness, and to become a Major-General in the Irish Army). He broke the news of the death of Michael Collins. Some news can be so devastating that the human will rebels against accepting it. Nerves cease to function rationally. The simple act of believing becomes suspended. The announcement of the death of Collins affected many in this way, even those who had never known him personally. It was not possible, they said, that God could visit Ireland like this with one woe after another in such fast succession. For those who knew the man personally, and admired his exceptional qualities, there was no word to fill their sense of loss. Brigid put it this way, 'I could not believe it, but I had to.'

She left for Dublin. The office was fully occupied again — organising another state funeral. Care had to be taken in working out the protocol of who took precedence in these processions — until suddenly it hit people again that this was the funeral of Mick Collins. Big, jovial, wrestling Mick — the last one anybody could associate with death. But indeed he was dead. Brigid had already seen him lying in state with a bandage around his head.

All their thoughts and sympathy turned to his bereaved fiancée, Kitty Kiernan, a frail tragic figure whose family had already suffered much for the Cause. She attended the Mass in the chapel of St Vincent's Hospital.

With Aunt Joe McGuinness and Mrs Eoin MacNeill, Brigid led the women's column in the funeral procession to Glasnevin. It was a hot day, and a long walk. There was still a sense of disbelief about all that was happening around them — to realise that they were there to bury Mick Collins. His successor as Commander-in-Chief, General Richard Mulcahy, gave an oration in words even more inspired than the inspiring call he had issued to the Army at 3.15 a.m. on the day after Collins' death.

> We bend today over the grave of a man not more than 30 years of age, who took to himself the gospel of toil for Ireland, the gospel of working for the people of Ireland and of sacrifice for their good and who has made himself a hero and a legend that will stand in the pages of history…

And as they turned from Glasnevin to face again the realities of civil war, a multitude of minds ruminated on its horror. As hatred thrives when it grows in the ruins of love, so, it seemed, the bitterness between Irishmen was worse than they had ever known against the British.

Dr Maurice Hayes, now a Major-General, was Director of the Army Medical Service, which had set up headquarters at 85 Merrion Square, with a small medical staff. In September 1922, Brigid received a message to report to Maurice Hayes in Merrion Square. They were recruiting nurses and doctors, and would like to consider her. She knew that this gesture had come as a result of Collins' interest in her professional future. She was accepted and therefore participated in the development of the Army Medical Service. She entered as a 1st Lieutenant on a pay of eight shillings a day, and worked with three successive directors: Maurice Hayes, succeeded by Colonel Tom O'Higgins (later Medical Officer of Health, Co Meath and father of Chief Justice O'Higgins), who in turn was succeeded by Mr Frank ('Pops') Morrin, afterwards a distinguished surgeon at St Vincent's Hospital.

For her service in the National Army, Dr Brigid Lyons held a record. She was the only woman ever to be commissioned in the Irish Free State Army. As a retired Army officer, she afterwards enjoyed the essentially masculine privilege of attendance at functions organised by old Army comrades associations.

The Civil War intensified. Bitterness and disillusion replaced the lofty idealism once the inspiration of young Irish men and women. Attack and reprisal became the pattern. There were inhuman incidents and bloody-mindedness on both sides. Nothing the British had done was worse than what the Irish were now doing to one another. In September, the Dáil empowered military courts to pass sentence of death on persons found in possession of firearms. In the following months, seventy-seven men were executed by firing squads, including Erskine Childers. Those executions were not to be forgotten. For many years, and even after peace had returned, the chilling slogan 'Remember the 77' could still be read, in faded paint, on walls and parapets throughout the country.

In December 1922, an Árd Fheis of Cumann na nGaedheal, the Free State Government party, was held. At lunchtime, Brigadier Seán Hales, a Cork TD, and Pádraig Ó Maille left, on a side-car, for lunch. They were attacked outside the Ormonde Hotel, Hales being shot dead, and Ó Máille wounded. Consternation reigned at the afternoon session of the Árd Fheis. It was significant that both men had voted for the resolution giving the Army powers to execute. Rumour had it that the shooting was the beginning of a campaign by the anti-Treaty forces to shoot all pro-Treaty TDs, in another effort to make the task of government impossible. Cabinet ministers were already living under guard in Government Buildings. All TDs were now issued with revolvers for self-protection and advised to go 'on the run'. Brigid's

Uncle Frank McGuinness, TD, had for months been living out of his constituency.

The Hales shooting brought swift Government reprisals. At dawn on the following day, 8 December 1922, Rory O'Connor, Liam Mellows, Dick Barrett and Joe McKelvey were executed in Mountjoy Prison 'as a solemn warning to those associated with them who are engaged in the conspiracy of assassination against the representatives of the Irish people'. Meanwhile, de Valera was writing from somewhere in Ireland, 'I have been condemned to view the tragedy here for the last year as though through a wall of glass, powerless to intervene effectively.' There had been a tide in the affairs of Ireland which had now ebbed beyond the far horizon.

For young Dr Brigid Lyons, the personal conflicts and tragedies became all too real when the Department of Justice posted her as Medical Officer to the female political prisoners in Kilmainham Gaol. They were, of course, mainly members of Cumann na mBan — for like most other organisations, the Cumann too had split on the Treaty issue. These women now regarded their late colleagues — people like Dr Lyons who believed in the Treaty — as 'less than the lowest British Tommy.'

Brigid remembered the assignment well:

Being sent as Medical Officer to Kilmainham was anything but a happy assignment for me. Many of those imprisoned there I had known in the Anglo-Irish War which made it sadder still for me and often extremely embarrassing. Grace (Gifford) Plunkett, Joseph Plunkett's widow, was brought in. Also Lil Brennan who had been in London with the Treaty delegation, and Mary Coyle, afterwards Mrs Todd Andrews. Then Annie MacSwiney, sister of Terence MacSwiney, went on hunger strike and nearly broke my heart. Her famous sister, Mary, was already a prisoner. Mary had previously been on hunger strike in Mountjoy Jail, and Annie, in protest, had camped on the footpath outside for weeks with blankets and hot bottles.

Annie was already a delicate girl. From the moment she arrived in Kilmainham, she refused everything. It was a frightful worry to me. I put her bed in a small ground-floor room with a fireplace. For what seemed like an eternity, she'd neither eat nor drink.

But the crowning tragedy came one night when I was called to see a new prisoner. Of all people, it was Mrs Tom Clarke. 'We meet in strange places,' she said. She was hurt to meet me there, and I was hurt to meet her. In every way, it was all too, too cruel. She was already in poor health, and twice before she had been brought into these awful dungeons to say goodbye, first to her husband, and then to her only brother, Ned Daly, before they were executed. I did all I could to make things easier for her. We'd always been such great friends, my aunt and my uncle, and while they sometimes disagreed politically, they always remained the firmest of friends. I was terribly upset. I will never forget the misery I felt that night. I reported next morning on medical grounds and she was immediately released. I believe her arrest was really accidental — done by somebody who didn't know her.

Sometimes, prisoners would ask Brigid to bring in things for them. Her desire was to oblige but she dare not. The measure of the confusion created by civil war is summarised in such prisoners' reactions. 'But you used to be a friend. Why can't you?' It was little use trying to explain. The Governor's warnings were all too explicit on that very matter. Such awkward situations occurred despite all efforts to be discreet. Returning to the prison one day, Brigid noticed a woman visitor waiting for admission. It was Margaret McEntee. Her husband, Seán, was a prisoner.

I was let in immediately with a salute from the orderly on the gate. Mrs McEntee had to go on waiting. I hated these embarrassments. They represented the sickening impact of civil war: brother against brother, father against son — even sister against sister.

The new state had had no opportunity to organise itself. The lack of administration was nowhere more evident than in Kilmainham Gaol, an out-of-date dilapidated prison re-opened at short notice to meet the needs of the time. Food supplies in bulk came in daily, but no arrangement existed whereby perishables might be used in the order of their delivery. Today's supplies of butter were dumped on top of yesterday's, and so it went on. The governor and army officers did not have so much as a table for meals. Cooking was appalling. Knives and forks were scarce. There was one teaspoon between them until that was lost. The prisoners, it need hardly be said, fared no better.

Once herself a prisoner in Kilmainham, Brigid Lyons, as an officer now, lived in conditions worse than any prisoner.

I had to sleep in a dreadful room across a yard. It was running with damp and in the past it had been a condemned cell. On the walls were scratched the last messages of people who had occupied it before execution. For light, it had one gas jet. It was bitterly cold and wet, and worse than any cell in the place. Colonel Shields brought me in his gramophone from Portobello to cheer me up. But nothing would cheer me at the time. My aunt was now living alone and was very upset by everything, including my position. Altogether, it was a period of gloom and heartbreak. The news from the country grew worse and worse, and the future looked desolate.

Occasionally a sense of humour flickered through the despondency. Seán T. Ó Ceallaigh was a prisoner. There had been an amusing description of that dapper little man being marched in after his arrest, with his rolled umbrella still on his arm. Brigid had first met him in 1915 with Uncle Joe. She had been impressed by his elegance and neatness, his culture and courtesy. He was a great raconteur, he played the flute expertly and he was a marvellous host. Joe McGuinness heartily approved when 'Seán T.' had been nominated as the Republic's first diplomat to Paris for the Peace Conference at the end of the Great War.

Seán Ó Muirthile had moved into Kilmainham to organise a busy office. One morning, in the middle of his turmoil, an orderly rushed in, saluted and said, 'Sir, Mr Seán T. Ó Ceallaigh's compliments, sir, and he complains there's a leak in the roof of his cell, sir, and the rain's coming down.' Looking up, Seán Ó Muirthile paused. 'Tell him put up his umbrella,' he said.

In later years, when he had become President of his country, nobody more than Seán T. enjoyed hearing such stories, however apocryphal they might be. His sense of humour was never-failing. Once, in an after-dinner speech to the University College Graduates' Club he expressed regret that he had not had the good fortune to be a graduate, 'But,' he added, 'I did the next best thing. I married two graduates.'

Amid the desolation of 1922, it was impossible for the active participants in the Civil War to foresee a day when they might once again sit down at the same dinner table and savour the humour of each other's postprandial speeches. For some, it came to pass, but not until they had purged hatred from their souls. For the rest, only death would end their bitterness.

# 22

# ANOTHER WAR

LIFE IMPROVED A little for Lieutenant Lyons when she was transferred back to Army Medical Services Headquarters in Merrion Square. True, reports of killings, shootings and burnings continued to fill the headlines. Bitterness on both sides had gone beyond the bounds of reason. The once-powerful Catholic Church was powerless. It was as if Ireland were intent on total self-destruction.

Depression had become a relative matter. To be free of that dripping cell in Kilmainham was at least something, but Brigid still felt a sense of doom — as if the end of the world were at hand. Ireland never would — never could — be the same again. Meanwhile, she had become interested in the new Army Comforts Fund, intended to help the National Army wounded and their dependants.

In Merrion Square, she met Michael Staines again. She had first met him in Longford in 1917 when he had helped to organise her Uncle Joe's South Longford by-election. Now he had been appointed first Commissioner of the new Garda Síochána. A uniform for the new police force was under consideration. A feminine opinion was sought. Whatever these young men were to wear, Dr Lyons exerted whatever little influence she had to make them appear as different as possible from the old and hated RIC. 'We were pleased with our choice — navy blue and silver buttons.'

In early 1923, she was transferred to St Bricin's Military Hospital. More clinically oriented, her job still embraced medical administration. Experience in organising elections and in office work stood her in good stead, as it did throughout her professional life.

February and March brought rumours of peace-feelers. Hopes were kindled one day and doused the next. On both sides, vindictive bloody-mindedness seemed, if anything, to have worsened. The Government was determined to govern and, short of total capitulation, would entertain no wordy peace conditions from the anti-Treaty faction. In March, an Italian prelate, Monsignor Luzio, arrived as a peace envoy from the Vatican. He talked to many people, including de Valera. Following the death of Griffith and Collins, W. T. Cosgrave had become President of the Executive Council. He and his ministers remained resolute. They represented the lawful Government of Ireland, and their authority was not to be impugned.

On 10 April, the death was announced of Liam Lynch, Chief of Staff of the Anti-Treaty Forces. A friend of Collins', Lynch was a man of determination, motivated by the highest ideals. His death was another tragic loss for Ireland. It was said that without him the anti-Treatyites (known as the Irregulars) could not carry on the war. However, at his funeral, de Valera said, 'You have to fling yourselves across the stampede of a nation… It is better to die nobly as your Chief has died than like a slave.'

Monsignor Luzio and the Pope had obviously been wasting their time. A once-popular catch-phrase became current again: 'The country isn't near settled yet.'

The Government was determined to break the resistance of those who had resolved to defeat the democratic process by force of arms. Throughout April, the Irregulars suffered repeated reverses. Officially, the Civil War came to an end at noon on 30 April 1923, with the issue of a proclamation by de Valera. He then made peace proposals to the Government. They were rejected. The order to 'cease fire' and 'dump arms' came on 24 May, and with it a message from de Valera to the anti-Treaty Forces. 'Military victory,' he said, 'must be allowed to rest for the moment with those who have destroyed the Republic. Other means must be sought to safeguard the Nation's right.'

In fact, a state of war continued for months — indeed years — and when the guns were silenced, the war of words went on for

decades. Sons and grandsons were inoculated with the virus of Civil
War incivility. Many a family prospered vastly while many another
endured deprivation imposed by men professing Christianity. Such
was the aftermath of a war needlessly and undemocratically
perpetrated on a country that had clearly yearned for peace.

The rewards for the idealists were scant. Lieutenant Lyons was
demobbed from the National Army on 26 January 1924. She received
a letter, dated 24 June 1924, from the President of the Executive
Council, Mr W. T. Cosgrave, who wrote:

> Your Commission as an officer in the Medical Service of the
> National Army having terminated, I desire to convey to you the
> thanks of the Executive Council for your valuable services to the
> Nation.

'… your valuable services to the Nation' — words, words, but at least
they were some consolation, if a little ironic, for by the time she
received that letter, Brigid's position as a doctor had become reversed.
She was already a long-term patient in the Richmond Hospital. A
diagnosis of pulmonary tuberculosis and a sentence of six months in
hospital might understandably add to the bitterness engendered by an
unnecessary civil war. Fortunately this was not so with Brigid. The
resilience that had made her a cheerful rebel for seven war-torn years
did not abandon her. With hindsight, and after years as a doctor, she
concluded, 'You can even become accustomed to chronic illness.'

She had only to look about her to see other young people in the
same position — many worse — all struck down in their prime, not by
bullets now, but by tuberculosis. This was the real aftermath of
guerrilla war, something of which the power-hungry politicians
neither knew nor cared. Even the doctors of the time accepted the
position with equanimity: there was nothing they could do to cure
tuberculosis. You got better or you didn't — and usually you didn't. In
Brigid's case, it soon became clear that it was up to the doctor to devise
her own treatment. And so she faced another challenge.

Months later, during her attempt to convalesce, Dan McCarthy
and Joe McGrath, then Director of Intelligence, and a member of the
Government, visited her. Well-meaning, they told how they'd heard of

marvellous cures in Leysin in Switzerland, the famous 'sun treatment'. Brigid told them how the matron at St Bricin's had recovered after a period in Nice. A southern climate was the great panacea of the time, but getting to the sun cost money. Her fortune had been a gratuity of three months' salary received on demob from the army, now long since spent on her illness.

Shortly afterwards, she received a message to see President Cosgrave at Government Buildings. Unknown to her, Dan McCarthy and Joe McGrath had spoken to him

'I believe you're very ill?' he enquired.

'I have been ill,' Brigid said. She minimised her condition. Ill or not, there might be a job in the offing.

Mr Cosgrave came to the point. 'Would you like to go abroad? I'm told it would help you.'

'Well, I've consulted various doctors, but apparently there's nothing to be done for me here. A stay in Nice has been suggested as a cure.'

The President explained. Many people had fallen ill as a result of war activity. They were in financial straits as a consequence. At the instigation of Larry Ginnell, a special fund had been set up after the State had become organised. 'There's very little in that fund,' Cosgrave concluded. 'But I can give you £200.'

Recollecting that moment, Brigid said, 'I was speechless. £200 was a fortune in those days'.

Then two fellow officers, Colonels Shields and Bennett, were also diagnosed. The three conferred. The decision was taken. In November 1924, they set out for Nice. That journey was to open up new horizons for the young doctor, struck down in her prime.

'Feeling pretty awful,' as she remembered, she glimpsed Paris for the first time. Then there was the tedious rail journey via Marseilles. They had a contact in Nice, a Mr and Mrs Fred Keogh who ran a restaurant called 'The Irish House' in the Rue de France. Mrs Keogh came from Cavan. They arranged rooms for the trio in a villa on the Promenade des Anglais. The proprietor was a pleasant Scot called Mrs McDonnell. There was a garden with tropical palms and the blue Mediterranean lapped the pebbly shore across the Promenade. It was a fascinating contrast to wintertime in Ireland.

Utterly without energy, Brigid sat in the garden, on the Promenade, and on the beach. As the weeks passed, she regained some strength. Lonesome, she lived for the post and the odd Irish newspaper. The Keoghs put on a lavish Christmas dinner, the three Irish officers as their guests. Afterwards, they sat on the beach in the sun, trying to convince themselves that it really was Christmas Day.

Mrs McDonnell's was a noisy place, sometimes bordering on insanity. Amongst the guests were four lively girls — two English, an American and an Italian. They were would-be operatic singers, pupils of the great Polish tenor, Jean de Reske, the man who once described John McCormack as 'the true redeemer of Bel Canto'. Now in his old age, the Maestro was surrounded by an international clientele of eager young singers. There was a piano in every room at Mrs McDonnell's and, from morning to night, the air was riven with scales and operatic arias. When artistic temperaments exploded, things went utterly berserk. But these outbursts passed as quickly as they had begun. Sometimes, the girls took the Irish doctor backstage at the Monte Carlo Opera and introduced her to fabulous singers with fabulous names, from the opera houses of Rome and Milan and New York. How could she not feel better, soaked, as she was, in sun and singing stars?

Early in 1925, President and Mrs Cosgrave arrived in Nice on holiday. Brigid had some happy and memorable excursions with them. It was the first break the President had enjoyed since assuming responsibility for a turbulent Ireland on the death of Griffith. In the meantime, and despite every opposition, he had managed to create a new democratic state.

Brigid received a message from Dublin. Commandant Nick Newport, a fine young man from Wexford, whom she knew, was very ill and was coming to Nice. The message requested that she would do what she could for him. Another of the casualties of war, he had been in St Bricin's Hospital with tubercular glands, and the Army was sending him to Nice to recuperate. Nobody had formally advised these people to go to Nice to the sun. They simply followed one another. As time and research confirmed, those who suffer from tuberculosis must treat the sun with respect. Sunbathing in the accepted sense can be fatal for pulmonary cases, but beneficial in certain other types. However, patients were confused on the matter.

Brigid was shocked when she met Nick at the station.

He was a wreck. I got him to the villa in a taxi, and put him to bed. I had to dress his wounds twice a day. I got a local doctor to see him. He said he was very ill, but he didn't know much about TB, nor indeed did any doctor in those days. But Nick was euphoric. He hoped that after a week or two he'd regain his strength. But I could see him going downhill from day to day. I wrote to Dublin stating the gravity of his illness and that I didn't think this treatment was right.

The colonels decided that they were now as well as ever they'd be, so they left for home. Then Nick received a letter. Another officer was coming out. Nick asked Brigid to meet this man at the station. Several trains arrived from Paris.

After two hours' wait, I saw somebody looking like an Irishman — very tall and thin and tired-looking. He proved to be the officer. He had come straight from St Bricin's Hospital, been sick on the boat and been travelling two days and two nights. I found him an apartment along the Promenade. That evening, he came to see Nick, and we heard the latest from Dublin.

His name was Captain Edward Thornton, and he was the man Brigid Lyons would marry. Captain Thornton was the first Irish officer to take a stand on the manner of his treatment by the National Army. When he fell ill, he spent several months in St Bricin's Hospital. Once, he happened to see his chart. Written in red ink was, 'This officer has extensive TB of his lungs and he is for immediate discharge.' That was a death sentence. It meant that there was nothing the doctors could do. He was to be removed from the ward to a hut at the rear of the hospital, next door to the mortuary. He became upset at this prospect, so he sent for his O.C. and told him in plain terms that no serving soldier should be treated like this. He pleaded that something be done to give him a chance to live. Colonel Dan Hogan, O.C. Eastern Command, stepped in and negotiated somewhere. And that was how

Eddie Thornton had arrived in Nice.

As a doctor, Brigid sought answers to the problem of treating tuberculosis. A southern climate did not seem to be the answer. Shortly after his arrival, Eddie had a haemoptysis (an episode of coughing up blood) after an afternoon in the sun on the beach. Brigid discussed it with an English doctor, a Dr Holt who lived in Nice. He agreed that the enervating effects of sun and heat were hardly appropriate, and suggested the sanatorium at Vence up in the hills, where perfumes are manufactured. It stood one thousand feet up and Picasso had once had his studio there. Dr Holt favoured the beneficial effects of altitude. He recommended that Brigid herself should go to Leysin, Fedey, high in the Swiss Alps, where Dr Roulier would not alone cure her, but he would educate her as a phthisiologist (an expert on pulmonary tuberculosis).

Still confined to bed, Nick Newport grew worse. His wounds never healed, but he was still the life and soul of the party, and Mrs McDonnell cared for him like a son. It was a mad, merry ménage with Italian opera alongside Irish tragedy. Brigid wrote a medical report to Colonel McKinney, Director of Medical Services in Dublin. In particular, she emphasised her worry about Nick's lack of progress. In reply, she was offered an honorarium for her medical attention to him. That had not been her point, so she wrote again to Dublin.

Nick continued to deteriorate. Alarmed at the responsibility she now carried as a doctor, Brigid wired Colonel McKinney. He replied that he was coming out immediately. But Nick's condition worsened. He died twenty minutes after the arrival of McKinney. In an effort to have his body returned to Ireland, they phoned the British Consul. 'He was a bitter man,' Brigid remembered.

> He had no time for us. All he gave was a tirade about Ireland breaking away from the Empire. The British had no obligation any longer to do anything to help us, and that was that.

There were many formalities for a funeral to Ireland and it took time. Brigid recalled:

> It was very sad. Nick's remains were two weeks waiting at Nice station before their transfer to Ireland. Eddie and I used to go

down and say a prayer by the coffin every day. Afterwards somebody told us the French Army would have seen to everything for us.

A decision about the immediate future had to be faced, particularly as the summer was on hand. By now, the relationship of Brigid Lyons and Eddie Thornton had become something more than friendship. It had perhaps not yet been articulated in so many words, but they were in love.

Brigid's decision to take Dr Holt's advice about Leysin was urged on by other events. In the summer months, Mrs McDonnell closed her villa in Nice, and moved to her villa in Le Touquet where she took paying guests until the autumn, when she would return south. Meantime, Maestro Jean de Reske had died. That broke up the party of opera pupils at the villa. Clearly, it was time to move on.

To Brigid's letter, Dr Roulier replied that yes, he would admit her to Leysin, he would treat her, and she could study too. Eddie had already gone to Vence and, understandably lonely, Brigid left Nice in June 1925. Seven months earlier, she had gone there in a state of deep depression, aggravated by chronic illness. She left with a new determination — life was sweet, the future hopeful. To live again was worth another fight. This time, she would fight illness — first her own and then that of others. And, as never before, she knew now that she had the will to succeed.

# 23

# PHYSICIAN, HEAL THYSELF

AFTER A STOPOVER in Lausanne and a lonely Sunday afternoon in Geneva, Brigid arrived by a dizzy funicular at Leysin Fedey, a village high in the Swiss Alps. The views extended over the Rhone Valley and away to Chamonix and Mont Blanc. They were indescribably beautiful — if only she were well enough to enjoy them. The clinic, a pleasant airy building, was on several levels, with many balconies. It seemed to cling precariously to the mountainside, and was set about with pines, so luxurious and so erect they might have been growing in the shelter of a hothouse. She was made welcome in many languages, for the fame of Leysin Fedey went far beyond Europe. And though at first she felt lonely and lost and listless, Brigid admitted, 'You couldn't but feel better once you got to Leysin.'

Dr Roulier laid down his treatment regime: absolute rest to commence with, together with exposure to the sun. On the first day, three minutes up to the ankles. On the next, five minutes on a greater area, and so on until gradually the patient had acquired a tan. He emphasised that the regime must be gradual. That, he explained, was all he could prescribe for the time being. But Brigid was a doctor, so he went further for her. He explained the new treatments they were now doing in Switzerland: plombage, phrenic crush, Gaffky Counts. Also, he talked about the mental attitude of the patient: response to discipline, will to get better, absolute co-operation. Dr Lyons was already learning things that she had never known before. Her mind went back to the wards of Dublin hospitals where even a revered consultant, faced with a case of tuberculosis, was too ready to shrug and reach for the book of death certificates.

The mental attitude of the patient was a new and fascinating concept. But as the weeks and months passed, Brigid saw it demonstrated amongst the patients at Leysin Fedey. There was a Latvian girl, a dark beauty called Renate Sarle. She had arrived, a fragile creature on the point of death, with surgical tuberculosis of her joints: hands, ankles and shoulders. Her friends had collected to send her to Dr Roulier, and she was convinced of her recovery. Fascinated, Brigid watched her progress. In two weeks, Renate was mahogany from the sun, every x-ray showed enormous improvement. Soon, she was on her feet, her exuberance overflowing to help the less optimistic. From the outset, the girl's attitude of mind had seemed to be the key to her progress. But as a doctor, Brigid also knew that surgical tuberculosis was more amenable to treatment than was the pulmonary disease.

She was herself already much improved. She found that there were other Irish people at Leysin Fedey, too:

I met two boys brought out by Mrs Darrel Figgis through the White Cross. Professor Theo Dillon was in the next clinic to me. Also Professor Gerard Murphy, the Gaelic scholar. They were all making marvellous progress.

Convinced that Dr Roulier had something to offer, Brigid wrote accordingly to Colonel McKinney. If Irish people were to be sent anywhere, Leysin Fedey was the place.

There had been no ulterior motive in her letter, but the first to be instructed to proceed to Switzerland was Eddie Thornton. He looked poorly on arrival, but Brigid was delighted to know that he was now to have the best possible treatment. And so the romance that had budded in Nice blossomed in Leysin Fedey. Eddie too was cheered. He found convivial Irish company in Ken O'Dea, a brother of Jimmy's. Ken's Dublin humour, if not entirely understood by the Swiss, was accepted with great hilarity. He would go for a walk every morning. Meeting Teshmon, a genial old retainer coming back with the patients' shopping, Ken would salute him loudly. 'Ah! The hard Tash!' With laughter, Teshmon accepted it as a happy Irish greeting.

Realising that she was so much improved, Brigid grew impatient. Dr Roulier counselled her. He arranged that, on a part-time basis, she could assist consultants in the clinic and take lectures on tuberculosis. But it was her financial position that she was thinking of. She could not pay her way indefinitely. Somebody suggested that she should apply for an Army pension.

I felt doubtful about that, and Eddie too was discouraging. He said they'd want an account of all the ambushes I'd been in. They all joked me, but anyway I decided to apply. The form had to be signed in the presence of a Peace Commissioner. There were no PCs in Switzerland, only *notaires publiques* and the nearest was in Geneva. So it was arranged he would come to the clinic. There was extra spit and polish for his visit. There were even more flowers planted. And then one day the poorest-looking man I've ever seen came trundling up the steep hill from the funicular. He was a disappointment to everybody. But we signed the application and sent it off to Dublin.

It was the little milestones that marked time's journey for the confined community high in the Alps at Leysin Fedey. Christmas 1925, for instance. With their carols and candles and Christmas trees, the Swiss made more of the festive trappings than the Irish. They were even ahead of Bing Crosby — they had real sleigh bells in the snow. Then there were the periodic excitements when a patient left cured.

We'd see them off, waving towels and napkins from the balconies as they went down by the funicular to rejoin the other world beyond the peaks.

And sometimes musicians came with their guitars and sang beneath the balconies. Brigid remembered that 'it was there I first heard "Valencia". We used to collect centimes and roll them in paper twists and throw them down with our requests.'

The doctor in Brigid found its greatest reward in monitoring the progress of children with surgical tuberculosis in Dr Roulier's 'School in the Sun'. Then there were the shared Irish newspapers, and the consolation that peace of some kind had come again at home. And always there was the crisp, clean Alpine air and the wonderful pink skies in the evenings, ending with a crimson sunset on the peak of some distant snow-clad mountain. These were the things which sustained them from day to day — these and, for Brigid, Eddie's company.

In September 1925, Brigid returned to Dublin. Leysin Fedey had done for her all she expected of it. She felt better than she had done for years. Then Eddie came home. Neither had received army pensions, but Brigid had at least been summoned to Portobello and been interviewed. The new State was niggardly, but she acknowledged that they had a lot to do. Very quietly, on 10 October, Eddie Thornton and Brigid Lyons were married in the Chapel of St Kevin at Dublin's Pro-Cathedral. Shortly afterwards, he returned to Switzerland, and she entered University College to study for a Diploma in Public Health. The State was about to develop the new public health services, and she felt attracted to such a career. Back again with Aunt Joe, she was soon immersed in study. But for the absent ones, it was like old times.

The year 1927 passed happily. In March, she passed the first half of her exam. Eddie was discharged from hospital, and the Minister for Defence had granted her a Military Service Pension backdated to 1924.

I went to Paris to meet Eddie. Paris was cheap then, and it was by way of being our honeymoon. When we returned after Easter, we took a flat. I resumed lectures and, with the assistance of a job in the Cumann na nGaedheal party office, Eddie began to study law. In October, I obtained the D.P.H. at University College.'

In early 1928, Eddie had to return to Switzerland. Brigid went to Dr Matt Russell, then Medical Officer of Health for the City of Dublin. She told him that she wanted a job — that was how things were done in the medical world in those days! Their conversation ended with him saying, 'There's only one other person I know who talks as much as you and he's Medical Officer of Health in Co Kildare and he wants an assistant down there. Go and tell him I recommend you for Kildare'

— all of which must read strangely to generations accustomed only to the scrutiny of the Local Appointments Commission.

However, Brigid went to the Custom House and Dr Stevenson, the chief there, advised her to write to Dr Austin Harbison in Kildare. She did, and got no reply. A few weeks later, she took a phone call from Belfast. She heard Dr Harbison, in his Northern accent, pronounce that she did not have enough experience in tuberculosis for the job. That was ironical, she told him. She enquired who in Ireland had better experience than one who had suffered it herself — and recovered? Her claim to unique experience made no impact, and that seemed to be that as far as Kildare was concerned.

Once on its feet, the Government had endeavoured to set up the best possible medical services in a country emerging from oblivion. To organise the public health aspect, they had appointed three Medical Officers of Health and sent them to the Rockefeller Foundation for training. They were Doctors Austin Harbison, Don Carroll (who had served with Brigid in the Army), and Robert Condy. Co Kildare was to be the pilot area.

Shortly afterwards, Brigid was summoned to Naas for an interview. Dr Harbison was charming. She was appointed temporarily and delegated to organise the local tuberculosis service.

I was most fortunate to have been sent to one of the three Rockefeller men, and Kildare was the pilot area, so, once again, I was in on the ground floor. I began in April 1928.

The attitude of Irish doctors to the age-old problem of tuberculosis must surprise their latter-day colleagues. A profession devoted to scientific enquiry, it seemed hopelessly to turn away from this, Ireland's greatest epidemiological problem. Knowing how Koch's bacillus was transmitted, and even in the absence of antibiotics, there was still much that might have been done by way of hygiene and isolation. Yet it was not until the introduction of BCG vaccination and of drug therapy in the 1950s, and when the problem had already become a political plaything, that the profession began seriously to deal with this once-terrifying disease.

What the position was like in the Irish countryside in 1928 is best described by Dr Brigid Lyons Thornton:

> There was an x-ray. The best we had was malt and cod-liver oil and creosote and a sanatorium at Peamount. It was difficult to get patients to go into the sanatorium and doubly difficult to prevent them coming out. They preferred to stay at home and cycle to the clinic to have their temperatures taken and cycle home again. And they were all in the bloom of youth. It was harrowing how little we could do. It was my personal experience made me keenly interested. I did my best to counter the prevailing idea that once you got TB you were written off: No cure, no hope, no anything. Only too well I knew the shock of being given that diagnosis. It had shattered me and I was a qualified doctor at the time.

Surgical tuberculosis, for which, even at the time, much could be done, was also glaringly neglected. Brigid related a typical instance.

> Periodically I had to visit a man too ill to leave his house. I'd been visiting the house for two months when he remembered casually: 'Pity you didn't come sooner — before Seán got so bad. He's a cripple in the back room'. I saw Seán, a handsome, highly nervous young man of twenty-seven, fit enough, but bed-ridden from a tubercular hip which had never been treated. The disease was obviously now quiescent, but his foot was turned totally backwards. He had been in bed from childhood with his mother nursing him and was frightened of seeing anybody. I got crutches from Fannin's and got him to the garden. It was a good summer. His whole outlook changed. Then I got Sir William Wheeler to take him into Mercers' Hospital. He corrected the deformity and, though a little stiff, the boy was able to lead a normal life. The gratitude of that family was something amazing.

Later in 1928, Brigid moved to Co Cork. There she worked with Dr Robert Condy. 'So I had the best of all worlds in public health training,' she said. 'I had the opportunity to work under two of the three Rockefeller men.'

As far as the prevalence of tuberculosis was concerned, Co Cork was no different from Co Kildare. There was a sanatorium at

Doneraile, but it was very difficult to persuade people to go there. If the doctor managed to persuade a patient, the sanction of the county council had then to be obtained — when the council met. More than likely, each councillor had his own voter/patient for the vacancy. Admission on medical needs was irrelevant.

Cork suffered from a particularly virulent strain of diphtheria. The death rate was high.

> We initiated the diphtheria scheme. It meant continuous inoculating every day with crowded clinics and long hours of driving. At the peak of this campaign, a certain councillor, far from encouraging all concerned, said publicly he'd run me out of the county because I'd introduced a new-fangled scheme for diphtheria and if it got going it would close all their fever hospitals and there'd be nothing for their little nurses to do but go to England. That councillor afterwards became a long-serving TD.

Asked if initiating public health schemes in Ireland in the teeth of such ignorant opposition ever discouraged her, Brigid had no doubt. 'Never,' she replied. 'It was another sort of fight.'

In September 1929, Brigid was appointed permanently to the Dublin Corporation Public Health Service. Meanwhile, Eddie had qualified at the Bar. He continued to winter in Switzerland until 1932, when that country went off the Gold Standard and it became financially impossible to live there. Practice at the Bar frequently brought him on circuit to the West. This work was too demanding. Inevitably his health broke down again. In 1933, on the advice of his brother in America, he went to Saranac Lake in the Catskill Mountains, a hospital with a high reputation. His letters were cheerful and he made great progress. Eventually he encouraged Brigid to visit him and his sister in Georgia. She went in November 1934, only to find that, in the meantime, Eddie had broken down again. To add to their demoralisation, news from Longford reached them to say that Uncle Frank was dead. A senator for five years, he had died on 30 November 1934, the very day on which he completed his term of office.

The father figure in Brigid's life, Frank McGuinness, was a big man in every way. Never doctrinaire, he adapted to the changing political needs of Ireland. When he ceased to be a Peace Commissioner under the British administration, he threw himself heart and soul into the Republican Movement. In Reading Gaol, he became close to Griffith and Cosgrave and subsequently he represented Longford in both the Dáil and the Seanad. It was Bríd McGuinness, one of the nieces he had adopted (she who had thrown herself between him and the Black and Tans), who nursed him through his last illness. Bríd later ran his business houses at 2 and 4 Main Street, Longford.

Brigid remained at Saranac Lake while Eddie had a thorcoplasty operation, after which he made an excellent recovery. They returned to Dublin in March 1935. As a less strenuous life, Eddie decided to qualify as a solicitor. He studied for another year and qualified and began to practise in Dublin. Eventually his operation scar broke down, though. Once again, he was faced with a tedious round of hospitals: from the Mater to Camberly and finally to Midhurst to the care of Dr (later Sir) Geoffrey Todd. A year later, he returned to Dublin. Now he was better than ever before. He remained well for a few years until Fate dealt its next blow. He developed hypertension. After a life of struggle to establish himself in three careers, as an Army officer, as a barrister and as a solicitor, Eddie Thornton died suddenly on 19 July 1947. In the same year, Aunt Frank died in Longford.

Aunt Joe, Brigid's other mother figure, had died in March 1938, her face destroyed by cancer. A founder-member of Cumann na mBan, she retained her love of Irish Ireland to the end. She and Joe McGuinness had been childhood sweethearts since they had grown up together in Tarmonbarry. And though war had sundered the happiness of their last years, she forgave it all because it was for Ireland. After Joe's death, she endured her loneliness with fortitude. 'Friends drift from a widow,' she would say sadly. Her photograph is on exhibition in Kilmainham Museum.

For Brigid Lyons Thornton, recollecting her career in the health service meant first recollecting the Civil War. Had it not been for that great political blunder, Ireland would have been building her health services at an earlier stage, instead of having to face, in 1923, the repair of a country needlessly ravaged. As a result, the health and welfare of the Irish people had to wait, and the introduction of a public health service was years later than it should have been.

She was proud of having served in the era that saw the elimination of those infectious diseases with high mortality rates. Diphtheria, for instance, the one-time scourge of the children of the cities of Dublin and Cork, is no longer seen. Doctors of today might find difficulty in recognising the ominous faucial membrane, or the 'bull-neck' which once spelt disaster. But her greatest satisfaction came from the achievements in dealing with tuberculosis.

Like all who were seriously concerned with that one-time Irish plague, Brigid recognised the credit due to Noel Browne who, as Minister for Health, retained his honest, shining idealism, refusing to be diverted from his purpose by hypocritical politicians or power-hungry priests. He it was who made possible the great assault of the 1950s on Ireland's most dreaded, most crippling and most killing disease.

Of those she knew as friends and as architects of the new state, she described William Cosgrave as a living dynamo, a tower of strength in creating the new Ireland. When Collins was killed and supreme responsibility fell on him, Cosgrave never flinched nor hesitated in ruthlessly imposing law and order. She remembered with gratitude an evening spent as the guest of President Cosgrave in his home. After dinner, she produced a cheque. Handing it to him, she said, 'I'm working now and I want to repay the money you so kindly lent me in 1922 to meet the expenses of my long illness.'

'There is no need to repay that money,' he told her. 'It was a grant.'

'But if that fund hadn't existed when I needed help so badly, I'd have been in a sorry state. Please let me make amends.'

'If you feel like that…' he said.

The other great architect of the new Ireland was, of course, Michael Collins. For Brigid, the words 'hero' and 'Collins' were synonymous:

There were many, many fine people but Michael Collins was like a colossus amongst them. He did so much for the country, he made his work immeasurable. He was so unselfish, so courageous, and at the grimmest moments, so cheerful, so reassuring. Children loved him, and he always spared them a moment. He used to jot down the little stories and sayings of the de Valera children. A man who loves children loves all mankind. There was nothing Michael

Collins spared himself to bring peace to the unfortunate people of
Ireland — not even his own young life.

Was it all worthwhile? Was modern Ireland the country that Brigid
Lyons Thornton and her compatriots lived and died for?

I'm not sure you can evaluate it that way. A lot more might have
been done but for that tragic Civil War. But look at it this way: if
my Fenian father could walk this land again, wouldn't he be only
astonished to see the freedom we've achieved? We're not on the far
side of the river yet, but we've crossed most of Collins' stepping
stones. I may not live to see it, but please God … there's only one
left.

LIMERICK
COUNTY LIBRARY

# EPILOGUE

DR LYONS THORNTON'S professional life as a child welfare paediatrician was spent in the service of Dublin Corporation at the Carnegie Centre in Lord Edward Street. For the greater benefit of the children, Bridgie recognised the need to educate the mothers in how to achieve a degree of hygiene, coming as they did from overcrowded, one-roomed slum dwellings, the only water available emanating from a single back-yard tap usually several floors down. Despite whatever the Public Health Service could do, disease flourished and vermin accumulated.

However, Bridgie never lost her faith, hope or charity. She did not often talk about that period of her life. Whenever she mentioned it, she always prefixed her remarks with an expression of regret about what might have been achieved years earlier but for the wastage of an unnecessary civil war.

Nevertheless, she lived to see the eradication of tuberculous meningitis in children, as well as the control, through vaccination and inoculation, of infectious and killing diseases like diphtheria, mumps and measles. In particular, improved feeding hygiene did away at last with a peculiarly lethal strain of gastroenteritis which had killed hundreds of babies in Dublin and Cork.

As a little girl, Bridgie had cherished an early wish to be a teacher. That wish manifested itself in the years she spent teaching hygiene to erring mothers. In 1947, as a postgraduate doctor, I took the Diploma in Public Health course, with some forty other postgraduate doctors, at

University College Dublin. These were experienced men and women who had served as doctors in many parts of the world during the Second World War. Bridgie lectured us in her subject, and I can testify that her impact was commonsense and practical and far exceeded that of many who paraded themselves as learned university professors.

When Bridgie retired, she did not seek rest. In fact, she expended as much, if not more, energy than at the height of her professional life. Not for her a restful twilight to a long day's strife in pursuit of her high ideals. Her membership of many learned and charitable organisations associated with the medical profession kept her busy. She was appointed as librarian to the Rotunda Hospital, a duty which took her across town every morning. And woe betide the bus conductor whose bad habits were revealed by his nicotine-stained fingers! Her lecture was always given and taken in the best of good parts. Overheard, it sometimes prompted a guilt-ridden passenger or two to stub their cigarettes.

As a hospital librarian, with access to all the current medical journals, she kept abreast of the newest developments. To less well-read doctors she was a fount of information. Indeed, she became the eyes and ears of the Dublin medical world.

Compassion had always played an essential part in Bridgie's life. It was never more in evidence than in her devotion to the affairs of the Medical Benevolent Fund. There is a popular notion that doctors are invariably well-off people. Some are, but some are not because of ill-luck or tragic circumstances: illness, accidents, addictions (drugs, more usually alcohol), and, of course, sudden death. They all bring catastrophe to the household of a struggling wife and, usually, a young family. Bridgie was never judgemental where the doctor concerned was the author of his own ruination. Her concern was his dependants, and she never ceased to raise funds to help alleviate the resulting distress.

In her old age, she feared loss of memory. It never happened. There was an occasion when she was invited to give a lecture at the Army Cadet School at the Curragh. She asked me to accompany her in case she got into a muddle. She was like a nervous actress about to go on stage without being too sure of her lines. The faces of those young officers reflected their total absorption as the lecturer flawlessly related the story of Commandant Edward Daly's heroic defence of the Four

Courts in 1916. Their interest resulted in a spate of thought-provoking questions. For Bridgie, the occasion was 'a sellout'.

Her indignation was roused when she heard Fianna Fáil people speak with pride of 'the Four Courts fight'. She knew that they never meant Daly's defence in 1916. She contended that, perverse or ill-informed, they foolishly meant their own takeover in 1922 when they were the cause of the destruction of the Four Courts, and of its Public Record Office containing the priceless National Archives of Ireland, the ashes of which rained down on Dublin for days.

In the 1950s, to supplement Noel Browne's assault on the age-old epidemic of tuberculosis, a national campaign of vaccination using BCG was launched. I was appointed its medical director. With fifteen teams touring the country, the job was a demanding one. Nevertheless, Bridgie had got me in her sights. Our campaign drew much scientific interest at home and abroad. Even the Department of External Affairs reported our activities through all Irish embassies. Of particular interest was the fact that we were years in advance of Britain, and that British doctors came to study our campaign.

At that time, Bridgie was secretary to the Public Health Section of the Royal Academy of Medicine. Pursued relentlessly by her, I contributed more than my fair share of papers to the Academy, and to similar medical groups.

She treasured a small collection of letters she had received from Michael Collins. One that was relevant she took to a celebratory dinner of old comrades. It was passed along the large dinner table. When the party was breaking up, Bridgie suddenly remembered her letter. 'My letter,' she called out. 'My Collins letter — who's got it?' There was no reply. Nobody owned up, then or ever after.

Two other Collins letters she had framed. They hung in her first-floor apartment. One day, a so-called American history student called at the front door. He was interested in the Irish Civil War, and in Michael Collins, and he had been directed to her. She went upstairs and brought down her framed Collins letters. The conversation continued until the milkman arrived with his weekly bill. She ran upstairs again, this time for her handbag. When she got back to the door, the American history student had gone, and so had her treasured letters. The milkman told her that the young gentleman had got into a car and driven away quickly.

Incidents such as these drained her confidence. Her outings she reduced to daily Mass at Clarendon Street, with coffee to follow, somewhere in Grafton Street. When she wanted to cross a street, she would raise her right arm, her stick or umbrella held high, like a mast pointing to the sky. She would then launch out on a perilous crossing, ignoring the hooting of irritated drivers.

As confidence waned and frailty invaded, her references to death grew frequent. 'I hope you get a fine day the day you're taking me to Mayo,' she would say referring to her funeral. These remarks were made not with depression, but with more than an element of humour. If you suggested that circumstances might keep you away, she'd respond with a laugh, 'Ah now, you won't let me down.'

Well, I didn't, and yes, we got a fine day. As it transpired, coincidence played a part in Bridgie's funeral. On Easter Monday in April 1987, we followed her flag-draped coffin from Dublin via Longford to Co Mayo. Exactly seventy-one years earlier, on Easter Tuesday in April 1916, the young Brigid Lyons had driven this same road, but in the opposite direction, when she joined her Uncle Joe in the defence of the Four Courts.

At Longford, where it had all begun, her funeral paused. It didn't seem quite right that Bridgie, wrapped in a tricolour, should be left in a hearse, like an exhibit for nationalism, in the car park of a hotel, while her mourning friends indulged themselves in luncheon, but that was the way of it.

At Toomore Cemetery near Foxford, a guard of honour from the Western Command was already on parade ready to do honour to their ninety-one-year-old distinguished veteran, and their first-ever woman officer. As she was laid beside Eddie, her soldier husband, a volley over the grave reverberated through the locality. It was a soldier's funeral — and Bridgie would have been pleased.

Could she have heard them, the voices of children at the nearby school would have pleased her too — voices that in the future years would call and be echoed across the breadth of Ireland, her beloved country to which she had helped bring freedom from domination and disease.

# BIBLIOGRAPHY

Barry, Tom, *Guerilla Days in Ireland*, Anvil Books, 1967

Béaslaí, Piaras, *Irish Independent*, 20 & 21 January 1953, 5 May 1965

Bourke, Marcus, *The O'Rahily*, Anvil Books, 1967

Caulfield, Max, *The Easter Rebellion*, Four Square, 1965

Crimmins, Tom, *Irish Independent*, 14 April 1966

*Daily Telegraph*, 10 July 1917

Feeney, William, *Evening Herald*, April 1966

Figgis, Darrell, *A Chronicle of Jails*, Talbot Press, 1917

Forester, Margaret, *Michael Collins: The Lost Leader*, Sidgwick & Jackson, 1971

Hally, Col. P. J., *The Irish Press* (supplement), 9 April 1966

Kilgannon, Tadhg, *Sligo and its Surroundings*, Kilgannon, 1926

Leland, Mary, *The Irish Times*, 5 January 1971

Longford, Lord & O'Neill, T. P., *Eamon de Valera*, Gill & Macmillan, 1970

Longford, Lord, *Peace by Ordeal*, New English Library, 1967

Macardle, Dorothy, *The Irish Republic*, Corgi Books, 1968

Macken, Henry, *Evening Herald*, 7 April 1966

McCormack, Lily, *I Hear You Calling Me*, W. H. Allen, 1950

McDonagh, Michael, *The Irish at the Front*, Hodder & Stoughton, 1916

Ní Chorra, Éilís, *The Irish Press*, 18 June 1969

Ó Briain, Prof. Liam, prsonal correspondence

O'Connor, Frank, *The Big Fellow*, Clonmore & Reynolds, 1965

O'Connor, Ulick, *Oliver St John Gogarty*, New English Library, 1967

Ó Luing, Seán, *I Die in a Good Cause*, Anvil Books, 1970

O'Malley, Ernie, *On Another Man's Wound*, Four Square, 1961

O'Neill, Patrick, *Evening Herald*, 13 April 1966

O'Shannon, Cathal, *Evening Press*, 8 March 1957

Robinson, Liam, *The Sunday Express*, 25 May 1969 and 1 June 1969

Ryan, Mark F., *Fenian Memories*, M. H. Gill, 1945

*Sinn Féin Rebellion Handbook* issued by the Weekly Irish Times
    contains a list of all prisoners and their sentences

*Sunday Independent*, 23 April 1916

Taylor, Rex, *Michael Collins*, Four Square, 1961

Walsh, Most Rev. William J., *Irish Independent*, 8 May 1917

White, Terence de Vere, *Kevin O'Higgins*, Anvil Books, 1966

Younger, Calton, *Ireland's Civil War*, Fontana Books, 1970

# INDEX

# INDEX